Ransoming the Waste Land

I0061500

Ransoming the Waste Land

Papers on C.S. Lewis's Space Trilogy, Chronicles of Narnia, and Other Works

Volume II

by

Nancy-Lou Patterson

Editors

Emily E. Auger

and

Janet Brennan Croft

Valleyhome Books

Copyright © 2016 Nancy-Lou Patterson

First published by Valleyhome Books in 2016. All rights reserved. No part of this publication may be reproduced, stored in a retrieval system, or transmitted, in any form or by any means, electronic, mechanical, photocopying, recording, or otherwise, without written permission, except for brief quotations in reviews, journals, and books.

Front cover and title page illustration credit: Nancy-Lou Patterson, "St. Anne's." First published as the cover of *Mythlore* 13.3 (Spring 1987). Further publication prohibited.

Back cover and last page illustration credit: Nancy-Lou Patterson, "The Destruction of Edgestow." First published as the cover of *Mythlore* 16.2 (Winter 1989). Further publication prohibited.

First Printing 2016
Ransoming the Waste Land Volume I
Hardcover ISBN 978-1-987919-00-4
Paperback ISBN 978-1-987919-03-5
Epub ISBN 978-1-987919-04-2

Ransoming the Waste Land Volume II
Hardcover ISBN 978-1-987919-01-1
Paperback ISBN 978-1-987919-05-9
Epub ISBN 978-1-987919-06-6

Table of Contents

Abbreviations for C.S. Lewis's Fiction

PR   *The Pilgrim's Regress*. 1933. Illus. by Michael Hague. 1981. Grand Rapids, MI: William B. Erdmans, 2000. [ISBN 0-8028-0641-4 with matching kindle edition.]

OSP   *Out of the Silent Planet*. 1938. Hammersmith, London: HarperCollins*Publishers*, 2005. [EPub Edition ISBN 0-00-715715-0, with page nos. matching print edition ISBN 0007157150].

ST   *The Screwtape Letters with Screwtape Proposes a Toast*. With a New Preface. New York: Geoffrey Bles, 1961. [New Preface 5-13. Original Preface 19-20. *The Screwtape Letters* (1942) 23-138. *Screwtape Proposes a Toast* (1959) 139-57.]

PER   *Perelandra*. 1943. Hammersmith, London: HarperCollins*Publishers*, 2005. [EPub Edition ISBN 0-00-7157169, with page nos. matching print edition ISBN 0684833654].

THS   *That Hideous Strength*. 1945. Hammersmith, London: HarperCollins*Publishers*, 2003. EPub Edition ISBN 978-0-007-33227-4, with page nos. matching print edition ISBN 0684833670].

LWW   *The Lion, the Witch and the Wardrobe*. 1950. Collector's Edition with Illustrations by Pauline Baynes. New York: HarperCollins, 2010. [E-Pub Edition 978-0-06-197415-1; with page nos. matching print edition ISBN 0064409422].

PC   *Prince Caspian: The Return to Narnia*. 1951. Collector's Edition with Illustrations by Pauline Baynes. New York: HarperCollins, 2010. [E-Pub Edition ISBN 978-0-06-197422-9 with page nos. matching print edition ISBN 0060234830].

VDT   *The Voyage of the Dawn Treader*. 1952. Collector's Edition with Illustrations by Pauline Baynes. New York: HarperCollins, 2010. [E-Pub Edition ISBN 9780061974267, with page nos. matching print edition ISBN 0064471071].

SC   *The Silver Chair*. 1953. Collector's Edition with Illustrations by Pauline Baynes. New York: HarperCollins, 2010. [E-Pub Edition ISBN 978-0-06-97423-6, with page nos. matching print edition ISBN 0064409457].

HB   *The Horse and His Boy*. 1954. Collector's Edition with Illustrations by Pauline Baynes. New York: HarperCollins, 2010. [E-Pub Edition 978-0-06-197413-7, with page nos. matching print edition ISBN 006023489X].

MN   *The Magician's Nephew* (1955). Collector's Edition with Illustrations by Pauline Baynes. New York: HarperCollins, 2010. [Epub Edition ISBN 978-0-06-197416-8, with page nos. matching print edition 0064409430].

LB   *The Last Battle*. 1956. Collector's Edition with Illustrations by Pauline Baynes. New York: HarperCollins, 2010. [E-Pub Edition ISBN 978-0-06-197414-4, with page nos. matching print edition ISBN 0060234938].

TWF   *Till We Have Faces: A Myth Retold*. Illus. Fritz Eichenberg. 1956. New York: Harcourt, Brace and Company, 1980. [ISBN 0156904365 with matching kindle edition].

Preface

Nancy-Lou Patterson's (b. 1929) many accomplishments include works of visual art, poetry, and fiction, and numerous scholarly papers published in *Mythlore* and other journals and anthologies. Of the Inklings, about whom she wrote most often, she particularly favored C.S. Lewis, whose work she read and enjoyed over a period of many decades.

> I have to admit to a very peculiar point of view. *That Hideous Strength* is my favorite book for adults. Not merely my favorite book for adults by C.S. Lewis, but my favorite book, period! Oddly, I don't remember exactly when I first read it. It must have been during the academic year 1953/1954 because that was when I read *Out of the Silent Planet* and *Perelandra*, but I have read it so often since then that I can't pinpoint the exact place where I first read it, as I so often can, having a powerful visual memory, with other books more seldom read. What I do remember is the impact of the book, its wonder, its delight, which for me—even after the word-for-word reading I gave it this year to prepare to discuss it with you—is what makes it the best of the trilogy. I say nothing against the cool masculine vision of *Out of the Silent Planet* and the warm feminine vision of *Perelandra*: these numinous "other" worlds are forever encoded in my memory as encounters with wonder. But my favorite book—not only of the trilogy, but of all books for adults, is *That Hideous Strength*. The more I read it, the more it speaks to me. I am here to tell what I think it says.[1]

Patterson's enthusiasm for the writings of C.S. Lewis is part of a widespread and long-lived flourishing of academic and popular studies of his work.[2] The strength of her analyses of Lewis's fiction derives from her recognition—perhaps inspired by her own creative work as a fiction author—that the power of his images, motifs, and symbols derives from his ability to use his extensive knowledge of literature and his own lived experiences to develop them in relation to broader cultural archetypes.

Patterson's most frequent approach is what is today popularly called "source criticism." When source criticism developed in the eighteenth century, it was called literary criticism and involved the analysis of texts in relation to probable antecedents. "Source criticism," E.L. Risden (2011) writes, "in current parlance implies different notions in different fields [...] It began as a subset of biblical criticism, to discern the various sources behind canonical (or non-canonical) books and stories, in part to understand the process of canonization and in part to understand the movement of story and the cultural influences of the ancient world."[3] Today, beyond its role in the actual preparation of books from manuscripts, source criticism generally

> considers relative chronology, authorship, and intention (if we can determine them), settings of the works, themes, patterns of organization of the whole works or of plot, common literary units such as borrowed characters, motifs, or "memes" (e.g., linguistic elements or even "narremes," repeated sections of narrative or similar digressions), parallel passages, points of view, and stylistic peculiarities. [...] Documenting sources provides readers a powerful tool to gain insight into authors, how they thought and worked, and to use in the interpretation of texts, so that we may find, enjoy, appreciate, and teach better and fuller (though not exclusive) readings. It helps us understand how all writers experience the pressures of the past as well as contemporary exigencies. [4]

Source criticism has become one of the most favored approaches to the study of Tolkien's fiction,[5] although, as Tom Shippey (1982) observes, Tolkien did not approve of it.[6] Numerous scholars have demonstrated the influence on him of "Beowulf and everything else in Old English [...]; medieval Romance, Arthurian and otherwise [...], but those examples only slightly less than the Bible [...]; fairy tales, fables, and folksongs [...]; Classical myth [...]; and the readings and discussions with his fellow Inklings."[7] Apparently Lewis, who drew on no fewer sources than Tolkien, sometimes disapproved of source criticism too;[8] yet he was without question interested in the approach, as papers such as his "What Chaucer Really Did to [Boccaccio's] *Il Filostrato*" indicate.[9]

Patterson comments on an "annotated Lewis" as a wonderful book yet to be written,[10] but her primary goal in studying and writing about Lewis's sources, both literary and biographical, was to show the importance of the themes he addressed. The papers included in the first volume of *Ransoming the Waste Land* examine Lewis's treatment of salvation in Arthurian and biblical forms, his hierarchy of beings from divine to inanimate, and his representation of the feminine in relation to a purportedly masculine divinity. Some of those in the second volume also address these subjects, but emphasize Lewis's representation of spatial and temporal realities, including directional symbolism, northerness, and environmentalism, and some of his character types, including anthropomorphized animals, deities, witches, and others.

Both volumes include papers that Patterson herself identified as part of a series on the representation of evil:

1. "'Banquet at Belbury': Festival and Horror in *That Hideous Strength*" (1981) Volume I
2. "'Halfe Like a Serpent': The Green Witch in *The Silver Chair*" (1984) Volume II
3. "Letters from Hell: the Symbolism of Evil in *The Screwtape Letters*" (1985) Volume II
4. "'The Bolt of Tash': the Figure of Satan in C.S. Lewis's *The Horse and His Boy* and *The Last Battle*" (1990) Volume II
5. "'Always Winter and Never Christmas': Symbols of Time in Lewis's Chronicles of Narnia" (1991) Volume II
6. "'This Equivocal Being': The Un-Man in C.S. Lewis's *Perelandra*" (1995, 1996) Volume I

The seventh paper, "The Holy House of Ungit" (1997), was not yet written in 1996 when Patterson identified this series. It is, as she describes it, about "Lewis's last novel *Till We Have Faces* [in which] no character specifically embodies or symbolizes evil, including the great goddess Ungit [...]"[11] By contrast, many of Patterson's papers outside this series are about Lewis's good or saved characters.

Patterson's approach to Lewis's fiction by way of the images that he brought to life is validated by Lewis's own creative process. Lewis believed that in writing stories "images always come first."[12] In a frequently cited passage, he wrote,

> All my seven Narnian books, and my three science fiction books, began with seeing pictures in my head. At first

they were not a story, just pictures. The *Lion* all began with a picture of a Faun carrying an umbrella and parcels in a snowy wood. This picture had been in my mind since I was about sixteen. Then one day, when I was about forty, I said to myself: "Let's try to make a story about it."

At first I had very little idea how the story would go. But then suddenly Aslan came bounding into it. I think I had been having a good many dreams of lions about that time. Apart from that, I don't know where the Lion came from or why He came. But once he was there He pulled the whole story together, and soon He pulled the six other Narnian stories in after Him.[13]

The starting point for *Perelandra*, he writes, "was my mental picture of the floating islands. The whole of the rest of my labours in a sense consisted of building up a world in which floating islands could exist."[14] This authorial sense of the importance of the image translated readily for Lewis into an understanding of symbolism: "It [symbolism] makes its first effective appearance in European thought with the dialogues of Plato. The Sun is the copy of the Good. Time is the moving image of eternity. All visible things exist just in so far as they succeed in imitating the Forms."[15] Whereas the allegorist "leaves the given [...] to talk of that which is [...] fiction. The symbolist leaves the given to find what is more real." In his own writing, Lewis specified that "the attempt to read that something else through its sensible imitations, to see the archetype in the copy, is what I mean by symbolism or sacramentalism."[16]

C.G. Jung's understanding of the archetype was interesting to Lewis, if not absolutely compelling, as he commented in his paper on science fiction: "I am not sure that anyone has satisfactorily explained the keen, lasting, and solemn pleasure which such stories can give. Jung, who went furthest, seems to me to produce as his explanation one more myth which affects us in the same way as the rest. Surely the analysis of water should not itself be wet?"[17] Of course Lewis greatly admired mythology, and his conversion to Christianity was, for him, very much about accepting that "the story of Christ is simply a true myth: a myth working on us in the same way as the others, but with this tremendous difference that *it really happened.*"[18]

He found the images in "Pagan" stories to be evidence of God working with what "He found there."[19] Readers may thus understand the emphasis and importance that Lewis placed on the "image" as what he "found" and as the starting point of all of his stories. Similarly, if, on a few occasions, some of Patterson's readers find the perspectives offered on the gender-specific aspects of archetypes and marriage a little old-fashioned, they might recall the recentness and changeability of modern perceptions related to these matters and that, like many literary critics, Patterson always begins with the text and what there is to be found in it. She shares her discoveries, particularly about Lewis's debt to biblical narrative, in thoughtful, in-depth, and beautifully written papers. Her explorations of other subjects and themes such as anti-semitism, environmentalism, evil, feminism, and Tarot, in the work of George MacDonald, Dorothy Sayers, and Charles Williams, are equally intriguing.

Her scholarly goals—unfortunately, in my opinion—never extended to the treatment of Lewis's work or the bible as sources for the tropes and conventions of more contemporary examples of fantasy and science-fiction genres, or the ease with which archetypes become stereotypes and stereotypes become the basis for misogynistic fantasy fiction. The essential aspects of Jane's character and story are certainly all too familiar today, as they are endlessly repeated and caricatured in today's novels, films, and television shows: she is the independent woman who must be tortured and burdened by associates with a widely exaggerated concern for her failure to procreate in a timely fashion:

> "Sir," said Merlin, "know well that she has done in Logres a thing of which no less sorrow shall come than came of the stroke that Balinus struck. For, Sir, it was the purpose of God that she and her lord should between them have begotten a child by whom the enemies should have been put out of logres for a thousand years."
>
> "She is but lately married," said Ransom. "The child may yet be born."
>
> "Sir," said Merlin, "be assured that the child will never be born, for the hour of its begetting is passed. Of their own will they are barren [...] For a hundred generations in two lines the begetting of this child was prepared; and unless God

> should rip up the work of time, such seed, and such an hour, in such a land, shall never be again."
>
> "Enough said," answered Ransom. "The woman perceives that we are speaking of her."
>
> "It would be great charity," said Merlin, "if you gave order that her head should be cut from her shoulders; for it is a weariness to look at her." (THS 275-76; ch. 13)

Jane ultimately relinquishes her pre-marital plans for her life entirely, and gives herself over to the demands of a heterosexual relationship, conceived of in the most conventional of terms. Patterson occasionally shows her awareness of the imperfections in Lewis's characters and plot developments—these may or may not coincide with the flaws perceived by her readers—but the definitions and implications of genre and cultural stereotyping obviously paled for her in comparison with the rich reverberations of biblical narratives in Lewis's fiction.

Further to the archetype (not the stereotype) in particular, rather than the image in general, Lewis acknowledged that "for Jung, fairy tale liberates the archetypes which dwell in the collective unconscious, and when we read a good fairy tale we are obeying the old precept, 'know thyself.'"[20] While Lewis might not have agreed with all of Jung's theory, he thought enough of it to suggest adding to it such non-human beings as talking animals for their power to convey "psychology, types of character, more briefly than novelistic presentation and to readers whom novelistic presentation could not yet reach. Consider Mr Badger in *The Wind in the Willows* [...]."[21] Lewis also specifically identified the image of God "as a grave old king with a long beard" as "a Jungian archetype [that] links God with all the wise old kings in the fairy-tales, with prophets, sages, magicians. Though it is (formally) the picture of a man, it suggests something more than humanity. At the very least it gets in the idea of something older than yourself, something that knows more, something you can't fathom."[22]

In December of 1938, Lewis responded to a fan letter: "I like the whole inter-planetary idea as a mythology and simply wished to conquer for my own (Christian) point of view what has always hitherto been used by the opposite side. I think Wells's *First Men in the Moon* the best of the sort I have read [...]"[23] Later, in 1944, he wrote that "The real father of my planet books is David Lindsay's *Voyage to*

Arcturus"; this was because it gave him "the idea that the 'scientific-tion' appeal could be combined with the 'supernatural' appeal."[24] Certainly, Lewis had no second thoughts about writing fantasy and science fiction, as opposed to a more "realist" fiction, as he believed that "Good stories often introduce the marvelous or supernatural,"[25] and admired its effects in H.G. Wells's *First Men on the Moon* and *War of the Worlds*,[26] and Walter Miller's *Canticle for Leibowitz*, as well as in Lindsay's novel, and others.[27] With regard to children's stories, which have an entirely "local and accidental" association with fairy tales and fantasy, he thought Tolkien's essay "the most important contribution to the subject that anyone has yet made."[28] He denied deliberately choosing fiction for didactic purposes, describing such assertions as "pure moonshine,"[29] and thought "that a book worth reading only in childhood is not worth reading even then."[30]

Although Lewis regarded much of the theology people later found in his stories to be of their own invention, he must have been pleased when readers of *Out of the Silent Planet*, such as the one Dorothy Sayers wrote to him about in 1953, recognized the Christian story it contained: "He said it was a most wonderful experience, as though two entirely different worlds had suddenly come into focus together, like a stereoscope, and it's a thing he can never forget."[31] Patterson's papers work on Lewis's fiction in a manner that is also much like a stereoscope, adding dimensions to the experience of reading that the reader—whether Lewis's work is new or familiar to them, whether his biblical sources are unfamiliar or already known to them—might have otherwise passed by without even knowing they existed.

——Emily E. Auger

Notes

[1] Nancy-Lou Patterson, "Ransoming the Wasteland: Arthurian Themes in C.S. Lewis's Interplanetary Trilogy, Part I," *The Lamp-Post of the Southern California C.S. Lewis Society* 8.2 (November 1984): 16. This statement was taken from the draft Patterson prepared for a proposed anthology on C.S. Lewis's fiction, which is the version presented in the first part of the present collection.

Notes

[2] William Calin counted "more than 150 books and hundreds of articles devoted to him, in whole or in part," as well as "three scholarly journals devoted entirely to the Inklings' current in modern literature plus four semi-scholarly journals published by the most important of the C.S. Lewis societies that came into existence after the writer's death and have grown in strength and in numbers ever since." The former include "*Seven* (ceased publication after 1991), *Mythlore*, and *Inklings Jahrbuch*." The latter include *CSL: The Bulletin of the New York C.S. Lewis Society*, *The Lamp-Post of the Southern California C.S. Lewis Society*, *The Canadian C.S. Lewis Journal* [OP], and *The Chronicle of the Portland C.S. Lewis Society* [OP]." "C.S. Lewis and the Discarded Image of the Middle Ages and Renaissance," *The Twentieth-Century Humanist Critics from Spitzer to Frye* (Toronto, ON: University of Toronto Press, 2007) 85, 202. C.S. Lewis's life has been made the subject of numerous biographies and his relationship with Joy Davidman the subject of a film *Shadowlands* (1994) with Anthony Hopkins and Debra Winger in the starring roles.

[3] E.L. Risden, "Source Criticism: Background and Applications," *Tolkien and the Study of His Sources*, ed. Jason Fisher (Jefferson, NC: McFarland, 2011) 22.

[4] Risden 24.

[5] Jason Fisher, "Preface," *Tolkien and the Study of His Sources*, ed. Jason Fisher (Jefferson, NC: McFarland, 2011).

[6] Tom Shippey, "Appendix A: Tolkien's Sources: The True Tradition," *The Road to Middle-earth: How J.R.R. Tolkien Created a New Mythology, Revised and expanded edition* (Hammersmith, London: HarperCollins*Publishers, 1982*).

[7] Risden 18.

[8] Richard B. Cunningham, *C.S. Lewis, Defender of the Faith* (Philadelphia, PA: Westminster Press, 1967) 91.

[9] C.S. Lewis, "What Chaucer Really Did to [Boccaccio's] *Il Filostrato*," *Selected Literary Essays by C.S. Lewis* (Cambridge: Cambridge UP, 1969) 27-44.

[10] Patterson wrote an enthusiastic review of Paul F. Ford's *Companion to Narnia* (1980), a book which some readers might consider coming

Notes

close to achieving the goal of an "annotated Lewis." See "From Adam to Zardeenah," *Mythlore* 8.1 (1981): 31-32.

[11] Nancy-Lou Patterson, "'This Equivocal Being': The Un-Man in C.S. Lewis's *Perelandra*," *The Lamp-Post of the Southern California C.S. Lewis Society* 19.3 (Fall 1995): note 1; see notes at the end of the second part of the article 19.4 (Fall-Winter 1995-96) 18.

[12] C.S. Lewis, "On Three Ways of Writing for Children," *Of Other Worlds Essays and Stories*, ed. Walter Hooper (New York: Harcourt Brace Jovanovich, 1966) 33.

[13] C.S. Lewis, "It All Began with a Picture" *Of Other Worlds Essays and Stories*, ed. Walter Hooper (New York: Harcourt Brace Jovanovich, 1966) 42.

[14] C.S. Lewis, Kingsley Amis, and Brian Aldiss, "Unreal Estates," *Of Other Worlds Essays and Stories*, ed. Walter Hooper (New York: Harcourt Brace Jovanovich, 1966) 87. See also Roger Lancelyn Green and Walter Hooper, *C.S. Lewis A Biography* (London: St. James's Place, 1974) 162-66.

[15] C.S. Lewis, *The Allegory of Love: A Study in Medieval Tradition* (1936; Oxford UP, 1967) 46-47.

[16] C.S. Lewis, *The Allegory of Love* 46.

[17] C.S. Lewis, "On Science Fiction," *Of Other Worlds Essays and Stories*, ed. Walter Hooper (New York: Harcourt Brace Jovanovich, 1966) 71. Jung also had a moment in the 1930s at which he recognized that the roots of his work lay in esoteric Christianity. See Gerhard Wehr, "C.G. Jung in the Context of Christian Esotericism and Cultural History," *Modern Esoteric Spirituality*, eds. Antoine Faivre and Jacob Needleman (New York: Crossroad, 1992) 386-87.

[18] Green and Hooper 118.

[19] Green and Hooper 118.

[20] Lewis, "On Three Ways of Writing for Children" 27.

[21] Lewis, "On Three Ways of Writing for Children" 27.

[22] C.S. Lewis, *A Grief Observed* (New York: Seabury Press, 1961) 27.

[23] Green and Hooper 163. He also wrote in this letter that Olaf Stapledon's *Last and First Men* (1931) was one of the inspirations for *Out of the Silent Planet* because it is one of those with "the desperately immoral outlook which I try to pillory in Weston" 163.

Notes

[24] Green and Hooper 164.

[25] C.S. Lewis, "On Stories," *Of Other Worlds Essays and Stories*, ed. Walter Hooper (New York: Harcourt Brace Jovanovich, 1966) 13.

[26] C.S. Lewis, "On Stories" 9, 11.

[27] C.S. Lewis, "On Science Fiction" 88-89.

[28] C.S. Lewis "On Three Ways of Writing for Children," *Of Other Worlds Essays and Stories*, ed. Walter Hooper (New York: Harcourt Brace Jovanovich, 1966) 26. See also J.R.R. Tolkien, "On Fairy-stories" (1947), *The Tolkien Reader* (New York: Balantine, 1966) 33-99.

[29] C.S. Lewis, "Sometimes Fairy Stories May Say Best What's To Be Said," *Of Other Worlds Essays and Stories*, ed. Walter Hooper (New York: Harcourt Brace Jovanovich, 1966) 36. See also, "Unreal Estates" 87.

[30] C.S. Lewis, "Sometimes Fairy Stories" 38.

[31] Green and Hooper 165.

Editorial Notes

In finalizing this collection I have followed Nancy-Lou Patterson's original anthology design for Volume I with regard to general content, organization, and thematic emphasis. I added later papers to the sections they obviously belong in, and altered some paper and section titles to eliminate repetition and improve clarity in the context of the updated collection. I chose the epigraphs from the original papers, from Patterson's revisions to those papers, and from the citations within the papers. The papers included in Volume II have been organized according to theme and subject matter. I added an abstract and a credit paragraph at the beginning of each paper.

I edited the previously published papers in Volume I in general accordance with the revisions Patterson herself worked on with only a few exceptions. I removed or revised a few statements of faith to improve the uniformity of the scholarly authorial "voice," which varied slightly according to the original publishing venue, to satisfy my own scholarly expectations as well as those of the reviewers and future readers. I restored some of the sections included in the published "Anti-Babels" that were edited out of the archive draft of "The Unfathomable Feminine Principle," either to the main text or the notes; but otherwise this paper follows Patterson's more recent work on the subject. I retitled that paper "Archetypes of the Feminine" in recognition of the restored content and to allow "The Unfathomable Feminine" to stand, as it appropriately does, as the concluding section title.

The other changes or corrections that I made were minor or of a technical nature. Among those worth noting are minor alterations to introductions and conclusions, including the removal of some extended and overly discursive paragraphs, as well as some that became redundant in the context of the collection; and slight revisions necessitated by the treatment here of papers originally published in parts as continuous essays. I added a few citations from the novels to support and clarify Patterson's arguments, as in the explanation of the "bent one" in "Thesis, Antithesis, Synthesis." I also changed the various references to C.S. Lewis's Trilogy as the Cosmic, Interplanetary, Ransom, and Space Trilogy to a uniform "Space Trilogy" or just plain

Trilogy.[1] I changed the various British, American, and Canadian English patterns applied in the papers in accordance with their original publishing venues to a uniform American English. I updated the citations to C.S. Lewis's fiction to the matching print and ebook (kindle) editions. There is currently—at the time of my writing of this preface—only one complete Space Trilogy matching print and ebook set and it is in British English; the only complete Chronicles of Narnia matching print and ebook set has been Americanized. I adjusted the quotations in Patterson's papers so that they are consistent with these volumes.

Wherever possible, I checked quotations and sources, with the exception of the Bibles and dictionaries, which have been left as Patterson gave them with her notes regarding the versions and editions used. The software for checking sources in ebooks is very good, but I did find that rechecking for a phrase sometimes resulted in different page numbers (by a variation of only one page), depending on which part of the quotation I put in the query box and whether or not the passage extended over two pages. I hope these or other discrepancies in source editions are not problematic for readers; the task of rechecking all of Patterson's references to the novels in particular, which she used in various editions, would have been more or less impossible without the ebook software. In the few instances where corrections to other citations and sources were required and editions were in doubt, I updated the edition or added citations to that which was available.

By way of acknowledgements, I want to thank my co-editor Janet Brennan Croft, editor of *Mythlore*: without her interest in Patterson's work and generous contributions this collection would simply never have come to publication. E Palmer Patterson and his daughters Fanny, Melanie, and Samantha have also been very supportive and generous with their time and interest. In addition, the Special Collections Librarians at the University of Waterloo (Waterloo, Ontario, Canada) provided access to the relevant papers, and all of the librarians with whom I came in contact at the Universities of Guelph, Waterloo, and Sir Wilfrid Laurier were extraordinarily helpful and interested in supporting this project. And last, but by no means least, I am very glad my nephew Mathew just happened to be available to brainstorm some pre-intel computer software into service when it was needed.

Notes

[1] The British collection is titled *The Cosmic Trilogy*. C.S. Lewis himself, however, frequently referred to the collection as the "Ransom Trilogy." See, for example, some of his letters in *The Collected Letters of C.S. Lewis*, including two to Sister Penelope. On September 6th, 1945, he wrote "Yes, I've finished another book wh. concludes the Ransom trilogy" (624); and on January 3rd, 1945, he wrote "Yes, I have written a story ... wh. concludes the Ransom trilogy" (635). The Collected Letters of C.S. Lewis Volume II: Books, Broadcasts, and the War, 1931–1949, ed. Walter Hooper (New York: HarperCollins, 2004). He also wrote to Rosamond Cruikshank on July 2nd, 1959, about "the Ransom trilogy." *The Collected Letters of C.S. Lewis, Volume III: Narnia, Cambridge and Joy 1950–1963*, ed. Walter Hooper (New York: HarperCollins, 2007) 1063.

From Here to There: Time, Travel, and Transformation

Then Aslan said, "Now make an end."
The giant threw his horn into the sea. Then he stretched out one
arm—very black it looked, and thousands of miles long—across the
sky till his hand reached the Sun. He took the Sun and squeezed it in
his hand as you would squeeze an orange.
And instantly there was total darkness.

——C.S. Lewis, *The Last Battle*

Nancy-Lou Patterson. "The Holy House of Ungit." First reproduced on the front
cover of *Mythlore* 21.4 (Winter 1997). Further reproduction prohibited.

1. Narnia and the North: The Symbolism of Northerness in the Fantasies of C.S. Lewis

Narnia impressed us as a "painted land," much like southern France.

—Group Discussion Report, *Mythprint*.[1]

Patterson considers C.S. Lewis's fascination with the north as a prelude to his conversion to Christianity. First, she documents the sources that inspired Lewis's treatment of the north in the Chronicles of Narnia: the writings of William Morris and his translation of The Volsunga Saga, *Longfellow's poem "Tegnér's Drapa," and illustrations by Arthur Rackham. She finds consistencies between this aspect of Lewis's work and the representations of northern elements and directional symbolism in shamanism and related mythologies (Finno-Ugric, Samoyed, Lapp, and Norse), in the Christian imagery and architecture of medieval Scandinavia, and in Chinese painting, as well as the writings of Charles Williams and J.R.R. Tolkien. In comparisons of Lewis's northern imagery with that in the fiction of Williams and Tolkien, she expands the discussion to include the symbolism of light and dark, and the importance of symbols as referencing a whole.*

Patterson considers the subject of northernness more briefly in "'Halfe Like a Serpent': The Green Witch in The Silver Chair." *She addresses other aspects of landscape in "The 'Jasper-Lucent Landscapes' of C.S. Lewis" and "The Green Lewis: Inklings of Environmentalism." All three papers are included in this volume.*

"Narnia and the North: The Symbolism of Northerness in the Fantasies of C.S. Lewis" was first published in Mythlore *4.2 (1976): 9-16.*

Roger Lancelyn Green and Walter Hooper (1974) tell us, in their indispensable biography of C.S. Lewis, that "When Geoffrey Bles, the publisher, received the story originally called *Narnia and the North,* he [...] disliked that title."[2] Lewis countered with several suggestions, and Bles replied, "I like best *The Horse and the Boy,* but what about the Horse and his Boy, which is a little startling."[3] Thus the title of one of the most popular volumes in Lewis's Narnian Chronicles was selected by his publisher. Apparently the titling of his books was not one of Lewis's strong points, for the above scenario recurs in Green and Hooper's account.

In most cases the published title, worn smooth by familiarity, seems the only right one, and *The Horse and His Boy* is indeed "startling." But *Narnia and the North* goes to the heart of the story, and Lewis's first choice reveals something central to his life. Corbin Scott Carnell has written extensively of *Sehnsucht,* the "troubling joy"[4] which presaged C.S. Lewis's conversion to Christianity, and devotes a number of pages in his excellent study *Bright Shadow of Reality* (1974) to Lewis's experience of "Northernness." Carnell writes, "Lewis believed that there was an erotic element in his response to 'Northernness.' But it was not a cheap or morbid eroticism." Rather, it was "the poetry of the flesh."[5] Carnell writes of Lewis:

> His interest in religion [...] was overshadowed by Northernness partly because it contained elements which his religion ought to have contained and did not. Northernness had a quality of aesthetic exaltation about it which Lewis had not found in Christianity and which he was seeking in the occult. Where religion had failed, Wagner and Norse mythology were able to awaken that strange excitement which at times he had experienced in his childhood.[6]

This excitement Carnell calls "that stab of Joy which came out of the North."[7] He finds that Lewis refers for the first time to "Northernness," "that exultant yet strangely tragic emotion,"[8] in his essay on William Morris in *Rehabilitations* (1939).[9]

Sources on the North

In that essay, Lewis defends Morris against charges of "fake medievalism." Morris's style is not florid, he says, but "consistently departs from that of modern prose in the direction of simplicity."[10] It is as Lewis attempts to account for the inexhaustible pleasures of Morris that he mentions northernness: "I knew one who could come no nearer to an explanation of Morris's charms than to repeat, 'It's the Northernness—the Northernness.'"[11] In expanding on this theme of Morris's simplicity of style, Lewis remarks: "Other stories have scenery: his have geography," and explains, "the effect is at first very pale

4

and cold, but also very fresh and spacious. We begin to relish what my friend called the 'Northernness'. No mountains in literature are as far away as distant mountains in Morris."[12] These remarks of Lewis come very close to the heart of the meaning which he attaches to the idea of the north and northernness.

It is no accident that Narnia and northernness are associated by Lewis: in his seven novels about Narnia the north is one of the basic elements in the symbolic structure. Interestingly, the same structure appears, with less emphasis, in the writings of J.R.R. Tolkien and Charles Williams. The northernness of Narnia is so essential that when I read in the Mythopoeic Society Group Discussion Report quoted in my epigraph, that someone could think of Narnia as being located in the south, I was moved to begin the research for this present essay. As Lewis began his lifetime of references to this theme with an essay on William Morris, I will begin at the same place. Morris wrote in his Preface to his translation of *The Volsunga Saga,* "'This is the great Story of the North', [...] 'which should be to all our race what the Tale of Troy was to the Greeks'."[13] We must remind ourselves that the British use the word "race" to mean something like what North Americans mean by "nationality" rather than in a strict genetic sense, and with the further suggestion of language as a determining factor. When my husband and I moved to Canada we were required to state our "race." We called ourselves "Caucasian," but this was not acceptable. My husband was recorded, at the officer's insistence, as "Scottish" because his last name is Patterson; I was called "German" because my maiden name was Gellermann, and our two children at that time were Scottish because they have their father's name. It was this sort of "race" that Morris had in mind. Nevertheless there is a certain "racial" element in these matters, as we shall see.

Morris was working on his translations of the Sagas—from the Icelandic—during the period when his marriage to his wife Jane, a magnificently beautiful woman who was a major prototype of the Pre-Raphaelite form of beauty, was strained and she was being pursued by his close friend Dante Gabriel Rossetti. Much of his pain at this Arthur–Guinevere–Lancelot situation he poured into his translations. At the worst point—when Mrs. Morris and Rossetti moved together into the new house, Kelmscott, which Morris had just purchased, Morris made a long-awaited trip to Iceland to see for himself the places where the events of the poems and stories of the Sagas had occurred. He departed early in July of 1871 on the journey which Philip Henderson (in his biography of Morris) calls "both a catharsis and an initiation into a new world."[14] Morris kept a journal of his experiences, which he found overwhelming, and wrote of his first view of the island:

> [...] a terrible shore indeed: a great mass of dark grey mountains worked into pyramids and shelves, looking as if they had been built and half-ruined; they were striped with snow high up, and wreaths of cloud dragged across them here and there, and above them were two peaks and a jagged ridge of pure white snow [...][15]

As each new prospect greeted him in his travels around Iceland, Morris had a similar reaction. On 22 July 1871, he wrote, "[...] surely it was what [I] 'came out for to see,' and yet for the moment I felt cowed, and as if I should never get back again: yet with that came a feeling of exultation too [...]"[16] When he returned to England, he wrote to a friend, "I am going to try to get to Iceland next year, hard as it will be to drag myself away from two or three people in England: but I know there will be a kind of rest in it, let alone the help it will bring me from physical reasons. I know clearer now perhaps than then what a blessing and a help last year's journey was to me; what horrors it saved me from."[17] The hell from which the purgatory of Iceland had saved him was of course the need to witness the love of Rossetti for Jane Morris. But what especially concerns us is the "feeling of exultation" in the face of the overpowering and desolate landscapes of the quintessential Northern Land.

Marghanita Laski has thrown light on this exultation in her *Ecstasy, A Study of Some Sacred and Religious Experiences* (1961). She compares numerous accounts of the ecstasies which she has recorded and studied: of special pertinence here are the "ecstasies of desolation." She describes one subject who "felt 'overpowered' by the mountains, as if 'they would come crashing down to crush me'," and another subject who "speaks of 'two enormous menacing peaks' that towered above her [...]"[18] Again, she reports that the subject "says the mountains looked dark and unfriendly," and that another subject "speaks of blinding rain, swirling mist."[19] She observes in discussing many similar examples, "I have the impression that in some cases feelings of desolation are themselves taken as indicating the presence of deity."[20] Laski herself does not believe that deity is actually present, and Morris's exultation (he calls it that, and not "exaltation") probably contained, like those of Lewis which Carnell calls "erotic," an element of sexual sublimation.

We must now see for ourselves what Lewis has written about his own first approach to these northern shores. These moments have been both quoted and paraphrased elsewhere (especially by Carnell) but for the sake of accuracy I will report the two most famous passages in full. I hope this will explain the error Carnell makes in referring to Longfellow's poem, "Tegnér's Drapa," as "Tegner's *Drapa,"* as if it were a translation by Longfellow of a work called *Drapa* by Tegnér, rather than the poetic encomium of Tegnér's death which Longfellow actually wrote.

Lewis had apparently acquired a book of Longfellow's poems: a number of editions were published in the late nineteenth century. The first work he refers to is a long sequence of poems in a number of different styles about the conversion of the north from the old Norse religion to Christianity: the series of poems is called *The Saga of King Olaf.* The Christian elements in this poem cycle and in the poem "Tegnér's Drapa" do not seem to have impressed any of the commentators on Lewis's experience, and probably Lewis himself was not caught so much by the Christian elements as by the evocations of the Norse religion which had gone before. Nonetheless, in view of what came of Lewis's intuitions of northernness—I mean his ultimate conversion to Christianity as an adult—which is the whole point of his including them and nearly everything else in *Surprised by Joy,* I think the point ought to be made. At any rate, Lewis wrote:

> I had become fond of Longfellow's *Saga* of *King Olaf* [...] But then, and quite different from such pleasures, and like a voice from far more distant regions, there came a moment when I idly turned the pages of the book and found the unrhymed translation of Tegner's Drapa, and read
>
> > I heard a voice that cried,
> > Balder the beautiful
> > Is dead, is dead—

> I knew nothing about Balder; but instantly I was uplifted into huge regions of northern sky. I desired with almost sickening intensity something never to be described (except that it is cold, spacious, severe, pale, and remote).[21]

One should note that Lewis refers to Longfellow's poem here as a "translation," so Carnell is merely following him. The second passage describes Lewis's second encounter with northernness:

> Someone must have left in the schoolroom a literary periodical: the *Bookman,* perhaps, or the *Times Literary Supplement.* My eye fell upon a headline and a picture, carelessly, expecting nothing. A moment later, as the poet says, "The sky had turned round."
>
> What I had read was the words *Siegfried and* the *Twilight* of *the Gods.* What I had seen was one of Arthur Rackham's illustrations to that volume. I had never heard of Wagner, nor of Siegfried. I thought the Twilight of the Gods meant the twilight in which the gods lived. How did I know, at once and beyond question, that this was no Celtic, or silvan, or terrestrial twilight? But so it was. Pure "Northernness" engulfed me: a vision of huge, clear spaces hanging above the Atlantic in the endless twilight of Northern summer, remoteness, severity [...] and almost at the same moment I knew that I had met this before, long, long ago (it hardly seems longer now) in *Tegner's Drapa,* that Siegfried (whatever it might be) belonged to the same world as Balder and the sunward-sailing cranes.[22]

In view of Lewis's later statement that his fantasies always started with his seeing pictures in his mind, it might be interesting to search the above mentioned publications to find the Rackham picture that played so powerful a role in Lewis's life. It isn't possible, from his account quoted above, to determine exactly which of Rackham's famous Ring paintings it was. Anyway, a motif from "Tegnér's Drapa" to which Lewis refers—"the sunward-sailing cranes"—is mentioned, and as Lewis does not quote it, I shall. It is not a very long poem but too long to give in full here. I will give the first two verses to suggest its descriptive powers.

> I heard a voice, that cried,
> "Balder the Beautiful
> Is dead, is dead!"
> And through the misty air
> Passed like the mournful cry
> Of sunward-sailing cranes.
>
> I saw the pallid corpse
> Of the dead sun
> Borne through the Northern sky.
> Blasts from Niffelheim
> Lifted the sheeted mists
> Around him as he passed.

The poem describes the death of Balder, the end of the age of the Gods, and the appearance of a new earth, which the poet associates with Christ's coming. The last verse, then, advises rather primly,

> Sing no more,
> O ye bards of the North,
> Of Vikings and of Jaris!
> Of the days of Eld
> Preserve the freedom only,
> Not the deeds of blood!

Longfellow could not foresee what "deeds of blood" were to be done in the name of Odin by Adolf Hitler when this whole range of thematic material became at least temporarily besmirched. But the poet obviously saw that the "days of Eld" could be given alternative readings.

Bishop Tegnér was a Swedish poet of whom Longfellow first became aware in 1828.[23] But it was not until 1835 during the first week of his arrival in Sweden that he read the actual poems and began, with his embryonic Swedish, to attempt translations. He traveled on to Holland and read *Frithiof's Saga* in translation, expressing in his Journal disapproval of the translator's style. Longfellow published a review (1837), which included some fragments of translation of his own.[24] These were praised by Tegnér himself. The Bishop wrote: "I have not been fully satisfied with anyone, except the Herr Professor's."[25] This encouraged Longfellow to go on with the project and his translations are considered among the finest in English. Andre Hilen said in 1947, "They still reveal a greater technical skill than possessed by any of the now numerous English translators."[26]

Longfellow published his poem "Tegnér's Drapa" ("Drapa" means ecomium or eulogy), which was originally entitled "Tegnér's Death,"[27] in 1846 when Tegnér died. He had made a note—"Balder the Beautiful is dead. A Monody on Bishop Tegnér"—in his "Book of Suggestions," and when the work was completed he referred to it in his Journal as "a mystic poem on Tegnér's death, in the spirit of the old Norse Poetry."[28] A major motif of the poem is expressed in this verse:

> The law of force is dead!
> The law of love prevails.
> Thor the thunderer,
> Shall rule the earth no more,
> No more, with threats,
> Challenge the meek Christ.

This concern with the conflict of Thor and Odin with Christ was fully expressed in Longfellow's poem cycle, *The Saga of King Olaf,* which Lewis mentions reading, above.

The North in Narnia

We have Lewis's own mention of the sunward-sailing cranes to show the long-lasting effects of the words of "Tegnér's Drapa." I wonder if the following passage from *The Voyage of the Dawn Treader* does not contain an expansion of this great image:

> Then something seemed to be flying at them out of the very center of the rising sun [...] They were birds, large and white, and they came by hundreds and thousands and alighted on everything. (VDT 223; ch. 14)

One bird places "something in its beak that looked like a little fruit, unless it was a little live coal" in the mouth of Ramandu the Star, and the others consume the splendid feast laid out on the Stone Table. Afterwards, "These birds rose from their meal in their thousands and hundreds," and "took their flight back to the rising sun" (VDT 224; ch. 14).

Having turned to the Narnian Chronicles for examples of the motif of Northernness, we will now examine the exact passages containing the phrase from which the title of this paper is taken. The book is *The Horse and His Boy,* as we have seen. When Bree, the Talking Horse, and his young companion, the unwilling slave boy Shasta, set off on their escape from bondage in Calormen, Bree instructs him in riding: "Don't look at the ground. If you think you're going to fall just grip harder and sit up straighter. Ready? Now: for Narnia and the North" (HB 18; ch. 1).

It proves to be a very long trip, and it is not until he is high up in the capital of Calormen, Tashbaan, that Shasta is able to gaze across the wide desert to catch a first glimpse of his goal (the mountains bordering Archenland, to the north of which Narnia lies); he looks down the northern slope of Tashbaan, past the northern wall, the river, and its gardens:

> But beyond that again there was something he had never seen the like of—a great yellowish-gray thing, flat as a calm sea, and stretching for miles. On the far side of it were huge blue things, lumpy but with jagged edges, and some of them with white tops. "The desert! the mountains!" thought Shasta. (HB 82; ch. 6)

He recognizes the scene because while in Tashbaan he has been mistaken by a group of Narnians for Prince Corin, and has over-heard Sallowpad the Raven, who advises that in order to get to Archenland and warn the occupants of Anvard, the guardian castle, that Prince Rabadash of Tashbaan is on his way to surprise them with an attack, someone should cross the desert by a "Western way," riding northwest towards Mount Pire, which will be known by its double peak.

While still mistaken for Prince Corin, Shasta is told by a Narnian faun—it is the very Mr. Tumnus who first meets Lucy in Narnia in *The Lion, the Witch and the* Wardrobe—to get some sleep before boarding the Narnian ship Splendour Hyaline: "I'll call you in plenty of time to get on board. And then, Home. Narnia and the North!" (HB 76; ch. 5). Shasta manages to slip away, and makes his way down the northern slopes of Tashbaan and out of the gate. There he must wait by the menacing tombs of ancient Calormene rulers until Aravis comes. His night alone there is made less terrible by the presence of a cat whom he later learns is Aslan in disguise. "There it sat down bolt upright with its tail curled round its feet and its face set to-wards the desert and toward Narnia and the North, as still as if were watching for some enemy" (HB 87; ch. 6).

Shasta is not the only one to have difficulties passing through Tashbaan; as Bree had exclaimed on first seeing the great city: "But I wish we were safely through it and out at the other side. Narnia and the North!" (HB 52; ch. 4). Aravis must make her own way through, and at one point she and Bree plan their escape together: "'And then, Narnia and the North!' whispered Bree" (HB 104; ch. 7). While await-ing her arrival, Shasta gazes across the desert to his goal, the moun-tains bordering Archenland, to the north of which, Narnia lies wait-ing:

> When he looked a little left and west, so that the sun was not in his eyes, he could see the mountains on the far side of the desert, so sharp and clear that they looked only a stone's throw away. He particularly noticed one blue height that divided into two peaks at the top and decided that it must be Mount Pire. (HB 90; ch. 6)

Clearly, these are to be mountains "as far away as distant mountains in Morris," and so they prove to be, in an exhausting ride across the desert. When at last the young Calormene Tarkheena Aravis arrives at the tombs with Hwin and Bree, they all set off across the desert with Mount Pire as their goal. Again, Bree takes charge: "Now. Are you ready, Hwin? Off we go. Narnia and the North!" (HB 127; ch. 9).

As they travel, "the double peak of Mount Pire, far ahead, flashed in the sunlight" (HB 129; ch. 9). Their terrible trip across the desert draws to a close when they arrive at a spot, predicted by the Raven and overheard by Shasta, where "a little cataract of water poured into a broad pool" (HB 133; ch. 9). They begin to travel up "the valley itself, with its brown, cool river, and grass and moss and wildflowers and rhododendrons" (HB 137; ch. 9). Their path leads them up among the mountains:

> To the right there were rocky pinnacles, one or two of them with snow clinging to the ledges. To the left, pine-clad slopes, frowning cliffs, narrow gorges, and blue peaks stretched away as far as the eye could reach. (HB 138; ch. 10)

This is the very landscape of Marghanita Laski's subjects' desolation ecstasies; and one may compare it with William Morris's first view of Iceland. The account culminates with a paean by Bree:

> "Broo-hoo-hoo, the North, the green North!" neighed Bree: and certainly the lower hills looked greener and fresher than anything that Aravis and Shasta, with their southern-bred eyes, had ever imagined. (HB 139; ch. 10)

In this passage the full symbolism of the north (and its opposing south) is suggested by Lewis, and it is to be among these mountains that Shasta encounters "the presence of deity" when he first knowingly meets Aslan. He has been sent on ahead, after the arrival of the four travelers in the mandelic enclosure of the Hermit of the Southern March, to find King Lune and warn him. This done, he has followed the riders to the rescue of Anvard, but becomes lost in the mountain fastness.

After a while he becomes aware of a companion in the darkness. "It darted into his mind that he had heard long ago that there were giants in these Northern countries" (HB 162; ch. 11). But the Thing beside him proves to be neither a giant nor a ghost. It is in fact a Lion, one who has already played many roles in Shasta's life. "Luckily Shasta had lived all his life too far south in Calormen to have heard the tales that were whispered in Tashbaan about a dreadful Narnian demon that appeared in the form of a lion" (HB 166; ch. 11). He does not know whom he is meeting, but "after one glance at the Lion's face he slipped out of the saddle and fell at its feet. He couldn't say anything but then he didn't want to say anything, and he knew he needn't say anything" (HB 166; ch. 11)

When his meeting with Aslan is over, Shasta finds that he is actually in Narnia, and that there lies at his feet a footprint left by the Lion. "As he looked at it, water had already filled the bottom of it. Soon it was full to the brim, and then overflowing, and a little stream was running downhill, past him, over the grass" (HB 167; ch. 12). He drinks, and rises refreshed, descending into the heart of Narnia where he meets a group of native Narnians, talking animals who live in the forest far from the doings of the court. There he eats his first real Narnian meal, bacon and eggs and mushrooms fried together by Duffle the Dwarf. Soon after, he is reunited with the Narnian court. He finds himself to be Prince Cor, brother of Prince Corin, and son of King Lune. He is soon after this to find that he is the future occupant of the throne of Archenland.

Bree, meanwhile, makes his own preparation to enter the north, an event he has long awaited. He takes a last roll in the grass, certain that such indignities are not indulged in by the talking Beasts of which he is now to become merely one more. "'Now I'm ready,' he said in a voice of profound gloom. 'Lead on, Prince Cor, Narnia and the North'" (HB 210; ch. 14). Shasta, or Prince Cor as we must now call him, comes to his home at last: "The next turn of the road brought them out from among the trees and there, across green lawns, sheltered from the north wind by the high wooded ridge at its back, they saw the castle of Anvard. It was very old and built of a warm, reddish-brown stone" (HB 180; ch. 15). He has come into the inheritance that Aslan has prepared for him. As Shasta said, "I'm a Narnian, I believe; something Northern anyway" (HB 80; ch. 5).

The North in World Culture

A popular dictionary defines "North" as "that one of the four Cardinal points of the compass which lies in the plane of the true meridian, and on the left hand of a person facing due east; the direction opposite south."[29] The definition of "south" is much more succinct: it is "the cardinal point directly opposite the north." It will be noted that north and south are here referred to their place on the compass. Something of the complexity and richness of meaning implied by this basic significance of directions is discussed by J.E. Cirlot in *A Dictionary of Symbols* (1962):

> The notion of orientation, taken in conjunction with the concept of space as a three-dimensional whole, plays a powerful part in the symbolic organization of space. The human anatomy itself, with its quasi-rectangular, symmetrical and bilateral pattern, in distinguishing between the front and back thereby designates two corresponding points of orientation. The natural position of the arms and shoulders completes this quadrangular scheme—a symbolic pattern which interpreted according to strictly anthropological and empirical criteria, would perhaps provide us with the key to the original conception of orientation as quaternary on the surface but septenary

three-dimensionally (embracing north, south, east and west, together with the zenith, the nadir, and the centre).[30]

North is then the first or primary direction, the one to which all others are related. It is in the position of the head, perhaps, I might suggest, actually of the superbrain or spiritual mind that in images of the Buddha protrudes from the top of his head. Thus, Cirlot tells us, "The Etruscans located the abode of gods in the north, and hence their soothsayers, when about to speak, would turn to face the south—that is, they would take up a position which identified them, ideologically, with the gods. To face the north is to pose a question."[31] Aslan in the form of a cat sits with his back toward Calormen, for he does not speak to them. Nevertheless, Shasta finds his back comfortingly warm.

A relationship of prophecy with the north is seen as a motif in shamanism, according to Mircea Eliade (1970). Eliade cites a Yakut legend, which "relates that shamans are born in the north. There a giant fir grows, with nests in its branches."[32] A great female eagle lays eggs there, and shaman souls are hatched, cut up, and reborn. Eliade explains:

> In all these examples we find the central theme of an initiation ceremony: dismemberment of the neophyte's body and renewal of his organs; ritual death followed by resurrection. We may also note the motif of the giant bird that hatches shamans in the branches of the World Tree; it has wide application in North Asian mythologies, especially in shamanic mythology.[33]

We may note that Henderson describes William Morris's trip to Iceland as an initiation, and that Shasta, after testing, becomes a new person, Prince Cor, when he finally arrives in the north. It is the particular trait of the shaman to be able, because of his or her initiation (and origin) to move between this world and the other world, the world of ordinary and the world of non-ordinary reality, to gain knowledge and to perform wonders. Thus, Eliade says:

> The Altaians conceive the entrance to the underworld as a "smoke hole" [like the hole at the top of a tipi] of the earth, located, of course, at the "Center" (situated, according to the myths of Central Asia, in the North, which corresponds to the Center of the Sky; for, as we know, the "North" is assimilated

to the "Center" through the whole Asian area, from India to Siberia).[34]

The shaman rises up the house pole to the roof hole—from the underworld to the overworld—which is associated with the North Star, so it is not for nothing that the Earth has "poles"! One is reminded that Lewis wrote in *The Last Battle,* "All the great northern stars were burning above the treetops. The North-Star of that world is called Spear-Head: it is brighter than out Pole Star" (LB 68; ch. 6).

In Finno-Ugric mythology (which has elements of shamanism) "there is said to be a monster who has devoured the sun or moon and these stars of light must be won back from him. This monster is often conceived as a giant, an incarnation of the North, land of darkness and cold."[35] We have already seen that Shasta fears to meet a giant in the north, and that the Calormenes of Tashbaan repeated rumors of a Narnian demon. In *The Silver Chair*[36] when Jill encounters Aslan in His own country, he tells her, "I have swallowed up girls and boys, women and men, kings and emperors, cities and realms" (SC 22; ch. 2). In *The Last Battle,* when Narnia comes to an end:

> [T]hey saw another patch where there were no stars: and the patch rose up higher and higher and became the shape of a man, the hugest of all giants. [...] He must be on the high moorlands that stretch away to the North beyond the River Shribble. [...] once long ago, in the deep caves beneath these moors, they had seen a great giant asleep and been told that his name was Father Time [...] (LB 171; ch. 14)

The giant winds a great horn, causing all the Stars to leap down from the sky.

> Then Aslan said, "Now make an end."
> The giant threw his horn into the sea. Then he stretched out one arm—very black it looked, and thousands of miles long—across the sky till his hand reached the Sun. He took the Sun and squeezed it in his hand as you would squeeze an orange. And instantly there was total darkness. (LB 180; ch. 14)

The giant, who has lain beneath "The Wild Waste Lands of the North" until the last hour of Narnia, thus does Aslan's bidding.

In another myth-cycle, this northern deity of "the land of dark and cold" possesses the *sampo*, a "talisman," which is "the column supporting the universe." These objects among the Samoyeds and Lapps "are generally situated on heights, even on mountains. Otherwise the cult took place in sacred woods containing the Tree of Life, which may have been a symbol for the column supporting the firmament."[37] I would suggest, in line with my Yogic notion of the north as located at the top of the head, that this column is not only a house pole, a universe-column, and a world tree, but the human backbone.

Readers who are familiar with Norse mythology will have begun to see a suggestion of shamanic origin for some of the elements in the great Eddaic stories. H.R.E. Davidson in *Gods and Myths of Northern Europe* (1964) describes the universe as the Eddas conceived it: "In the beginning there were two regions: Muspell in the south, full of brightness and fire; and a world of snow and ice in the north."[38] From this "realm of fire, the heat from which helped in the creation of the world, the sons of Muspell ride out against the gods at Ragnarok."[39] *Ragnarok* is the word usually translated as "Twilight of the Gods," to which Lewis refers. The "sons of Muspell" were followers of Surt, whose name is associated in Iceland with "the gloomy and impressive caverns of the volcanic region,"[40] and Davidson makes it her suggestion that Ragnarok, with its battle of ice and fire which destroys the earth, may be related to Icelandic volcanic eruptions in an icy Sea. Surt is then the southern giant.

This dichotomy of hot and cold is found in the Bible—the poets who actually wrote down the poems of the *Elder Edda* were Christians—in Job 37.9: "Out of the south cometh the whirlwind; and cold out of the north." And in Isaiah 21.1 (perhaps as a source of Lewis's desert in *The Horse and His Boy*): "As whirlwinds in the south pass through; so it cometh from the desert, from a terrible land." It is interesting to note that in the great Stave Churches of Norway, the place usually taken by the Old Testament in Christian art is taken by images from the Dragon Myth and the Sigurd Saga.[41] "Christianity brought not only a new faith but also the challenge: change your way of thinking! […] Transform revenge into forgiving love!"[42] Dan Lindholm (1969) concludes, "This was the state of affairs at the time of the arrival of Christianity. A reminder of this, of the dragon which must always be conquered anew, was there for everyone who entered the doorway of a Stave church."[43] Most of these churches were built during the twelfth century, and provide us with concrete evidence to match with that of the Sagas, that Christianity was welcomed and naturalized in the north.

To continue with our discussion of the meaning of the south, which must be understood in order to gain a complete grasp upon the meaning of its opposite, the north, we may turn to the writings of Aldous Huxley. Huxley (1954) has made use of the other major association of the south, that of its role as the Antipodes (and not necessarily hot). He uses the word "antipodes" to stand for the visionary mode: in discussing Chinese painting and its ability to produce what Laski calls desolation ecstasy, he writes:

> all the rest of the vast landscape is emptiness and silence. This revelation of the wilderness, living its own life according to the laws of its own being, transports the mind towards its antipodes: for primeval Nature bears a strange resemblance to that inner world where no account is taken of our personal wishes [...][44]

He explains his use of this term:

> A man consists of what I may call an Old World of personal consciousness and, beyond a dividing sea, a series of new Worlds—the not too distant Virginias and Carolinas of the personal subconscious and the vegetative soul; the far West of the collective unconscious, with its flora of symbols, its tribes of aboriginal archetypes; and, across another, vaster ocean, at the *antipodes* of everyday consciousness, the world of Visionary Experience.[45]

It will be noted that east, west, and south are accounted for in this system: perhaps the north represents the anagogical function, the direct intuition of the divine, which comes from the very center of the human consciousness, or from above it or outside it entirely, depending upon whether one wishes to use immanence or transcendence as the mode of divine operation.

Comparisons with Charles Williams and J.R.R. Tolkien

Charles Williams and J.R.R. Tolkien also made use of north/south in their symbolic structure. In the interest of succinctness

I will turn to Robert Foster's *A Complete Guide to Middle Earth* (1971) for part of my proof.[46] Readers who have examined Tolkien's maps will notice that while the action of *The Hobbit* moves from west to east (and back again), that of *The Lord of the Rings* moves from north to south. The ring-bearer comes from the Shire, in the northwest of his world, and moves as steadily south as he can, toward the land which Sauron has darkened, to throw the Ring, appropriately, into the chasm of a volcano. The map of Middle-earth (Midgard is the part of the world tree midway between the roots in the underworld and the branches above) shows at its top a region called the "Northern Waste."[47] Foster defines this area as "the lands north of the Misty Mountains and the Ered Mithrin."[48] He also locates "Norland" as "a northern land of Middle-earth in the First Age."[49] Elsewhere he tells us that "FORODWAITH (S.: 'north–people') [were] Men of the First Age, the inhabitants of Forochel and other areas in the extreme north of Middle-earth."[50] I must admit that none of this takes us very far, but when we turn to the south, we find that "HARADWAITH (S.: 'south-folk')" refers to both the "Haradrim and the land where they lived."[51] Haradwaith was also called Harad—in reference to the land south of the River Harnen, which included a near and a far Harad. Hobbits also called the region Sunlands, as well as Sutherland and Haradwaith.[52] Haradwaith and Sutherland were thus equivalent geographically, and perhaps also linguistically," and this leads us to my point: Foster tells us of the "HARADRIM (S.: 'south-people')" that they are "the primitive and savage men of Harad." Here we come to the crux of the matter:

> The Haradrim were tall and dark-skinned, with black hair and eyes. They loved bright clothing and ornaments, and some tribes of Haradrim painted their bodies. In battle they used all weapons, and were noted for their use of Oliphaunts.[53]

He continues: "Called in Westron Southerns and Southrons. Also called the Swarthy Men (by Hobbits) and the Swertings."[54] These dark southerners may be compared, then, with the "NORTHMEN Men related to the Rohirrim and the Edain."[55] We find that the "ROHIRRIM (S.: 'horse-lord people') [...] were tall and blond, with fair faces; they lived to be about eighty [...] The Rohirrim loved their horses above all else [...] were culturally conservative."[56]

Needless to say, blond and conservative (as opposed to dark and savage) horsemen play a large role in *The Lord of the Rings*.

With this in mind, we return for a moment to the Narnian Chronicles, where we find the same color and costume symbolism associated with the north and south. The natives of the southern nation of Calormen are exemplified by the description of the Tarkaan who attempts to buy Shasta from his foster-father Arsheesh and thus precipitates his flight to the north (Bree is the Tarkaan's horse):

> His face was dark, but this did not surprise Shasta because all the people of Calormen are like that; what did surprise him was the man's beard which was dyed crimson, and curled and gleaming with scented oil. (HB 6; ch. 1)

One may compare him with the dark skinned Haradrim who "loved bright clothing and ornaments." In marked contrast to this is Shasta's first sight of the Narnians in a delegation to Tashbaan:

> [T]hey were all as fair-skinned as himself, and most of them had fair hair. And they were not dressed like men of Calormen. Most of them had legs bare to the knee. Their tunics were of fine, bright, hardy colors—woodland green, or gay yellow, or fresh blue. Instead of turbans they wore steel or silver caps, some of them set with jewels, and one with little wings on each side of it. A few were bare-headed. The swords at their sides were long and straight, not curved like Calormene scimitars. And instead of being grave and mysterious like most Calormenes, they walked with a swing and let their arms and shoulders go free, and chatted and laughed. (HB 57; ch. 4)[57]

In view of the charges of racism leveled at Lewis from time to time, we should remind ourselves that Aravis is a Calormene, and she becomes the wife of Shasta, while Emeth (whose name means "truth" in Hebrew) is a lover of Tash who learns in Aslan's country that it is Aslan who had actually accepted his devotion. The scimitars and florid language, the turban and dark skins, are derived from the Saracens, the noble adversaries of medieval literature, and stock character of the British mummer's play performed at Christmas. We can wish Lewis had not used this motif, but it is a venerable one in European literature. Anyway, a European going in a southerly direction encoun-

20

ters North Africa with its Islamic culture, so it is not surprising that with the blond Norsemen in the actual north of Europe and with the dark North Africans to the south, the color associations seem to British writers to be so obvious as to be unquestionable.

An even more southerly trek will bring the traveler south of the Sahara into black Africa, which is also Islamic in its Sudanic regions (becoming Christian, and/or traditional as one travels into the forested regions, Africa having now become one of the strongest areas of indigenized Christianity in the world). This observation brings us to the writings of Charles Williams, who uses some of these same symbols of "southernness" in his poems and novels. The first example is to be found in his prophetic *Shadows of Ecstasy* (1933), which was his first novel, written in the thirties but not published until his later books had won him acceptance. In Chapter I, "Encountering Darkness," we meet Mr. Nigel Considine, "a rich man [… who] gave a collection of African images to the anthropological school."[58]

Nigel Considine gives a lecture, in which he declares, "you may not yet sit at the feet of the natives of the Amazon or the Zambesi; […] the fakirs, the herdsmen, and the witch doctors may not enter the kingdom of man before you."[59] There is talk of "simultaneous native risings in the interior of Africa,"[60] and "pressure on Egypt,"[61] and the next chapter reveals that "something very unusual was happening in Africa."[62] The book turns upon this rising, which ultimately threatens Europe, and upon Nigel Considine, a man who has enjoyed a preternatural length of years. The gentle Zulu Prince, Inkamasi, figures in the story as Considine's adversary. He says, "I do not want to help Considine, though I long for Africa to be free."[63] In the end, he dies, but Considine dies with him. The novel concludes with a visionary passage in which the book's hero, Roger Ingram, imagines Considine's body returning to life beneath the sea (into which it had been carried by submarine) while "The creatures of the deep, octopus and shark, greed and ferocity, fled before it."[64]

This last motif, the octopus of greed, suggests the later development of Williams's antipodean Empire, P'o-l'u, of which he wrote in his poem, "The Prayers of the Pope":

> even those wizards hid their eyes where some few, their chief,
> the beastliest and chilliest in blasphemy, called farther on the
> powers of P'o-l'u, on the antipodean octopods, on the slime

that had been before the time of Merlin and below the trees and seas of Broceliande.[65]

The fullest expression of the idea of P'o-l'u is found in the play, *The House of the Octopus*: Williams writes in its Preface, "The name of P'o-l'u and the title of its Emperor were taken from certain earlier poems published before the outbreak of war."[66] Thus P'o-l'u is not Japan, for "It is rather a spiritual threat than a martial dominion." The story tells of Christianized indigenes of a Pacific island threatened with invasion by the malignant Empire of P'o-l'u: "of P'o-l'u— P'o-l'u, the thick-tentacled octopus, the empire of mastery within the waters." It is a watery, voracious Hell, "where some, whom the Infinite Mercy after a week bade the monsters release, wander mindless."[67] The play concludes with the triumphant martyrdom of the Christians, in care of the Flame, the "Lingua Coeli," who is "that energy which went into the creation and was at Pentecost (as it were) redelivered in the manner of its own august covenant to the Christian Church."[68] This figure, of course, represents the Holy Spirit, who appears in a number of Williams's plays in various guises.

The region of P'o-l'u lies beneath the sea into which the roots of the forest of Broceliande extend. As C.S. Lewis explains, "Broceliande, if you follow it far enough and in a certain direction, will bring you right round the world to the 'antipodean ocean.'"[69] He explains further, "Broceliande is what most romantics are enamoured of; into it good mystics and bad mystics go: it is what you find when you step out of our ordinary mode of consciousness."[70] Lewis, one notes, already knew that Carlos Castaneda had to learn from his Yaqui shaman, about "non-ordinary reality." P'o-l'u is an aspect of it: the antipodean aspect. It is, in a polar sense, at the southernmost part of the earth, in those very antipodes to which Aldous Huxley refers, and which belongs to the same globe that bears a North Pole too. All of the southerly symbols ranged above—the noble but ferocious Calormenes of Lewis, the gaudy primitives of Tolkien, the turbulent Africans and menacing P'o-l'uans of Williams—represent not specific groups of people, but aspects of the mind of everybody. The northerners and the northern regions, including Narnia, are also part of the mind: regions of Aslan's Country.

We are all familiar with the destructive reverberations of European racism, but we must avoid projecting it backwards into an imagined past, and finding it in every piece of writing constructed on antique models. The use of color as a racist symbol is described feelingly by Frantz Fanon (1952):

> In Europe, the black man, whether physically or symbolically, represents the dark side of the personality. [...] A beautiful blond child—how much peace there is in that phrase, how much joy, and above all how much hope! No comparison with a beautiful black child: the adjectives literally don't go together.[71]

But in contrast with this, the medieval world did not use color symbolism with a racial intention. Eulalio Baltazar (1973) writes, "In terms of the Aristotelian categories of substance and accident, the color and shape and form of the body were not essential to being a man but rather were accidental, that is, nonessential. It was for this philosophic reason, it would seem, that the medieval white Christian did not make much of skin color."[72] An example of this is found in the Mummer's plays, to which I referred above. The term "Saracen" means firstly a nomad of the desert between Syria and Arabia, but by extension, a Muslim, especially as hostile to the crusaders. I have used it as a generic term. According to E.O. James (1961), "The central feature in the Mummer's play is the fight between Saint (or King) George and his adversary who is killed or wounded and then restored by the Doctor." This adversary, "Bold Slasher in the guise of Turkish Knight"[73] is thus not finally defeated, but rather goes through death and resurrection. He is dressed in a costume resembling that used by Lewis for his Calormenes. According to the interpretations of folklorists, he is the Old Year, the King (or King's Son), and, some think, originally Dionysus himself, the dying and resurrected god.[74] These exceedingly primitive motifs are found in the play performed yearly at Christmastime in rural England, and surviving separate from and beyond the medieval religious plays showing the Creation-Incarnation-Resurrection cycle and the morality plays which have their origin within the Christian liturgy. Baltazar can throw some light on the mystical significance of these motifs:

> Thus in mystical theology, darkness is a symbol not only of the negative but also and above all of the supremely positive—God. It is toward the Divine Darkness that man must

tend and away from the sub-darkness or nether darkness of ignorance, sin, evil. The great religions as we have noted earlier always symbolized God as Darkness ...

The mystical theology of Dionysus [that is, Dionysian as opposed to Apollonian] is known in the Christian tradition as negative theology.[75]

In a final extension of my Yogic model, the south lies in the region of the lower chakras—those of the bodily organs, where the passions and heats of the flesh are located, and likewise those Dionysian intuitions which represent a significant part of psychic life; but the spinal column and the kundalini path extend from those southerly regions to the northernmost, the sphere of intellect, mind, the rule of Apollo; and they are all part of the whole person: body and mind, unconscious and conscious. At their center is the divine Center. Archenland is to be ruled during Narnia's golden age by dark-skinned Aravis and fair-skinned Shasta together, for "when they were grown up they were so used to quarreling and making up again that they got married so as to go on doing it more conveniently" (HB 224; ch. 15). They represent the *hieros gamos,* or sacred marriage, of which Cirlot says, "The King and Queen together comprise the perfect image [...] of the union of heaven and earth, sun and moon, gold and silver, sulphur and mercury; and—according to Jung—they also signify the spiritual 'conjunction' that takes place when the process of individuation is complete, with the harmonious union of the unconscious and consciousness."[76] The son of Aravis and Shasta/Cor is "Ram the Great, the most famous of all the kings of Archenland" (HB 224; ch. 15).[77]

We have seen, then, that "the Northern hemisphere is regarded as that which represents light, corresponding to the positive principle *Yang;* the southern is linked with that of darkness and corresponds to *Yin.*[78] One cannot be expressed without including the other. The whole includes all aspects of human experience, and God is more than the whole of all that is. For C.S. Lewis, the way to God lay through the north yet even for him it only pointed a direction, and in others of his stories God is found beyond the planets.

Notes

[1] Chris Whitaker, "Group Discussion Report of ROKE, Baton Rouge, La. (Feb. 19 1974)," *Mythprint* 10.5 (Nov. 1974): 5.

[2] Roger Lancelyn Green and Walter Hooper, *C.S. Lewis, A Biography* (London: Collins, 1974) 245.

[3] Green and Hooper 245.

[4] Corbin Scott Carnell, *Bright Shadow of Reality: C.S. Lewis and the Feeling Intellect* (Grand Rapids, MI: William B. Eerdmans, 1974) 36.

[5] Carnell 42.

[6] Carnell 42.

[7] Carnell 47.

[8] Carnell 78.

[9] C.S. Lewis, "William Morris," *Selected Literary Essays,* ed. Walter Hooper (Cambridge: Cambridge UP, 1969) 219-31. Reprinted from C.S. Lewis, *Rehabilitations and Other Essays* (London: Oxford UP, 1939).

[10] C.S. Lewis, "William Morris" 220.

[11] C.S. Lewis, "William Morris" 219.

[12] C.S. Lewis, "William Morris" 221.

[13] Philip Henderson, *William Morris: His Life, Work and Friends* (London: Thames and Hudson, 1967) 109.

[14] Henderson, *William Morris* 119.

[15] Henderson, *William Morris* 119, entry by Morris, 13 July 1871.

[16] Henderson, *William Morris* 123.

[17] Henderson, *William Morris* 135-36.

[18] Marghanita Laski, *Ecstasy, A Study of Some Sacred and Religious Experiences* (London: The Cresset Press, 1961) 209.

[19] Laski 209-10.

[20] Laski 212.

[21] C.S. Lewis, *Surprised by Joy* (1955; New York: Harcourt, Brace, Jovanovich, 1966) 17.

[22] C.S. Lewis, *Surprised by Joy* 72.

[23] The discussion of Longfellow and Tegnér follows Andres Hilen, *Longfellow and Scandinavia, A Study of the Poet's Relationship with the Northern Languages and Literature* (New Haven, CT: Yale UP, 1947) *Yale Studies in English* 107 (Archon Books, 1970) 47-51.

Notes

[24] Henry Wadsworth Longfellow, rev. "Frithior's Saga (The Legend of Frithiof) by Esaias Tegnér," *The North American Review* 45.96 (July 1837): 149-85.

[25] Hilen 52.

[26] Hilen 53.

[27] Hilen 61.

[28] Hilen 61.

[29] *Webster's New Collegiate Dictionary* (Springfield, MA: G. and C. Merriam Co., 1956).

[30] J.E. Cirlot, *A Dictionary of Symbols,* trans. Jack Sage (New York Philosophical Library, 1962) 233.

[31] Cirlot, *A Dictionary of Symbols* 233.

[32] Mircea Eliade in *Shamanism: Archaic Techniques of Ecstasy* (NY: Bollingen Foundation, Princeton UP, 1970) 37.

[33] Eliade, *Shamanism* 38.

[34] Eliade, *Shamanism* 278-79.

[35] A Sauvageat, "Finland-Ugria: Magic Animals," *Larousse World Mythology*, ed. Pierre Grimal (London: Hamlyn, 1973) 424.

[36] "The Wild Waste Lands of the North" is the title of Chapter 5.

[37] Sauvageat 424. The *sampo* is usually understood as a mill which grinds out wealth. The rotating pole may be seen as an analogy of the vertical pole around which the universe spins.

[38] H.R.E. Davidson, *Gods and Myths of Northern Europe* (Harmondsworth, UK: Penguin, 1964) 27.

[39] Davidson, *Gods and Myths of Northern Europe* 235.

[40] Davidson, *Gods and Myths of Northern Europe* 208.

[41] Dan Lindholm, *Stave Churches in Norway* (London: Rudolf Steiner Press, 1969) 48.

[42] Lindholm 64.

[43] Lindholm 64.

[44] Aldous Huxley, *The Doors of Perception and Heaven and Hell* (1954; Harmondworth, UK: Penguin, 1959) 104.

[45] Huxley, *The Doors of Perception and Heaven and Hell* 72; Patterson's italics.

[46] Editor's note: Patterson used this earlier edition of Foster's book. I have updated the quotes, information, and page numbers to match the

Notes

revisions in his more recent *Tolkien's World from A to Z: The Complete Guide to Middle-Earth*, 1971, Revised and Expanded Edition (New York: Random House, 1978).

[47] When a Branch of the Mythopoeic Society, now called Esgaroth, was formed in Toronto, I suggested that it ought to be called "Northern Waste," because Canada is referred to in our national anthem as "the True North strong and free," but nobody liked the idea.

[48] Foster 372.

[49] Foster 372.

[50] Foster 190.

[51] Foster 239.

[52] Foster 238.

[53] Foster 238.

[54] Foster 238. Interestingly, "southron" is a Scottish term for "Englishman."

[55] Foster 373.

[56] Foster 425.

[57] By a bit of synchronicity at just this point in completing this paper, my husband brought the following quotation to my attention:

"The *Quarterly Paper's* Christmas number in 1849 contained, among other things, a small and sketchy map of the world which was intended to show the deployment of missionary forces and the division of the globe into different religions and religions sects. This was illustrated by the use of varying shades and combinations of cross-hatching. The totally heathen world was demonstrated in black; Protestant Christianity came pure white. Islam was picked out in a dark shade and both the Roman Catholic and Orthodox world were depicted in a light shade. This deeply offended Mr. Gladstone's sensitivity to sectarian distinctions. The Orthodox, he believed, should have been demonstrated in a lighter shade than that applied to the Roman Catholics." Geoffrey Moorhouse, *The Missionaries* (London: Eyre Methuen, 1973) 163.

There is suggested here something of the somewhat (to our sensibilities) ingenuous attitude toward some of the subjects touched upon in this paper which is found in the writings of many fantasists

Notes

who were born and received their educations in the late Victorian and Edwardian era.

[58] Charles Williams, *Shadows of Ecstasy* (1933; New York: Pellegrini and Cudahy, 1950) 6; ch. 1.

[59] Williams, *Shadows of Ecstasy* 8; ch. 1.

[60] Williams, *Shadows of Ecstasy* 16; ch. 1.

[61] Williams, *Shadows of Ecstasy* 16, 20; ch. 1.

[62] Williams, *Shadows of Ecstasy* 22; ch. 2.

[63] Williams, *Shadows of Ecstasy* 129; ch. 7.

[64] Williams, *Shadows of Ecstasy* 259; ch. 14.

[65] Charles Williams, *The Region of the Summer Stars* (London: Oxford UP, 1950) 53.

[66] Charles Williams, *The House of the Octopus* (London: Edinborough House Press, 1945) 5.

[67] Williams, *The House of the Octopus* 50.

[68] Williams, *The House of the Octopus* 5.

[69] C.S. Lewis, "Williams and the Arthuriad," *Arthurian Torso* (London: Oxford UP, 1948) 99.

[70] C.S. Lewis, "Williams and the Arthuriad" 100-101.

[71] Frantz Fanon, *Black Skin, White Masks* (1952; English trans. New York: Grove Press, 2008) 166. Cited in Eulalio P. Baltazar, *The Dark Center: A Process Theology of Blackness* (New York: Paulist Press, 1973) 61.

[72] Baltazar, *The Dark Center* 28.

[73] E.O. James, *Seasonal Feasts and Fasts* (London: Thames and Hudson, 1961) 273.

[74] James, *Seasonal Feasts and Fasts* 275.

[75] Baltazar, *The Dark Center* 164.

[76] Cirlot, *A Dictionary of Symbols* 160.

[77] One cannot know, of course, whether Ram takes his name from Rama, the hero of the great Hindu epic, the Ramayana, and type of the "completely moral man." See J. Herbert, "Hindu Mythology," *Larousse World Mythology*, ed., Pierre Grimal (London: Hamlyn, 1965) 217.

[78] Cirlot, *A Dictionary of Symbols* 89. Cirlot's description of the Yang/Yin symbol is as follows: "activity, or the masculine principle

Notes

(Yang), is represented by a white circle (depicting heaven), whereas passivity, the feminine principle (Yin) is denoted by a black square (portraying earth) ... The interaction implicit in dualism is represented by the famous symbol of the Yang-Yin, a circle divided into two equal sections by a sigmoid line across the diameter, the white section (Yang) having a black spot within it, and the black (Yin) a white spot. These two spots signify that there is always something of the feminine in the masculine and something of the masculine in the feminine" (45). The complementarity in the portrayal of Aravis, the warrior maiden, and Shasta/Cor, the helpless foundling who is guided to kingship by Aslan, is one of the most attractive elements in *The Horse and His Boy*.

2. "Always Winter and Never Christmas": Symbols of Time in C.S. Lewis's Chronicles of Narnia

> While he lay dreaming his name was Time. Now that he is awake he will have a new one.
>
> ——C.S. Lewis, *The Last Battle*

Patterson demonstrates how a narrative pattern of thesis, antithesis, and synthesis is developed in the representation of time in the Chronicles of Narnia, with an emphasis on The Lion, the Witch and the Wardrobe. *She shows how time is symbolized by characters associated with good: Father Christmas (LWW) and Father Time (SC, LB); and evil: Jadis the White Witch (LWW). She concludes by drawing attention to the role played by anamnesis, which in this story means the recovery of cyclic time in Narnia through Father Christmas.*

Many of the themes addressed here are also examined in other papers in Ransoming the Waste Land, Volumes I and II. *For example, Patterson demonstrates how the narrative pattern of thesis, antithesis, and synthesis is developed in The Space Trilogy in "Thesis, Antithesis, and Synthesis in the Space Trilogy"; the relationship of the White Witch to the Snow Queen and Father Christmas is also discussed in "The Host of Heaven"; and the salvational aspect of time associated with Father Christmas is treated in "Miraculous Bread ... Miraculous Wine." These papers may be found in* Ransoming the Waste Land Volume I. *The role of the Green Witch is further discussed in "Halfe Like a Serpent" included in this volume.*

"'Always Winter and Never Christmas': Symbols of Time in Lewis's Chronicles of Narnia" was first published in Mythlore *18.1 (Autumn 1991): 10-14. It is Patterson's fifth paper on the representation of evil in Lewis's fiction.*

Time, both cyclical and linear, and eternity, both durational and simultaneous, are symbolized in the Narnian Chronicles by figures of Good: Father Christmas and Father Time, and evil: Jadis the White Witch. The origins, parallels, and developments of these symbols in Western culture, and their theological implications in the

Narnian Chronicles, are the subject of this paper. Its thesis is that, despite Clyde S. Kilby's (1964) opinion that the "appearance of Father Christmas in *The Lion, the Witch and the Wardrobe"* is "incongruous,"[1] this figure holds the key to Lewis's understanding of the theological significance of time.

A number of writers have discussed the element of time in the Narnian Chronicles.[2] In these seven books, Lewis describes parallel times which are so disparate in duration that what occupies a lifetime on Earth is the entire history of the creation of Narnia. The action of *The Magician's Nephew,* which although not the first written or the first published, is chronologically first in terms of the human timeline of the Chronicles, describes the origins of Narnia, while the final book, *The Last Battle,* not only describes the end of Narnia, but sets the entire duration of Narnian time into the context of the lives of Digory Kirke, Polly Plummer, and the other child visitors to Narnia. The history of a world from beginning to end is a figure for a human lifetime, and the myths of origin and doom, found in so many religions, can be seen as metaphors for the human experience of life, which comes from mystery and goes to mystery. The central salvational event is, in the Christian idea of time, singular, and it operates both forward and backwards: Jesus is born, dies, descends to hell/death, rises, and ascends to heaven, and in so doing, determines the ultimate outcome of the lives of all people of both past and future.

This infinitely efficacious sequence, enacted in the single human/divine lifetime of Jesus, presents the grand salvific program as a dialectic process, thus: *Thesis:* Earth is made; *Antithesis:* Earth is marred; *Synthesis:* Earth is remade and/or renewed. In each of the Narnian Chronicles the same pattern appears, and each book ends with the restoration or renewal of good elements from the past. Lewis set forth this pattern first and most powerfully in *The Lion, the Witch and the Wardrobe,* with the story of the death and resurrection of Aslan, and in that book Lewis uses a set of very potent images of time, exactly described in the phrase, "Always Winter and Never Christmas," which I have chosen as the title of my paper. Father Christmas, whose coming heralds the arrival of the savior Aslan, is Lewis's first symbol of time in the Narnian Chronicles.

A peculiarity of the books is that they can be read in two orders: either as they appeared in order of publication, with *The Lion, the Witch and the Wardrobe* first, or as they are ordered in accordance with the internal sequence of events, with *The Magician's Nephew* first. As Lewis wrote the novels, Paul Ford (1980) perceptively says, he sets forth "a redemption story" first. After telling a series of these stories, "he was able to tell the story not only of Narnia's beginnings but also of its consummation."[3] A key image of this consummation, and Lewis's second symbol of time is found in *The Silver Chair,* in the figure of Father Time, who makes a re-appearance in *The Last Battle.* My essay will discuss these twin symbols of time as representing in Father Christmas both the individual salvational event and the cyclical element of time, and in Father Time both the general creation-to-consummation sequence, and the linear element of time.

In the book Lewis based on his World War II BBC broadcasts, *Mere Christianity,* he discusses time as a phenomenon. "Almost certainly God is not in Time,"[4] he said, implying that time is an aspect of creation rather than of creator. He compares time with a written narrative possessing its own internal time, set against the time of an author: "I could think about Mary […] for as long as I pleased, and the hours I spent […] would not appear in Mary's time […] at all."[5] Thus, Lewis concludes, "If you picture Time as a straight line along which we have to travel, then you must picture God as the whole page on which the line is drawn."[6] Note that time is specifically defined here as a linear process or sequence.

Very late in his apologetic career, *in Letters to Malcolm,* Lewis returned to the theme of time, introducing some emendations. "I certainly believe that to be God is to enjoy an infinite present, where nothing has yet passed away and nothing is still to come."[7] This corresponds to his earlier image of God as "the whole page." But Lewis continues, "The dead might experience a time which is not quite so linear as ours—it might, so to speak, have thickness as well as length."[8] Indeed, he adds, "I *feel* […] that to make the life of the blessed dead strictly timeless is inconsistent with the resurrection of the body.[9]

The relationship of time and eternity for Christians is given a malign expression in Alan W. Watts's (1968) study, *Myth and Ritual in Christianity.* At first, Watts seems to agree with Lewis: "the life of the soul-and-body in Heaven will be at once eternal […] and everlasting."[10] He explains, "the soul will see time as God sees it—all at once, past, present, and future,"[11] but "It will contemplate the 'moment' of eternity for an everlasting time."[12] For Watts, "Taken literally, the state of the blessed in Heaven is actually no less frightful than that of the damned in Hell."[13] This, he tells us, is because the blessed will suffer "the terrible monotony of everlasting pleasure."[14] A frozen Hell is no more terrible than an infinitely extended Heaven. This is precisely the dilemma that Lewis's fantasy series addresses.

Father Christmas and the White Witch

When Lucy enters Narnia in *The Lion, the Witch and the Wardrobe,* her first physical sensation is of "something soft and powdery and extremely cold" (LWW 8; ch. 1), in a word, snow. "A moment later she found that she was standing in the middle of a wood at night-time with snow under her feet and snowflakes falling through the air." On the next page, the idea of Christmas is introduced, as Lucy sees her first Narnian: "What with the parcels and the snow it looked just as if he had been doing his Christmas shopping. He was a faun" (LWW 10; ch. 1). Thus, winter (snow) and Christmas (parcels) are central elements encountered by Lucy as by the reader in Lewis's first book about Narnia. Note that the concepts—winter, Christmas— are presented in physical form—snow and parcels—from the outset.

When Lucy joins the Faun in his cozy cave to share a wonderful tea, the Faun confesses that he is a kidnapper, working under the orders of "the White Witch" (LWW 19; ch. 2). In answer to Lucy's question, he explains, "Why, it is she who has got all Narnia under her thumb. It's she that makes it always winter. Always winter and never Christmas; think of that?" Lucy immediately replies, "How awful!" (LWW 19; ch. 2) in response to this terrible state of affairs.

With the five words "always winter and never Christmas," Lewis presents a fundamental structure in which every word is significant. "Always" here means continuously, in the sense of duration, or an on-running, linear state of being, which takes place in time. "Winter" means a time of severe cold, heavy snow, frozen streams, and long nights. "And" connects or relates two sets of paired terms. "Never" means that within this endlessly continuing winter, there is no moment when the possibility of spring is anticipated, when the nights begin to shorten and the light begins to return. "Christmas" means that the central focus of human history, the moment when the creator enters his own creation, to which the cycling years return again and again, is kept outside of Narnian time, and does not bring its yearly gifts of renewal, its (to use that untranslatable Greek term employed in theological discourse) *anamnesis.* Anamnesis means not only to recall in the sense of remembering, but to recall in the sense of calling back, bringing something from the past into the present.

Narnia is a frozen world. Its "always" implies a "never." In this symbolism, winter is used as a negative image, embodied not only in the landscape and season, but in an evil personage, the White Witch. This personage, who appears in the book's title, appears first not to Lucy, but to Edmund, the potential traitor; her coming is announced by the distant sound of sleighbells, and "at last there swept into sight a sledge drawn by two reindeer" (LWW 30; ch. 3). Riding "in the middle of the sledge" (LWW 31; ch. 3) is a great lady," who is "covered in white fur up to her throat." Moreover, "Her face was white—not merely pale, but white like snow," a face not only "beautiful [...] but proud and cold and stern." Like the Snow Queen in Hans Christian Andersen's fairy tale, upon which she is modeled, the White Witch is as white and as cold as snow; and like the Snow Queen with her Kay, the White Witch carries a boy, Edmund, away on her sledge to a castle. It is significant that in the Snow Queen's castle, "in the midst of the endless, empty hall there was a frozen lake."[15] One thinks immediately of the frozen sea in which Satan is plunged forever in Dante's *Inferno.* Here, Gerda at last finds Kay, "quite blue with cold," desperately trying to solve the "Great Mental Ice Puzzle" by assembling fragments of ice: "He put together patterns to form a written word; but he never could succeed in putting out the exact word that he wanted, which was 'ETERNITY'."[16]

The frozen sea in *The Snow Queen* is not, then, a symbol of eternity, but of some terrible opposite. The Snow Queen has told Kay that "if you can find me that pattern, you shall be your own master, and I'll make you a present of the whole world, and a pair of new skates."[17] Whatever the whole world may mean, skates change winter's frozen rivers into speedy roads, and frozen lakes or seas into vast vistas of freedom. Narnia's winter lacks the Christmas gift of freedom, or to put it another way, the perspective of eternity.

Snow is a true symbol, in the Jungian sense that it is ambivalent, capable of expressing both evil and good. The Snow Queen, unlike the White Witch, is not evil. Like the North Wind in George MacDonalds's *At the Back of the North Wind,* she is about her father's business even when she brings snow. "Now I'm going to whisk off to the hot countries," she tells Kay, as she flies off to visit Etna and Vesuvius; "I shall go and peep into the black pots [… and] whiten them a bit: that's my job, and besides, it'll be good for the lemons and vines."[18] In the same way, snow reappears in *The Silver Chair* when Jill and Eustace return with the rescued Prince Rilian from Narnia's Underworld. Jill's experience echoes Lucy's: "The air seemed to be deadly cold, and the light was pale and blue," and there were "a lot of white objects flying about in the air" (SC 216; ch. 15). It comes to her that "the pale, blue light was really moonlight, and the white stuff on the ground was really snow." And the white flying objects are snowballs, thrown in the complex movements of "the Great Snow Dance […] done every year in Narnia on the first moonlight night when there is snow on the ground" (SC 217-18; ch. 15). This figure of the dance is Lewis's favorite derived from medieval and Renaissance thought, and it symbolizes the dance of all creation in its orderly round.

The White Witch is evil not because she brings cold and snow, but because she will not relinquish her power and allow the stately rotation of the year to proceed. Like Satan, she would rather reign in a frozen Hell, than serve in a fecund Heaven. She does not want to take her place in the stately dance of creation. She is like the Green Witch of the Underworld in *The Silver Chair,* who urges her captives to choose illusion over reality—the unseen sun.

Lewis returned to the Witch in *The Magician's Nephew,* describing how, in a previous existence in the world-city of Charn, she has been Queen Jadis, and has chosen to pronounce the Deplorable Word (which undoubtedly is *not* "Eternity") rather than allow her own sister to occupy the throne. Lewis describes her "white, beautiful hand" (MN 59; ch. 5) and her "large cold finger and thumb" (MN 71; ch. 6), reiterations of snow and freezing, both used to grasp and control Polly and Digory, the children who, through a quarrel, have released her from her long self-chosen oblivion. At the climax of the book, Aslan creates Narnia, and the Witch Jadis takes up residence in this perfect creation through Digory's fault. Aslan sends Digory and Polly to get an apple in order to plant a tree in a garden "that she will not dare to approach" (MN 154; ch. 12), but when the children arrive, Jadis is there ahead of them.

Digory enters the gate of this holy place, and, with Aslan's permission, picks an apple. And "There only a few yards away from him stood the Witch," and "her face was deadly white, white as salt" (MN 174; ch. 13), white, that is, as Lot's wife, who became a pillar of salt through disobedience. She tempts Digory to join her in her disobedience, to steal an apple for his own use (to heal his dying mother) rather than take it to Aslan as he has been told to do. With a terrible effort, and putting right what he had previously put wrong, Digory resists. The apple is eventually planted, the protective tree of Narnia grows and bears yet more fruit. Digory is bidden by Aslan to pluck a new apple, and with this, his mother is indeed healed. What is more, its apple core, planted in England, grows to a great tree from which wood is taken to make the Wardrobe which forms the door "That was the beginning of all the comings and goings between Narnia and our world" (MN 202; ch.15). Obedience brings joy and freedom, disobedience brings sorrow and enslavement, to the worst of all masters and mistresses, one's self.

Turning people to stone is the White Witch's forté, and stone, like ice, is a state of being frozen. The freeing of the Witch-enchanted persons, such as animals, giants, and longaevi, by Aslan is a major event in *The Lion, the Witch and the Wardrobe.* The intention of the Witch to thwart the on-running movement of the year is most poignantly expressed when she turns to stone a charming little party of Narnians who have begun to celebrate Christmas with an outdoor feast.

The White Witch, Jadis, and the Green Witch are associated with a cold duration, a sterile fixity, and a lightless illusion. These figures of Hell, death, and evil, in the context of time, are countered in the Narnian Chronicles by two images of time as good. These are Father Christmas and Father Time. Before discussing these figures, a little analysis of their historic origins and development will be given, based upon the study of "the gods and patriarchs who are or who have been personifications of time in the Western World"[19] by Samuel L. Macey (1987). He calls Father Time and Father Christmas the "two 'sons'" of Saturn-Cronus.[20] Father Time takes Saturn-Cronus's sickle and Father Christmas takes the Saturnian gift-giving aspect.[21]

The character of Saturn-Cronus is "influenced in many ways by the gods of the Indo-Iranian pantheons and in particular by their several twin gods, who represent benevolent infinite time and malevolent finite time."[22] Saturn-Cronus "represents concurrently the Saturnalian values of past golden days but also the sickle of Time, the future destroyer."[23] These are the twin roles played by Father Time in the Narnian Chronicles, where the giant Time is a king who sleeps after a long rule, only to awake at the end of the world, and, borrowing a symbol from Gabriel's tool for announcing the last judgment, blows his horn to announce the end of Narnia.

Like Father Time, Father Christmas is concerned with the annual cycle of time. But his iconography tallies the ongoing years "for a whole family or people"[24]:

> [I]t is Father Christmas, in his role as the Old Year, who helps us to celebrate the regeneration of life and the continuation not only of the sun itself but more immediately of our family and our people."[25]

Macey speaks of "the English Father Christmas of the seventeenth century who is simultaneously lauded by Anglicans and damned by Puritans,"[26] presumably the Father Christmas intended by the Anglican Lewis. This gift-bearing figure originally appeared as a precursor, harbinger, or herald of Christmas, still preserved in the Continental Saint Nicholas, who is "involved in the dualism of being both judge and benefactor"[27] and whose feat occurs early in December. The English Father Christmas is essentially a "Rewarder"[28] and is "not concentrated on the feat of Saint Nicholas but rather derived from his role in the Mummers' Play, in which, in several versions, '"In comes I, Father Christmas', is the opening sentence."[29] The Mummers' Play is a depiction of "the annual death of the year [...] and its annual resurrection in spring,"[30] and this resurrection, central to *The Lion, the Witch and the Wardrobe,* in which Aslan's arrival breaks the Witch's artificial winter with a sudden spring, makes the presence in that book of Father Christmas absolutely appropriate.

In announcing Aslan, Father Christmas is a kind of Elijah who heralds the return of the creator to his own world. I said above that "parcels" are used as a figure for Christmas when Lewis first represents the Narnian situation. Father Christmas, the gift-bearer, arrives like the Witch on a sledge drawn by belled reindeer. True to his complex mythological sources, he makes the children and beavers feel "very glad, but also solemn" (LWW 107; ch. 10). His first gift is an announcement about the Witch: "She has kept me out for a long time, but I have got in at last. Aslan is on the move. The Witch's magic is weakening" (LWW 107; ch. 10). This passage makes Father Christmas's role as an annunciator perfectly explicit. His gifts are all practical—"tools not toys"—a sewing machine for Mrs. Beaver, a finished dam for Mr. Beaver, a shield and sword for Peter, a bow, quiver of arrows, and ivory horn for Susan, and for Lucy a bottle of healing cordial and "a small dagger" (LWW 109; ch. 10) and, as a climax, "a large tray containing five cups and saucers, a bowl of lump sugar, a jug of cream, and a great big teapot all sizzling and piping hot" (LWW 109; ch. 10).

Father Time

This jovial, practical figure of Father Christmas, whose arrival marks the recovery of cyclical time in Narnia, is joined in *The Silver Chair* by Father Time, whose role embodies the more absolute cycle of creation from beginning to end. In a cave "about the shape and size of a cathedral [...] filling almost the whole length of it, lay an enormous man fast asleep." Although he is large, "his face was not like a giant's, but noble and beautiful. His breast rose and fell gently under the snowy beard which covered him to the waist. A pure, silver light [...] rested upon him" (SC 146; ch. 10). When Puddleglum enquires about his name, the Warden (a gnome) replies, "That is old Father Time, who was once a King in Overland [...] They say he will wake at the end of the world" (SC 146; ch. 10). The snowy beard images the sleep of vegetation and other life under the winter snow.

Katherine Briggs (1976) points out that "The throne of a sleeping champion in a cave under a hill is common through Europe"[31] and she mentions Charlemagne, Barbarossa, Holger the Dane, and King Arthur, among others, as examples of the type/motif "King Asleep in Mountain." Readers of Lewis will of course think of the sleeping Merlin, roused in *That Hideous Strength* to help put right an England gone wrong. The point is the return to the present of a good sleeper from the past, reawakened and renewed. True to his special role, it is

Father Time who comes not to restore but to complete the world by heralding its "consummation."

In the chapter of *The Last Battle* appropriately entitled "Night Falls on Narnia" (LB 171; ch. 14) this return is described. "Out on their left they saw [...] the shape of a man, the hugest of all giants" (LB 171; ch. 14). His position in the Narnian landscape causes Jill and Eustace to remember

> how once long ago, in the deep caves beneath those moors, they had seen a great giant asleep and been told that his name was Father Time, and that he would wake on the day the world ended. (LB 141-71; ch. 14)

Aslan expresses their thoughts: "while he lay dreaming his name was Time. Now that he is awake he will have a new one." Perhaps, in this new role, his name is to be Eternity! Father Time blows his horn, and the end of Narnia begins, in a long panoply of last things. Finally, Aslan commands him to "make an end" and the giant, casting his horn into the sea, reaches out to the Sun and crushes it in his immortal hand.

The end of Narnia does not, however, signal an end to everything. The dead Narnia is replaced by a new, everlasting Narnia where "morning freshness was in the air" (LB 192; ch. 15). Aslan's country is perceived to include not only this "real" Narnia but "the England within England" (LB 208; ch. 16), another idea repeated from *That Hideous Strength*. The book concludes as the children and all their restored companions from their various visits to Narnia begin "Chapter One of the Great Story [...] which goes on forever, in which every chapter is better than the one before" (LB 211; ch. 16), that story which all readers of the Narnian Chronicles would most like to read.

Anamnesis

The combination of repeated cycles and the single cycle of beginning to end is found in myths because it is found, first, in the physical world. In his study, *Time's Arrow, Time's Cycle* (1987), Stephen Jay Gould surveys the Western understanding of time: "Something deep in our tradition requires, for intelligibility itself, both the arrow of historical uniqueness and the cycle of timeless immanence—and nature says yes to both."[32] These two elements—cycle and arrow—he characterizes thus: "The metaphor of Time's cycle captures those aspects of nature that are either stable or else cycle in a simple repeating (or oscillating) series because they are direct products of nature's timeless laws,"[33] and "The essence of time's arrow lies in the irreversability of history, and the unrepeatable uniqueness of each step of a sequence of events."[34]

The majestic and interlocking phenomena of the natural world, movements within the cosmos in general and the solar system in particular, create time in both cycle and arrow. These phenomena, especially lunar and solar cycles, were observed and recorded by humankind as early as the Upper Paleolithic, and even in that early era served not only a notational, but also a symbolic role. In this paper we are concerned with time as a figure for the divine order of creation and as a metaphor for the human experience of life (which includes, in Christian thought, birth, death, and resurrection). The dialectic structure of birth, death, and resurrection is celebrated in the twin cycles of the Christian year—Advent, Christmas, Lent, Easter, Ascension, Pentecost—and the Christian week, which begins with a celebration of the Resurrection on Sundays; and in the paired linearities of Christian life: birth/death/resurrection, and Christian Eschatology: Creation/Christ/Consummation.

It is in this context that the word *anamnesis* forms the interpretive key of my argument. E.L. Mascall (1972) in *A Dictionary of Christian Theology* says, "the Hebrew notion behind the Greek term signifies the bringing in the present of a chronologically past act with all its original efficacy."[35] The anamnesis is "a literal 're-calling' in the sense of 'calling back'." We see this in the recovery of cyclicality by Narnian time as Father Christmas arrives to herald the return to Narnia of its creator, Aslan. The same motif in its more absolute or linear sense is expressed in the figure of Father Time, who at Aslan's command comes back to bring an end to Narnia, whereupon Aslan reveals that the real Narnia is now available.

In its specific Christian application, the *anamnesis* is that segment of the eucharist in which is recited the command of Jesus to "Do this in remembrance of me," with the word "remembrance" an inadequate rendering in English of the Greek (and Hebrew) meaning defined above. The eucharist is for Christians—it was for Lewis—the foretaste of the resurrection in the present. Its central feature, in sacramental theologies, is the making present again and again of what has been done once for all, by the one who says, "Behold, I make all things new" (Revelation 21.5).

If our present life is, as Lewis in his Platonic way called it, a Shadowlands, what is foreshadowed in the eucharist, which is repeated in the cycles of the week and year? Exactly this: eternal renewal. Eternity is not, in this symbolic structure, an endless duration, but neither is it an infinite moment. Rather, it is an eternal renewal, an everlasting arrival at a place or time that is ever fresher, newer, more central, and more complete, not through novelty but through renewal of what is and always has been best. A profound understanding of time (as both cycle and arrow) and eternity (as neither infinite stasis nor utter timelessness but as eternal renewal) is vividly expressed in the Narnian Chronicles, as Lewis weaves together his symbols of time.

Notes

[1] Clyde S. Kilby, *The Christian World of C.S. Lewis* (Grand Rapids, MI: Wm. B. Eerdmans, 1964) 145.

[2] See Martha E. Sammons, "Time," *A Guide Through Narnia* (Wheaton, IL: Harold Shaw Publishers, 1979) 63-64; Paul F. Ford, "Time," *Companion to Narnia* (San Francisco, CA: Harper and Row, 1980) 289-90; and in most detail, Michael Murrin, "The Multiple Worlds of the Narnia Stories," *Word and Story in C.S. Lewis,* eds. Peter J. Shakel and Charles A. Huttar (Columbia, MO: University of Missouri Press, 1991) 248-251; reprinted from VII: *An Anglo-American Literary Review* 3 (1982): 93-112.

[3] Ford xxxix.

[4] C.S. Lewis, "Time and Beyond Time," *Mere Christianity: A revised and amplified edition* (1952; HarperSanFrancisco, 2001) 167.

[5] C.S. Lewis, *Mere Christianity* 168.

[6] C.S. Lewis, *Mere Christianity* 168.

[7] C.S. Lewis, *Letters to Malcolm, Chiefly on Prayer* (1963; New York: Harcourt, 2002) 109.

[8] C.S. Lewis, *Letters to Malcolm* 109.

[9] C.S. Lewis, *Letters to Malcolm* 110.

[10] Alan W. Watts, *Myth and Ritual in Christianity* (Boston, MA: Beacon Press, 1968) 225.

Notes

[11] Watts, *Myth and Ritual in Christianity* 225.

[12] Watts, *Myth and Ritual in Christianity* 226.

[13] Watts, *Myth and Ritual in Christianity* 225.

[14] Watts, *Myth and Ritual in Christianity* 227.

[15] Hans Christian Andersen, *The Snow Queen*, ch. Story the Seventh (1844; Gutenberg ebook # 442).

[16] Andersen, "The Snow Queen," ch. Story the Seventh.

[17] Andersen, "The Snow Queen," ch. Story the Seventh.

[18] Andersen, "The Snow Queen," ch. Story the Seventh.

[19] Samuel L. Macey, *Patriarchs of Time: Dualism in Saturn-Cronus, Father Time, the Watchmaker God, and Father Christmas* (Athens, GA: University of Georgia Press, 1987) xi.

[20] Macey xi.

[21] Macey 111.

[22] Macey xi.

[23] Macey xii.

[24] Macey 135.

[25] Macey 139.

[26] Macey 140.

[27] Macey 140.

[28] Macey 145.

[29] Macey 145.

[30] Macey 145.

[31] Katherine Briggs, *A Dictionary of Faeries* (London: Allen Lane, 1976) 370.

[32] Stephen Jay Gould, *Time's Arrow, Time's Cycle* (Cambridge, MA: Harvard UP, 1987) 200.

[33] Gould 196.

[34] Gould 194.

[35] E.L. Mascall, *A Dictionary of Christian Theology,* ed. Alan Richardson (1969; London: SCM Press, 1972) 7.

3.   "Halfe Like a Serpent": The Green Witch in
The Silver Chair

Halfe like a serpent horribly displaide,
But th'other halfe did womans shape retaine.
——Edmund Spencer, *The Faerie Queene*[1]

Patterson argues that the villain and the heroine of The Silver
Chair—*the Green Witch and Jill Pole—are part of a descent quest
comparable to that of the Mesopotamian goddess Inanna. She reviews
comparisons of the Green Witch made by other scholars to Circe,
Lilith, Morgan Le Fay, Spenser's monster Errour, Persephone, and
finally Spenser's Duessa, before turning to her own nominations for
prototypes of the Green Witch's role: Astarte, Hel, the Sumerian Kur,
the Babylonian Tiamat, and others. She then discusses the story of
Inanna and Ereshkigal and its relevance to Lewis's novel.*

*Patterson also discusses associations between Lewis's charac-
ters and plots and astrology in "The Host of Heaven," and the role of
Jill as seeress in "'Guardaci Ben': The Visionary Woman in* That
Hideous Strength *and the Chronicles of Narnia." Both papers are included in* Ransoming the Waste Land Volume I. *The subject of northerness in Lewis's fiction, raised briefly here, is treated at greater
length in "Narnia and the North: the Symbolism of Northerness in the
Fantasies of C.S. Lewis" included in this volume.*

"'Halfe Like a Serpent': The Green Witch in The Silver Chair"
was first published in Mythlore *12.2 (Autumn 1984): 37-47. It is Patterson's second paper on the representation of evil in Lewis's fiction.*

The Green Witch of *The Silver Chair* is, as John Cox (1977)
describes her, "the femme fatale in poisonous green who is repeatedly
identified as Queen of the Deep Realm or Queen of the Underland."[2]
The Green Witch is certainly the principal element in what Paul A.
Karkainen (1979) describes as the "sophisticated picture of evil"[3]
conveyed in this novel. However, *The Silver Chair* also conveys a
complete feminine structure, in which the polyvalent symbol of
woman receives full expression. The Green Witch is the villainess of
The Silver Chair but Jill Pole is its heroine.

The structure of the narrative is a descent-quest, carried out by a female to rescue a male. The motif of the heroine, while less common than the hero, is not unknown in mythology. Its most famous form is certainly the descent of Inanna/Ishtar into the Underworld, where she encounters her sister, the goddess Ereshkigal. Inanna is a full-fledged goddess, however, and Jill is a young girl, a Kore or maiden.[4] Jill Pole is a heroine figure who is sent into the underworld in place of the Star's daughter to rescue that dead queen's son, Prince Rilian. The Star's daughter has been killed by the Queen of Underland in the form of a serpent and her son is kept in enchanted captivity below the earth. He is rescued by Jill, who goes down to him armed with the four Signs of Aslan and accompanied by two male companions (an amphibian and a metamorph), and is brought back to his true kingdom in the overworld. The other captives of the underworld Queen are the Gnomes (earth beings) who return to their true ruler, the Salamander (fire being), in the true and uttermost depths of Bism. In this structure there are a Star-Queen, an Underworld Queen, a heroine and her male companions, and a male captive. It is significant that in this novel, Aslan the divine Lion does not enter his creation—Narnia—but sends Jill to carry out the rescue as his emissary.[5] This task is to be accomplished by means of four Signs:

1) to greet "an old and dear friend" of Eustace's "at once";
2) to journey "out of Narnia to the north" to the "ruined city of the ancient giants";
3) to find "a writing on stone in that ruined city" and to do what it tells her to do; and
4) to "know the lost prince" by the fact that he is the first "in your travels" to ask her to do something in "my name, in the name of Aslan" (SC 25; ch. 2).

It is generally said that the four Signs have no symbolic significance, and indeed, they are all exact descriptions of situations that Jill and Eustace will meet in their quest for Prince Rilian. But a list of commandments written on stone has resonance in Western culture. In particular, the instruction to "know them by heart" and to "pay no attention to appearances," but to "remember the signs and believe the signs" (SC 27; ch. 2) calls upon so many echoes of religious practice—the use of phylacteries and the recitation of the *Shema* in Judaism, based on Deuteronomy 6.4-8, and the memorization of passages of Scripture, the Lord's Prayer, and the Creeds in Christianity—as to be highly suggestive. These instructions seem to involve

1) *recognition*, re-knowing, specifically recognizing an old friend;
2) *exploration*, (traveling "north," and specifically traveling to an unknown or undiscovered place of ancient knowledge) as a venture inward;
3) *interpretation*, recognition (knowing again) of a partially obliterated place and decipherment of a written inscription; and
4) *response* to the one most central word (or Word): Aslan, the name of the creator, ruler, and judge of Narnia.[6]

Several motifs which are used significantly by Lewis elsewhere recur in these signs. These motifs are the journey to the north, which forms the central narrative structure of *The Horse and His Boy*, and the ruined city, which reminds us of the ruins of Cair Paravel in *Prince Caspian*, and of Charn, the city ruined by Jadis's pronouncement of the Deplorable Word in *The Magician's Nephew*. North is a direction of very strong resonance for Lewis. It represents a movement out of ordinary reality into the endless emptiness of a mysterious realm and suggests the object of Romantic desire for Lewis— mediated to him at first through Norse mythology.[7] The ruined city or castle is another motif from Romantic thought, which appears in works by William Morris and other writers who influenced Lewis. It appears in *The Silver Chair* not only in the ruined city of the giants, but in the ruinous tower where Glimfeather holds his Parliament of Owls. It suggests great distances in time in the same way that Northernness suggests great distances of space. In general terms, these motifs are figures for the journey into the Unconscious. All four signs require a journey to a new form of understanding or knowledge, like the one implied by T.S. Eliot in *The Four Quartets*:

> [...] the end of all our exploring
> Will be to arrive where we started
> And know the place for the first time.[8]

The Star Queen

In *The Silver Chair*, an "old owl" recounts a tale which, while not immediately understood by the children, proves to contain essential information in the end, and introduced the Green Witch. The old owl begins: "When Rilian, the son of Caspian, was a very young knight, he rode with the Queen his mother on a May morning in the north parts of Narnia" (SC 57; ch. 5). North again, you see. "In the warm part of the day they came to a pleasant glade where a fountain flowed freshly out of the earth" (SC 57; ch. 4). Freshly-flowing fountains are recognized all over the world as gates to the Underworld.[9]

"And so, presently," the narrator continues, "a great serpent came out of the thick wood and stung the Queen in her hand" (SC 57; ch. 4). This "worm" is described as "great, shining, and as green as poison, so that we could see it well: but it glided away into the thick bushes and we could not come at it" (SC 58; ch. 4). The motif of the "thick woods" and "thick bushes" carries the significance of a remote and dangerous place where it is hard to move freely, and is a strong clue to at least one identity of "that venomous worm." We read in *The Faerie Queene* of an encounter of the Red Cross Knight with Errour: "This is the wandring wood, this *Errour's den*."[10] The "poison" element will be discussed below in relation to the identity of this serpent; here it is the identity of the poisoned victim that concerns us.

The owl says of her that "She had been a great lady, wise and gracious and happy, Prince Caspian's bride whom he had brought home from the eastern end of the world. And men said that the blood of the stars flowed in her veins" (SC 58; ch. 4). The death of the Queen is described in some detail: her cry, the look on her face, her attempt to speak, and her expiration within ten minutes of the attack. This death is not a peremptory or convenient event to Lewis, but a reprise of the death of his mother in the fullness of her life. She was always idealized in his thought. The Queen's associations with the east and the stars are significant. The east in Narnia (at least from the vantage-point of the "Caspian Trilogy") is the closest approach to Aslan's Country, probably because Christ, addressed in the Advent antiphons as "O, Orient," is associated with the sun rising in the east. It is because of this association that Christian churches are orientated to the east; that is, their altars are (or are said to be, wherever their location) at the east end. The west in that symbolic structure is the position of the Last Judgment, and the western door faces the place of the dead. In *The Silver Chair*, Jill and Eustace face the east while invoking Aslan (SC 10; ch. 1), and Aslan sends Jill "due west" (SC 29; ch. 2) toward Narnia.

The Queen from the east, who lives on the "island of the Star," is a kind of Stella Maris, "Star of the Sea," a title of the Blessed Virgin Mary, and a title of Near Eastern goddesses before that: Ishtar's name *means* "Star." The fact that this Queen is nameless—being called only "Ramandu's daughter" (VDT 234; ch. 14) or "the girl." She is described as "a tall girl, dressed in a simple long garment of clear blue," and she carries "a tall candle in a silver candlestick" (VDT 215; ch. 13). Significantly, she emerges from "a door opened in a hillside" (VDT 214; ch. 13). She is a complex figure, both stellar and chthonic. Caspian addresses her as "Madam" (VDT 215; ch. 13) and Reepicheep calls her "Lady" (FDT 217; ch. 13). Her advice to Edmund is also significant: when he suggests that "When I look in your face I can't help believing all you say: but then that's just what might happen with a witch too" (VDT 217; ch. 13). This is her reply: "You can't know," said the girl. "You can only believe—or not" (VDT 217; ch. 13).

These words are a prefiguration of the encounter between Aslan and Jill in *The Silver Chair* (SC 17; ch. 1). This girl, Lady, Queen, and daughter of a Star is a figure like that of "the Morrigan," the Celtic goddess whose name means simply "Great Queen." One thinks of the apparition which emerged from the grotto at Lourdes, whom St. Bernadette consistently referred to as "*Aquero*"—"that," or "that one," until That One gave herself a name.[11] She is, perhaps, not capable of being named by profane lips. Lewis says of her, "She became a great queen and grandmother of great kings" (VDT 270; ch. 16).

The Green Serpent Murderer

In contrast to this Star-Queen who in her first epiphany emerged from a hillside on an island (combining images of darkness, underworld, sea, emergence, light, and stars for reasons to be discussed below) is her killer, a serpent from the thick woods who is green as poison. In his search through the "Northern woods" for "the worm" the bereaved son of the Queen, Prince Rilian, returns to "that same fountain where the Queen got her death." There, "at noon Drinian [his companion] looked up and saw the most beautiful lady he had ever seen; and she stood at the north side of the fountain and said no word but beckoned to the prince with her hand" (SC 59; ch. 4). Her position "at the north side of the fountain'" in a passage in which the phrase "Northern woods" occurs twice underscores the symbolism Lewis attached to the north, which in this novel emphasizes its danger as well as its potentially fatal attraction. "And she was tall and great, shining, and wrapped in a thin garment as green as poison" (SC 60; ch. 4). This garment is presumably her serpent-self's skin: she shifts her form from serpent to woman and from woman to serpent as readily as common snakes shed their skins.

Both serpent and woman are "shining" and "green as poison." Lewis adds, "It stuck in Drinian's mind that this shining green woman was evil" (SC 60; ch. 4). He has not been seduced, unlike the Prince, who "stared at her like a man out of his wits" (SC 60; ch. 4). On hearing this story, Jill, as the resident seeress,[12] exclaims, "I bet that serpent and that woman were the same person" (SC 61; ch. 4). But her perceptions do not protect her when she meets the shining green woman face-to-face! The "oldest owl" says, "Long, long ago, at the very beginning, a White Witch came out of the North and bound our land in ice and snow for a hundred years. And we think this may be one of the same crew" (SC 61; ch. 4).

Companions on the Quest: Jill, Eustace, and Puddleglum

Jill now sets out to pursue her quest with Eustace as her companion. She also obtains a guide: Puddleglum the Marsh-wiggle. Eustace is Jill's strength: he tires less easily than she because "the Narnian air was bringing back to him a strength he had won when he sailed the Eastern Seas with King Caspian" (SC 64; ch. 5). He is also well qualified as the pursuer of a shape-shifting serpent, for he has been a Dragon himself. His dragon-self was stripped from him by Aslan in *The Voyage of the Dawn Treader*. He has thus undergone metamorphosis, has seen reality from two bodily points of view, like Tiresias. The Marsh-wiggle too is a boundary crosser. Many of his attributes are those of an amphibian—a frog, in fact[13]—and he lives in a marsh, an area neither all land nor all sea, but partaking of both. In the same manner, "the fingers of his hands were webbed like a frog's, and so were his bare feet which dangled in the muddy water" (SC 69; ch. 5). From his generic name, Marsh-wiggle, one infers that he may have passed through a tadpole phase! In any event he has the nature of one equally at home, or at least in varying phases having been at home, on land or sea, combining in himself attributes of both worlds. Lewis has given him a memorable personality: he is Jill's wisdom. While constantly playing the Cassandra and foretelling doom, he is actually a canny and sweet-tempered being who understands with extraordinary clarity the real nature of any situation. With her two metamorphic companions, one a Narnian native and the other a Narnian verteran, Jill is well equipped to attempt the hazardous route.

They begin by crossing the River Shribble—-shrivel? nibble? rib? shrive? There is a certain Stygian sound to the name of this "shallow, noisy stream" (SC 78; ch. 6). Ettinsmoor itself is a playground for ettins, for giants. Here, at the edge of "the wild waste Lands of the North," the great stupid creatures are playing at cockshies, oblivious of the intruders. It is like a game played with stones *by* stones. The effect is to shift scale, making the little party smaller still. Giants were equated with features of the northern landscape in Norse mythology.[14]

A far more terrible stream awaits the travelers beyond the moor: "They looked down from the top of the cliffs at a river running below them from west to east" (SC 84; ch. 6). Obviously this is the absolute demarcation between south and north. "It was walled in by precipices on the far side as well as on their own and it was green and sunless, full of rapids and waterfalls" (SC 84; ch. 6). In *The Silver Chair*, greenness and sunlessness are images of malignancy. There is a further element of underworld imagery here as well: *The Elder Edda* describes some of the streams that fall from the cauldron of the upper world:

> Gjoll and Leift, they gush down to men
> And afterwards down to Hel.[15]

At the edge of this awesome symbol of separation, the travelers see "the last thing they were expecting." It is "a huge, single arch," as tall as "the dome of St. Paul's," which Puddleglum suspects of being a "sorcerer's" (SC 84; ch. 6). Its stones are "as big as those at Stonehenge" (SC 86; ch. 6), and its balustrade is carved with "giants, minotaurs, squids, centipedes, and dreadful gods." The two figures of huge size come not from modern skyscrapers, but from structures out of the deep and recent past that are replete with numinous and emotional associations. The bridge, which like the precipitous river is a motif from Norse mythology, is in the shape of an arch, a large and perfect form of which both Stonehenge with its circular structure and St. Paul's with its awesome dome are suitable figures.

This bridge, however, is not to be trusted, as Puddleglum points out. It is full of holes. The dangerous bridge is an image from many parts of the world's mythology, and Lewis has made its malignant nature clear by its decorations, which are drawn from motifs of repugnance to him: giants, already introduced in this sequence (and quite different from dear old Giant Wimbleweather of *Prince Caspian*); minotaurs, which suggest the "bull-headed men" (LWW 152; ch. 14) who are listed among the tormentors of Aslan (along with "ettins") in *The Lion, The Witch and the Wardrobe*; squids, which suggest the denizens of P'o-l'u in the poems and plays of Charles Williams; centipedes, which are one of the shapes taken by Screwtape in a moment of angry forgetfulness; and "dreadful gods," which perhaps depict the Calormene deities of *The Horse and His Boy*, which Lewis had already written but not yet published,[16] and to which a bard refers in a song sung at Cair Paravel before Jill and Eustace start north (SC 47; ch. 3).

Meeting the Black Knight and the Green Witch

On the far side of this ominous structure there stands a knight in black armor on a black horse, with his visor down and "no device on his shield" (SC 87; ch. 6). This figure resembles many a knightly challenger in Malory and elsewhere; in particular, one might think of the Black Knight in "The Lady of the Fountain" in *The Mabinogion*.[17] In this dire company we now meet the Green Witch face-to face. She rides side-saddle and wears "a long, fluttering dress of dazzling green." She speaks "in a voice as sweet as the sweetest bird's song" (SC 88; ch. 6)—like the Underworld birds of Rhiannon?—and sends the children before her to the Autumn Feast of the "gentle giants of Harfant" (SC 74) who, she says, "are as mild, civil, prudent, and courteous as those of Ettinsmoor are foolish, fierce, savage, and given to all beastliness" (SC 89; ch. 6). This is of course false counsel, since the giants of Harfang feature Man-pies at this particular feast!

The lady gives her name: "She of the Green Kirtle." On her promises of "hot meals and warm rooms" (SC 90; ch. 6) the children are deflected from their real goal, the ruined city which actually lies before the Castle of Harfang. When they are finally awakened to the dangers they face, the hunt is on. "Jill gathered up her long skirts—horrible things for running in" (SC 135; ch. 9) and runs, correctly oriented at last, back toward the ruined city.

The place where the final descent begins is most unpropitious:

> It was an unattractive hole—a crack between the earth and a stone about three feet long and hardly more than a foot high. You had to fling yourself flat on your face and crawl in. (SC 136; ch. 9)

In this posture of absolute abasement, Jill, preceded by Puddleglum and Eustace, enters the underworld. There the three travellers meet "the Warden of the Marches of Underland" (SC 140; ch. 10) who greets them:

> "Many fall down, and few return to the sunlit lands," said the voice. "Make ready now to come with me to the Queen of the Deep Realm." (SC 140; ch. 10)

This quisling (who is not telling the truth about the depth of this realm, since there is a truly Deep Realm under Narnia called Bism) is accompanied by a multitude of sad-faced gnomes, who, despite horns and "three-pronged spears" are not devils (SC 141; ch. 10). The mysteriously inactive denizens of Underland—fungiform trees, dinosaur-like creatures dozing like fossils in their rocky chambers, long-bearded Father Time sleeping his patient sleep—and the vast cavern-sea across which the travelers and their escorts are rowed, combine images of Stygian night and the dusty underworld of Homer[18] where the dead live a feeble, twittering existence like that of a guttering candle in a closely curtained room.

In the city of sad, silent gnomes, the travelers meet again the Black Knight, and discover another identity for the lady: "the Queen of Underland" (SC 171; ch. 12). The Prince, as the Black Knight later proves to be, calls her "this all but heavenly Queen" (SC 156; ch. 11) in ironic contrast to the truth, which is that she has killed his own mother, to whom that title might accurately have been given. He is in fact the prisoner of the Queen of Underland, only free from her power over his mind for one hour in twenty-four, during which he is bound to a silver chair but knows himself. Thus bound, but fully awake, the

Prince tells his visitors that the lady is "the most devilish sorceress that ever planned the woe of men" (SC 165; ch. 11). He now utters the word foretold by the fourth Sign: "by Aslan himself, I charge you—" (SC 166; ch. 11).

> They all stood looking at one another with bright eyes. It was a sickening moment. "All right!" said Jill suddenly. "Let's get it over." (SC 167; ch. 11)

Puddleglum and Eustace set the Prince free and immediately, and unexpectedly, the witch enters the room. In two paragraphs her title changes permanently from "the Lady of the Green Kirtle, The Queen of Underland" to "the Witch" and the "Witch-Queen." The scene in which she attempts to place all four of her unwilling visitors under a new spell has been quoted many times and is a pivotal event of the novel.

> Now the Witch said nothing at all, but moved gently across the room [...] When she had come to a little ark set in the wall [...] she opened it, and took out first a handful of a green powder. This she threw on the fire. (SC 173; ch. 12)

We are not surprised to learn that it is a *green* powder. The "sweet and drowsy smell" of this powder she accompanies by "a steady, monotonous thrumming" upon her mandolin and begins to speak "in a sweet, quiet voice."

Characteristically for Lewis, her speech takes the form of a debate, which she comes close to winning, while all the time "the witch's voice" continues "cooing softly like the voice of a wood-pigeon from the high elms in an old garden at three o'clock in the middle of a sleepy, summer afternoon" (SC 177; ch. 12), surely one of the most evocative images of drowsy enchantment in literature! Puddleglum saves the day by stamping out the fire with his naked foot. The enchanted smoke begins to clear and what remains "smelled very largely of burnt Marsh-wiggle, which is not at all an enchanting smell" (SC 181; ch. 12).

Puddleglum, having restored an atmosphere of sanity by his sacrificial act, now pours forth his famous retort that if Aslan and the overworld are not real, they are nonetheless a "play-world which licks your real world hollow" (SC 182; ch. 12). The "real world"— Underland—proclaimed by the Witch, is precisely hollow, a labyrinth of caverns scooped out between Narnia and the true depths below. The Witch, defeated in magic and argument alike, now turns to naked power (evil becomes physical in the last resort, just as does good). "Her legs were intertwined with each other, and her feet had disappeared. The long green train of her skirt thickened and grew solid, and seemed to be all one piece with the writhing green pillar of her interlocked legs" (SC 183; ch. 12). In a word, she turns into a "great serpent [...] green as poison" (SC 183; ch. 12),[19] and in this form she is killed.

At this point, it is revealed that just as the "White Witch came out of the North and bound our land in snow and ice," so Underland has also been bound. Its freeing allows Lewis to add yet another scene of liberation and renewal. The gnomes, whose real home is the Land of Bism in the depths below Narnia, are freed. A chasm opens into the deeper depth, revealing "fields and groves of an unbearable, hot brilliance," where gems are alive, and the salamanders, "wonderfully clever with their tongues; very witty and eloquent" (SC 206; ch. 14) call the rejoicing gnomes back home.

There is no Hell in Narnia! Even its fiery depths are good. The children too return to their own place—the surface of Narnia, where they find a delight of their own—a joyous snow-dance, suitable to a Midwinter's Eve celebration, performed to "wild music, intensely sweet and yet just the least bit eerie too, and full of good magic as the Witch's thrumming had been full of bad magic" (SC 217; ch. 15). The gloriously hot Bism and the delightfully cold Narnia provide a pleasant, mutually enhancing contrast, quite different from the contrast of the numinous music of Narnia and the stupifying music of the Queen of Underland. All the attributes of the Green Witch have been equally good things perverted to false use, except perhaps her serpent form, which is used by Lewis as a figure for the truth about her.

Who is the Green Witch?

We may now turn to a consideration of this truth. Who is the Green Witch? A number of candidates for the source of this figure have been suggested, all of them useful. There can be no single answer in a discussion of an archetype. If I propose a few candidates of my own, I do not do so in contradiction to those proposed by the writers I am about to discuss. Peter J. Schakel (1979) remarks of the

Green Witch that "She is a figure of evil in this fairy story, but that evil is handled in the manner of romance, not theology."[20] He compares her with Circe, pointing out that "on a holiday which celebrates the return of fertility, she kills a mother and makes plans to [...] enslave her son. The use of the May element, the traditional European celebration, is indeed suggestive. Beltaine, celebrated on the first day of May, featured fertility rituals related to the "waxing power of the sun."[21] The celebration of May-Day in *The Silver Chair* is based upon the evolved form of Beltaine in British medieval life, which featured not only the well-known maypole with its circular sun-symbolizing wreath, but delicious green foods.[22] These ritual attempts to ensure the coming of spring by sympathetic magic are contrary to the behavior of the serpent in *The Silver Chair*. She is, despite her skin of green, opposed to life. That is why Lewis identifies her green color repeatedly as "green as poison."

In comparing this lady with Circe we are following Lewis's own lead, as Schakel points out: Lewis wrote "the witch [...] is of course Circe [...] the same Archetype we find in so many fairy tales. No good asking where any individual author got *that*. We are born knowing the witch, aren't we?"[23] Circe was one of the daughters of Helios, the Greek god of the Sun.[24] In this mythologem of the Sun-daughters in the *Odyssey*, Circe is "beautifully alluring" as well as "frighteningly powerful."[25] Through her, men "can be transformed and disappear into a pig-existence."[26] The pig is the sacred animal of Demeter and Persephone, goddesses of the Vegetation cycle and the Underworld: a pig-existence is an underworld, unconscious existence. This pig-imagery is made explicit in *The Silver Chair* when Jill, ever the seeress, thinks of the enchanted Prince: "He's the silliest, most conceited pig I've met for a long time" (SC 159; ch. 11).

To the modern reader, the plight of Circe's pigs is like that of Prince Rilian, transformed into a "selfish, self-centered pig" (SC 161; ch. 11) and deprived of his identity. But this work of Circe's is a reflection of "a still greater goddess," who exercised the "all-transforming power of love," Aphrodite. Prince Rilian is in love, as besotted as Romeo, but his Lady, patterned after certain medieval ladies, is false. The explanation given by Karl Kerenyi (1979) of the difference, is extremely important:

> In a fortunate love encounter, power and love are balanced; moreover, the one is also the other. What produces unfortunate love is that disturbance of balance which appears as love-magic, as a wish to arouse love through power, rather than through the impersonal awakening of love as a power over the lovers. Every other kind of sorcery, indeed the whole of magic, stands under the sign of the simple will to power and in relation to love-magic is secondary.[27]

These words—"sorcery, indeed the whole of magic, stands under the sign of the simple will to power"—exactly define the evil to which Lewis points again and again. The Green Witch compels the *love* of Rilian, not that she might enjoy his love, but that she might have him in her power, in order to work her own will.

The name Circe is related to "circle"—her magic is the power to encircle, just as the "solar movement is circling."[28] Circe is a weaver who sings seductively at her loom. In this she resembles the "mythological field of the north" where the Lay Sun spins the sun's rise, while in the *Kalevala* another sun's daughter weaves "at the border of the wide horizon."[29] The horizon is the place of the sun's visible activities, its source when it rises, and its goal when it sets. The spinning and weaving of the sun's action creates the structure of time as the sun moves back and forth upon the circle of the horizon like a shuttle, tracing the pattern of the seasons. As so much of the structure of *The Silver Chair* depends upon the seasons, it is appropriate that the famous encounter between the Green Witch and Prince Rilian's rescuers turns upon the subject of the sun.

At the height of her efforts to convince them that Narnia does not exist, wise Puddleglum declares:

> "I've seen the sun coming up out of the sea of a morning and sinking behind the mountains at night. And I've seen him up in the midday sky when I couldn't look at him for brightness." (SC 176; ch. 12)

The enchanted listeners are aroused by these vivid images, and the Witch redoubles her efforts. She declares their sun to be a dream, and accuses them of basing it upon the reality of a lamp; she sets them all to chanting the falsehood, like the devotees of a religious cult: "There is no sun," and "There never was a *sun*" (SC 178-79; ch. 12). At this moment Puddleglum resorts to physical sacrifice, but the point has been made: the sun is a figure of the Real. Even the Witch is a creature of the only deity there is: even her powers, used for falsity, are derived from her creator.

Another candidate for the witch is suggested by Glen Good-Knight (1970): "In a tone quite different from his mentor, MacDonald, Lewis uses the Lilith mythos within the Narnian cosmos."[30] A very full treatment of the nineteenth-century Lilith states that "She represents a source of evil, a siren who destroys those who fall under her spell."[31] Wrestling with the wealth of uses of the Lilith figure, Meredith Price (1982) sees a dichotomy between a stellar Lilith and a chthonic Lilith.[32] I think this problem is resolved in understanding that another deeper deity underlies the Lilith image, the goddess of love, who in ancient Mesopotamia was a celestial goddess with a chthonic sister, forming a complete mythologem.

Lilith appears in Isaiah 34.4: "The wild-cat shall meet with the jackals and the satyr shall cry to his fellow, Yea Lilith shall repose there and find her a place of rest." Everything in this passage suggests that Lilith will find her rest in a derelict place, a desert place, far from human habitation, in a word, a place like the Wild Waste Lands of the north in *The Silver Chair*. In the *Zohar*, the sacred book of Kabbalism, Lilith is the feminine aspect of Samael; "the female of Samael is called Serpent."[33] Originally a wind-spirit, she became associated in Talmudic thought with a night-spirit. In the Middle Ages these figures coalesced in the Jewish folkloric figure of *Lilit*, who pursued newborn babies and lay with men in their sleep. The poisonous serpent beside the well in *The Silver Chair* well accords with yet another aspect of the Lilith myth: "it is blood, rather than poison, that pollutes the wells"[34] during a moment at each of the four quarters of the year when special angels change their watch over sources of drinking water. The Kabbala suggests that "Lilit's menses are the source of these drops of blood."[35]

At this point we are very close to that point of view which finds the mysteries of feminine fertility a source of danger to masculine power. We might think we had strayed very far from the subject of a children's novel, had we not the word of Lewis himself that the White Witch, with whom the Green Witch is said to share the same race, is a descendant of Lilith. But before exploring this Near Eastern divinity to her full origin I will treat other candidates for the Green Witch.

Meredith Price has suggested that she "embodies aspects of Morgan Le Fay. Her relationship to Rilian (enchantress to her captive knight) is distinctly Arthurian, reminding one of the green-girdled lady under Morgan's direction in [...] *Sir Gawain and the Green Knight*."[36] Some scholars regard Morgan Le Fay as The Morrigan, the Irish goddess of battle and death, a figure associated with the Underworld.[37] The Morrigan could take the form of a snake. The lady who does the bidding of Morgan Le Fay in *Sir Gawain and the Green Knight* carries out her work with a green belt given as a token to Sir Gawain. She tells him:

> For whoever goes girdled with this green riband,
> While he keeps it well clasped closely about him,
> There is none so hardy under heaven
> > that to hew him were able

Gawain lives to regret this gift and its meaning, associated with its color, becomes clear:

> He took then the treacherous thing and untying the knot
> Fiercely flung the belt at the feet of the Knight:
> "See there the falsifier, and foul be its fate!"[38]

This green girdle is "the falsifier," and this is the significance of the green garment worn by the Witch in *The Silver Chair*.

Cox has another source to nominate: "Spenser's monster Error, half woman and half serpent." This reference to Spenser brings us very close to an immediate source of Lewis's central imagery in *The Silver Chair*, *The Faerie Queene*. In his great early study *The Allegory of Love*, Lewis proposed to use "romance" for that tendency in the late sixteenth century toward a "widening and deepening of the allegorical *terrain* [...] to shift the interest from the personifications to the whole world in which such people and such adventures are plausible."[39] As "An English branch of that excellent Italian *genre* the romantic epic,"[40] *The Faerie Queene* is filled with images that were immediately recognizable to readers familiar with small town pageants and country pulpits. In such imagery, "A dragon's mouth is the 'griesly mouth of hell' as in a medieval drama."[41]

A dragon of this type is implied by Cox's first candidate, the half woman and half serpent of my epigraph. This monster is "Errour," who winds her serpent body around the Knight, pours out "A flood of poyson," and receives a fatal blow in return: "He raft her hateful heade without remorse," whereupon her own repulsive offspring devour their mother's body, burst asunder from their copious meal, and die themselves.[42]

In keeping with his source-hunting in *The Faerie Queene*, Cox identifies the silver chair itself with that in the Cave of Mammon encountered by Sir Guyon. Mammon shows Guyon a garden which is "really a demonic perversion of the earthly paradise, a garden of death rather than life":[43]

> The Gardin of Proserpina this hight;
> And in the midst thereof a silver seat[44]

This garden is full of plants which are images of sleep and death: "mournfull Cypresse," "Heben sad," "Dead sleeping Poppy, and black Hellebore," and other plantations suitable to a witch's garden.[45] The sadness and mournfulness are perhaps reflected in the cavern of Underland in *The Silver Chair*, which "was very sad, but with a quiet sort of sadness" (SC 145; ch. 11). On the basis of this use of the silver chair and its associations, Cox nominates Proserpina as the "archetype of Lewis's Queen of Underland."[46] I think there is a relationship between Persephone/Proserpina and *The Silver Chair*, but it lies not only in her role as the Queen of the Underworld, but in her role as the Kore or descending maiden, a part played by Jill, not by the Green Witch.

There is one more candidate for the Witch, nominated by Donald E. Glover (1981), who writes that "Rilian [...] seduced by the beauty of the Witch [...] reminds us of Spenser's Duessa and her Red Cross Knight."[47] A commentator on *The Faerie Queene* points out that "The Red Cross Knight gets into trouble partly because he takes Duessa at face value, as a lady to whom he had knightly obligations."[48] Lewis himself says that Duessa is a child of Night who can only reflect light: she "is but pretended, reflected light!"[49] This false, reflective lady, is

> one Duessa, a false sorceresse
> That many errant knights hath brought to
> wretchednesse.[50]

She is false because her beauty is a magical facade covering an ugly reality, expressed by Spenser as the body of an old woman with the feet of a taloned bird. Her power is wrought by "wicked herbes and oyntments," "charmes and magicke might," which render her lover helpless even when he has seen her in her ugliness: "That all my sense were bereaved quight: Then brought she me into this desert waste."[51] The desert waste is the haunt of Lilith in the Old Testament. This is precisely Rilian's plight.

In discussing the meaning of this underworld setting and the descent/ascent structure which it embodies, I shall add two final candidates of my own to the list of sisters, cousins, and aunts of the Green Witch. I shall begin by discussing the whole schema of the Feminine, of which these negative figures represent only a part.

The central symbolism of the feminine has been said to be the *vessel*: "a body-vessel whose inside always remains dark and unknown."[52] A descent to the underworld is thus a descent to the "inside," to that which is dark and unknown. Cave, vessel, belly, and earth, all belong "to the dark territory of the underworld."[53] Animals with a uterine form associated with this complex are pig, squid, shellfish, and owl, a list that will sound familiar to readers of *The Silver Chair*. These images of "negative transformation" form one polarity of the feminine: the mysteries of drunkenness belong here, with their implications of ecstasy, madness, impotence, and stupor, which lead in descending order to transformation, dislocation, rejection, and deprivation, in Erich Neumann's (1955) terminology. The Prince has been transformed from a vigorous young man to a prating booby; he has been dislocated from his own kingdom to an underground prison; he is in a state in which he would be rejected, were he to return to that kingdom, and he has been deprived of his mother, his true throne, his country, and his sanity.

Goddesses whose names are associated with this gloomy polarity include Lilith, Circe, and Astarte. We are fully familiar by now with the first two names, but why Astarte? Constellated here is the "symbol group of the Terrible Mother—night, abyss, sea, watery depths, snake, dragon, whale."[54] Darkness is the source alike of the "night sky, earth, underworld, and the primeval water that preceded the light."[55] It is because of the "waters above and waters below" of the Mesopotamian cosmos, reflected in Genesis, that there is a starry element in this system. Constellations, sun, moon, and planets, all emerge from below the horizon; thus, these bodies were presumed to spend as much time in the underworld as they did in the overworld.

Waters below the earth were known through springs, wells, and marshes; waters above the earth sent down rain; and the whole was surrounded by the encircling waters of the sea. A special "northern" aspect of this system is found in the tradition that the Milky Way is the "Path of Hel," the goddess who is the "northern ruler of the night."[56] This figure thus presents herself as a source of the idea of the *northern* witch: Hel is "the mistress of the sinister abode where the dead will go that are not welcome at Odin's Valalla."[57] She is Loki's daughter, sent by Odin "down into the realm of mist and darkness, Niflheim."[58] This dark underworld is described by Snorri in *The Prose Edda*:

> He threw Hel into Niflheim and gave her authority over nine worlds. [...] She has a great homestead there with extraordinarily high walls and high gates. Her hall is called [Damp-with-sleet]; her plate, Hunger; her knife, Famine, her man-servant [Slow-moving]; her maid-servant [Slow-moving]; the stone at the entrance; Drop-to-destruction; her bed, Sick-bed; its hangings, Glimmering Misfortune. Hel is half black, half flesh-colour, and is easily recognized for this; she looks rather grim and gloomy.[59]

Loki's awesome daughter has two brothers: "the first was the wolf Fenrir, the second, Jormundgard—that is the Midgard Serpent,"[60] as the *Prose Edda* explains. Lewis used the Wolf in *The Lion, the Witch and the Wardrobe* as the agent of the White Witch. In *The Silver Chair* he gives one attribute of the serpent to the Green Witch: as described in the *Prose Edda*, at Ragnarok, "the Midgard serpent will blow so much poison that the whole sky and sea will be spattered with it."[61] This poisonous quality is a peculiarity of the northern worm: "In Anglo-Saxon England it was the fiery dragon, breathing out fire and passing over the habitations of men like a dangerous comet shedding fire [...] But in the Scandinavian stories it is on the serpent aspect of the dragon that most stress is laid,"[62] and the serpent is often poisonous: The *Volsunga Saga* tells of the dripping venom of Fafnir "snorted forth [...] on all the way before him as he went."[63] At

Ragnarok, "the world serpent emerged from the waves blowing out poison over the world."[64] It is a serpent of this sort that emerges beside the fountain in Narnia to poison the Star's daughter.

Shapeshifting women who become snakes are part of an image system of eternally-living beings who continuously renew themselves as they change: they are forms of the long-living beings whom Lewis called the "Longaevi" in *The Discarded Image*. Puddleglum remarks to the enchanted Rilian "that this Lady of yours must be a long liver," and the Prince replies. "She is of divine race, and knows neither age nor death" (SC 154; ch. 10). The moon too renews itself periodically, as does the uterus in menses, so "moon-goddesses are usually represented as serpents."[65] In mythology, moon-goddesses often bring fertility and life, but Lewis used the moon in two of his books as an image of infertility and death. In *That Hideous Strength*, the moon is Sulva, an interplanetary body upon which the residents practice evil forms of birth control. In *Surprised By Joy*, the moon appears in several boyhood incidents, where during "those moonlit nights in the dormitory at Belsen," the "tyrannous noon of revelation"[66] became a figure for a stern, demanding guilt. And in Lewis's science-fiction story, "The Form of Things Unknown," the Medusa, with the serpents writhing about her head, turns an unsuspecting astronaut to stone, functioning as a prototype of the White Witch.

The serpent image is used by Lewis as an agent of death rather than as a symbol of ever-renewing life. And of course there are numerous sources in literature for this kind of serpent. Underlying them are some very archaic forms indeed, including the Sumerian Kur, the Babylonian Tiamat, and the Old Testament Rahab and Leviathan. The serpent in these ancient interpretations is an image of the primaeval, boundless, all-fertile, all-devouring, and bottomless sea of the unconscious, out of which selfhood emerges, and into which it is ever summoned to return. Were it not for revelations to the contrary selfhood would seem inevitably fated to re-submerge and disappear. If this were the whole of this image-structure in the ancient Near East, we should see Lewis as having depicted exclusively a negative female image of evil.

Inanna and Ereshkigal

Another myth touching on these matters is that of Inanna and Ereshkigal. It was Inanna who brought the elements of human culture to the Sumerians from her father Enki, god of wisdom. She enticed him to give them to her while he lay drunk at table, the very image of a repressive father and a self-reliant daughter.[67] In a further effort to obtain control over her own affairs, she descends from her throne in the sky to the underworld to visit her sister Ereshkigal. Ereshkigal had ruled originally in "the wilderness at the world's end,"[68] but now ruled the underworld with her husband Nergal, sleeping naked and black-haired in a palace of lapis lazuli.

This myth in its written form includes some elements that appear in *The Silver Chair*. In "Inanna's descent to the Nether World," the "queen-of heaven, the goddess of light and love and life," determines to visit the nether world in search of her lover Tammuz. Gathering all the needed divine decrees and wearing all her "queenly robes and jewels," she arranges to have messages sent for help to various gods, should she fail to return in three days.[69] She fears that Ereshkigal may try to kill her. "At the gate she is met by the chief gate-keeper."[70] Like Jill in Underland, and at each of the seven gates of the nether world she loses one of her ceremonial garments: the crown upon her head, the rod in her hand, the necklace of lapis lazuli, the sparkling stones upon her breast, her gold ring, her breast-plate, and the garments of ladyship.[71] Naked and kneeling, she encounters her terrible sister and seven judges, before whose gaze she falls dead and is hung upon a stake. When she fails to return, each god is appealed to and Enki sends "two sexless creatures" to bring the food of life and the water of life to the dead goddess. Revived, she returns suitably accompanied by various shades, bogies, and harpies, to the upper world.

There is a catch, however. Anyone who has visited the underworld must send a substitute to replace herself. Inanna makes a tour of Sumerian cities where her ghostly entourage terrifies the inhabitants. At last she reaches Erech, where her long-sought husband is found making merry and quite oblivious to the suffering she has undergone. Despite his appeals for divine aid, he is taken to the nether world in his wife Inanna's place.

The descending sky goddess has been interpreted as the moon, stripped day after day of her seven bright accoutrements as she wanes, and acquiring them again as she waxes to become "Queen of Heaven."[72] The moon's phases require twenty-eight days, four phases of seven days each. The dark of the moon is usually reckoned as lasting three days. The seven bright images of divine power put on and taken off are figures of this process and the three days the goddess hung impaled on the pole in the nether world represent the dark of the moon. The moon in the sky is thus an image of the basic process of the world in which female power waxes and wanes, ever renewing herself, bringing forth life from death and death from life along that spiraling line, time. This royal and divine lady is the archetype behind the Star's daughter in *The Silver Chair*.

The divine decrees, the most important of Inanna's prerogatives, are suggested in the four Signs given by Aslan to Jill, when he sends her to the underworld as a surrogate for the slain Star-Queen. Jill goes into the underworld girded with the Armor of God. Unlike Inanna, she is neither confined there nor forced to send a substitute to replace herself. Instead of finding the straying Prince in the upper world, she finds him where she seeks him, and brings him release. Sent by Aslan, she becomes an *alter Christus*, one who resembles Jesus who descended into Hell and, after three days, released the souls of those who had been unjustly bound there. By cooperating freely with Grace, in obeying the four signs, Jill and her companions are able to do the redeeming work of Aslan. When Rilian returns to his own world,

> Instantly every head was bared and every knee was bent; a moment later such cheering and shouting, such jumps and reels of joy, such hand-shakings and kissings and embracings of everybody by everybody else broke out that the tears came to Jill's eyes. Their quest had been worth all the pains it cost (SC 225; ch. 15)

Ereshkigal, the queen of the nether world who is reflected in the many other goddesses mentioned in this paper—Circe, Lilith. Morgan Le Fay, Errour, Proserpina, Duessa, Hel, Tiamat—is one half of the full mythologem of Woman. She is, as it were, that "Halfe like a serpent" which lies beneath the surface of life, invisible but filled with power. This is the power which the Green Witch, falsely dressed in the garments of fertility and renewal, uses to kill the Star-Queen and compel the love of Prince Rilian, dragging him below the level of consciousness. When he calls upon Aslan (to whom all times are alike) Aslan sends a rescuer. Girded with royal commands that might have been worn by a sky-queen on a divine quest, and companioned by two metamorphs, Jill Pole descends the Polar Way from overworld to underworld. There she meets the guardian of Underland and the host of under land-dwellers. The Witch does her worst, attempting to strip away Aslan's gifts by sorcerous seduction, but the rescuers counteract her magic with a profound dose of physical and spiritual reality: self-sacrifice and faith. The Witch is killed in her true snake-form.

Nothing in Narnia is evil in itself; the northern witches are intruders: the underworld, too, is good. As we have seen. Lewis presents the complete mythologem of the feminine:

The Queen of Heaven—the Star's daughter;
The Heroine on a descent-quest—Jill Pole;
The Queen of the Nether World—Green Witch

By this means, Lewis allows the power of this archetype to manifest itself completely. The Green Witch can only function by falsification of what is really true, and privation of what is really good. These northern witches always mean the same thing.

Notes
[1] Edmund Spenser, *The Faerie Queene*, intro. by Graham Hough vol. I (London: The Scolar Press, 1976).
[2] John D. Cox, "Epistemological Release in *The Silver Chair*," *The Longing for a Form: Essays on the Fiction of C.S. Lewis*, ed. Peter J. Schakel (Kent State UP, 1977) 161.
[3] Paul A. Karkainen. *Narnia Explored* (Old Tappan, NJ: Fleming H. Revell, 1979) 105.
[4] The figure of a girl who goes into the underworld to rescue a captive boy is found in George MacDonald's *The Princess and the Goblin* (Gutenberg ebook #708), where she meets a queen of the underworld, the Goblin Queen, who dies with one shoe off, revealing that she has toes like a "sun-woman" and the other on, a shoe of stone, presenting

Notes

her chthonic identity. I have written extensively of the *Kore* motif embodied in Princess Irene, in "Kore Motifs in George MacDonald's *The Princess and the Goblin*," an unpublished essay presented before the Second Annual Conference on the Fantastic at Boca Raton, Florida in 1981. [Editor's note: This paper is now available in *For the Childlike: George MacDonald's Fantasies For Children*, ed. Roderick McGillis (Metuchen, NJ: Scarecrow, 1992) 169-82.]

I have discussed the moon and star goddess who sends the Princess on this underworld quest in "Archetypes of the Mother in the Fantasies of George MacDonald," *Mythcon I Proceedings* (Los Angeles, CA: The Mythopoeic Society, 1971).

[5] Jill is not an unlikely or unexpected heroine. We learn right away of her forceful nature: "for the moment she looked like a tigress" (SC 7; ch. 1) when she fears that her schoolmate Eustace Scrubb has only invented Narnia as an exit from Experiment House, a place of hopelessness under the rule of a female Head which is a prefiguration of the situation in Underland. When Aslan appears to Jill crouched beside "the stream, bright as glass, running across the turf" (SC 21; ch. 2), this description of the stream resembles that of MacDonald describing the stream in the land *At the Back of the North Wind*, which borders the Earthly Paradise as in *The Divine Comedy*: "He said the river—for all agree that there is a river there—flowed not only through, but over grass: its channel […] was of pure meadow grass, not over long." George MacDonald, *At the Back of the North Wind* (1868; Gutenberg ebook #225) ch. 10. This stream forms a benign image counteracting the malignant fountain and evil rivers associated with the Green Witch, and is the source of the resurrection of Prince Caspian at the end of the book. This image of water—both life-giving and life-taking—is complete.

[6] An Anglican reading this passage will likely be reminded of a familiar Collect in the *Book of Common Prayer*, that for the Second Sunday in Advent, in which a worshipper asks: "Blessed Lord, who has caused all holy Scripture to be written for our learning: Grant that we may in such wise hear them, read, mark, learn, and inwardly digest them, that by patience and comfort of thy holy Word, we may embrace and ever hold fast the blessed hope of everlasting life."

Notes

[7] "Pure 'Northerness' engulfed me: a vision of huge, clear spaces hanging above the Atlantic," C.S. Lewis, *Surprised by Joy* (1955; New York: Harcourt, Brace, Jovanovich, 1966) 73.

[8] T.S. Eliot, "Little Gidding," *Four Quartets* (London: Faber and Faber, 1959) 240-242.

[9] There is a fresh-flowing stream in the garden enjoyed by Irene in springtime in MacDonald's *The Princess and the Goblin* that becomes her escape route when she re-emerges with the rescued Curdie at the climax.

[10] Spenser, *The Faerie Queene* Book I, Canto I, Stanza 13. The motif of the "thick woods" as a symbol of dangerous territory associated with kidnapping reminds me of the vocabulary used to describe the site where the Lindburgh baby was buried by his kidnapper, the resonance of which is developed by Barbara Goldsmith in *Little Gloria; Happy at Last* (New York: Dell, 1981) 233. "Special phrases became part of the kidnap vocabulary that children of the thirties understood like a secret language. The victim's body was often placed in a *shallow grave* in a *densely wooded area*" (Goldsmith's italics).

[11] René Laurentin, *Bernadette of Lourdes* (Minneapolis, MN: Winston Press, 1979) 242-43. Laurentin remarks: "This term used by Bernadette [...] is somewhat shocking. It expresses Bernadette's respect for the ineffable. It is completely in accord with what we call negative theology (*theologia negativa*)" (243). The name which the apparition gave to herself was expressed in "French, which Bernadette did not know": "*Que soy era Immaculada Councepciou.*" This is translated, "I am the Immaculate Conception" (75-76).

[12] In *The Silver Chair* it is Jill Pole who first sees Aslan. Does her name, Pole, suggest the world-axis motif with its top in the starry heavens and its serpent-attended base in the underworld? She travels this route from Aslan's Country to Underland below, and back again, in *The Silver Chair*.

[13] Margaret Blount, *Animal-Land* (New York: Avon, 1977), writes that Puddleglum has "serious saurian views of life" (297), and "has the reptilian virtues of being cold-blooded and reliable" (298), but I think Lewis meant to suggest a frog-like amphibian rather than a reptile.

Notes

[14] H.R. Ellis Davidson, *Scandinavian Mythology* (London: Hamlyn, 1969) 117.

[15] *The Elder Edda*, trans. Paul B. Taylor and W.H. Auden (New York: Viking Books, 1970) "The Lay of Grimnir," stanza 28.

[16] Paul F. Ford, *Companion to Narnia* (San Francisco, CA: Harper and Row, 1980) 314.

[17] "And thereupon, behold, a Knight on a black horse appeared, clothed in jet-black velvet, and with a tabard of black linen about him." *The Mabinogion*, trans. Lady Charlotte Guest (John Jones, Cardiff, 1977) 9.

[18] Martin P. Nilsson, *A History of Greek Religion* (New York: Norton Library, 1964) 212. Nilsson calls it a place of "empty nothingness."

[19] The scene of metamorphosis used here owes something to the changes of the thieves to various saurian monsters in the Seventh Bowge of Hell in *The Divine Comedy*:

> The shade's feet clave together, till by and by
> Legs, thighs, and all so fused that never a sign
> Could be discerned of seam, or junction scarred […]

The Divine Comedy of Dante Alighieri the Florentine, Cantica I, Hell, trans. Dorothy L. Sayers (Harmondsworth, UK: Penguin, 1949) Canto xxv, lines 105-107. It is echoed in the change of Miss Wilmot: "Her body was writhing into curves and knots where she lay," so that "No longer a woman but a serpent indeed surged before him" in Charles Williams, *The Place of the Lion* (London: Faber and Faber, 1931) 153.

[20] Peter J. Schakel, *Reading With the Heart: The Way into Narnia* (Grand Rapids, MI: Eerdmans, 1979) 69.

[21] Nora Chadwick, *The Celts* (Harmondsworth, UK: Penguin, 1970) 181.

[22] Madeleine P. Cosman, *Medieval Holidays and Festivals* (New York: Charles Scribners and Sons, 1981) 51: included are green salads, green peppermint rice, minted green whipped cream, and a gingerbread figure called Jack-in-the-Green whose edible head was decorated, like the celebrants who enjoyed him, with sprigs of green.

[23] Schakel, *Reading With the Heart* 9.

Notes

[24] Karl Kerenyi, *Goddesses of the Sun and Moon* (Irving, TX: Spring Publications, 1979) 3.

[25] Kerenyi 6.

[26] Kerenyi 8.

[27] Kerenyi 10.

[28] Kerenyi 11.

[29] Kerenyi 12, 13.

[30] Glen Goodknight, "Lilith in Narnia," *Narnia Conference Proceedings* (Los Angeles, CA: The Mythopoeic Society, 1970) 16.

[31] Roderick F. McGillis, "George MacDonald and the Lilith Legend in the XIXth Century," *Mythlore* 6.1 (Winter 1979): 3.

[32] Meredith Price, "All Shall Love Me and Despair, the Figure of Lilith in Tolkien, Lewis, Williams, and Sayers," *Mythlore* 9.1 (Spring 1982) passim.

[33] Raphael Patai, *The Hebrew Goddess* (New York: Avon, 1978) 193.

[34] Joshua Trachtenberg, *Jewish Magic and Superstition: A Study in Folk Religion* (New York: Atheneum, 1970) 257.

[35] Trachtenberg 255.

[36] Price 7.

[37] Patricia Monaghan, *The Book of Goddesses and Heroines* (New York: E.P. Dutton, 1981) 207.

[38] "Sir Gawain and the Green Knight," *Sir Gawain and the Green Knight, Pearl, and Sir Orfeo,* trans. J.R.R. Tolkien (London: George Allen and Unwin, 1975) 79-81, 113-115.

[39] C.S. Lewis, *The Allegory of Love* (1936; New York: Oxford UP, 1958) 294.

[40] C.S. Lewis, *The Allegory of Love* 305

[41] C.S. Lewis, *The Allegory of Love* 312.

[42] Spenser, *The Faerie Queene*, Book I, Canto I, Stanza 19. The passage on Errour is from Spenser, *The Faerie Queene*, Book I, Canto I passim. This figure may be said to reappear in the character of "Sin" in *Paradise Lost*:

> The one seemed woman to the waist, and fair,
> But ended foul in many a scaly fold
> Voluminous and vast, a serpent armed with mortal sting.
> (Book II, lines 650-652)

Notes

[43] Cox 162.

[44] Spenser, *The Faerie Queene*, Book II, Canto VII, Stanza 53.

[45] Spenser, *The Faerie Queene*, Book II, Canto VII, Stanza 52. Dorothy Jacob, *A Witch's Guide to Gardening* (New York: Taplinger, 1964): Hellebore (Helleborus niger) is known today as the "Christmas rose" but it "was a real standby for witches" (55). *Hebe* is one of the foxgloves, which contains digitalis: Jacob says of the witch, "Her scrap of ground would certainly have contained aconite, endive, foxgloves, belladonna, henbane, moonwort, and many more" (20-21). Harold A. Hansen, *The Witches Garden* (Santa Cruz, CA: Unity Press, 1978): Poppy (Papaver somniferum and Papaver rhoeas) were used in witch's "flying ointment" (93) and is of course a featured image in *The Wizard of Oz* as a causer of enchanted sleep. J.E. Cirlot, *A Dictionary of Symbols* (New York: The Philosophical Library, 1962): Cypress is "A tree dedicated by the Greeks to their infernal deity. The Romans confirmed this emblem in their cult of Pluto [...]" (72).

[46] Cox 163.

[47] Donald E. Glover, *C.S. Lewis: The Art of Enchantment* (Athens, OH: Ohio UP, 1981) 166.

[48] Paul J. Alpers, *The Poetry of the Faerie Queene* (Princeton, NJ: Princeton UP, 1967) 148.

[49] Lewis, *The Allegory of Love* 314.

[50] Spenser, *The Faerie Queene*, Book I, Canto II, Stanza 34.

[51] Spenser, *The Faerie Queene*, Book I, Canto II, Stanza 42.

[52] Erich Neumann, *The Great Mother* (Princeton, NJ: Princeton UP, 1955) 39-40.

[53] Neumann 44.

[54] Neumann 187.

[55] Neumann 212.

[56] Neumann 224.

[57] Georges Dumezil, *Gods of the Ancient Northmen* (Berkeley, CA: University of California Press, 1973) 58.

[58] H.R. Ellis Davidson, *Gods and Myths of Northern Europe* (Harmondsworth, UK: Penguin, 1964) 32.

[59] Snorri Sturleson, *The Prose Edda*, trans. Jean I. Young (Berkeley, CA: University of California Press, 1954) 56.

Notes

[60] Sturleson 56.

[61] Sturleson 87.

[62] Davidson, *Scandinavian Mythology* 119.

[63] *Volsunga Saga*, trans. William Morris (New York: Collier Books, 1962) 142.

[64] Davidson, *Scandinavian Mythology* 122.

[65] Robert Briffault, *The Mothers* (New York: Atheneum, 1977) 142.

[66] C.S. Lewis, *Surprised by Joy* 60.

[67] Monaghan 149.

[68] Monaghan 97-98.

[69] Samuel Noah Kramer, *Sumerian Mythology* (1944; Philadelphia, PA: University of Pennsylvania Press, 1969) 83, 86.

[70] Kramer, *Sumerian Mythology* 87.

[71] Samuel Noah Kramer, *Mythologies of the Ancient World* (Garden City, NY: Anchor Books, 1961) 108.

[72] Monaghan 154.

4.　The Holy House of Ungit

> The girl, you remember, had to marry a monster for some reason. And she did. She kissed it as if it were a man. And then, much to her relief, it really turned into a man and all went well. The other story is about someone who had to wear a mask; a mask which made him look much nicer than he really was. He had to wear it for years. And when he took it off he found his own face had grown to fit it. He was now really beautiful.
>
> ——C.S. Lewis. *Mere Christianity*

Patterson corrects what she believes are widespread misunderstandings of Ungit and Orual attributable to their interpretation in terms of dichotomies, rather than transformations. Her analysis of Ungit is both a study of Lewis's sources and a reaffirmation of his preference for thesis–antithesis–synthesis in narrative and image structure. She considers Ungit's existence as a black stone, her seated posture, and her parental relationship to Eros with reference to the bible and ancient religions. In addition, she discusses Orual, her tutor, and the priest of Ungit as sources of information about practices associated with Ungit, such as live sacrifices, the wearing of veils, and the use of myrtle, as well as her tendency to jealousy.

This paper, like "Thesis, Antithesis, and Synthesis in the Space Trilogy," included in Ransoming the Waste Land Volume I, *is an argument against interpreting Lewis's fiction in terms of dichotomies. Patterson studies some of Lewis's other dark deities in "'The Bolt of Tash': the Figure of Satan in C.S. Lewis's* The Horse and His Boy *and* The Last Battle*" and in "Letters from Hell: The Symbolism of Evil in* The Screwtape Letters*," both included in this volume; in "'This Equivocal Being': The Un-Man in* Perelandra*" available in* Ransoming the Waste Land Volume I*; and other papers in both volumes.*

"The Holy House of Ungit" was first published in Mythlore *21.4 (Winter 1997): 4-15. It is Patterson's seventh and final paper on the representation of evil in Lewis's fiction.*

Better than anybody else, Doris T. Myers (1994) has explained what *Till We Have Faces* is about. It concerns, she says, the fact that Lewis has interpreted the God of Love in the Greek myth of Psyche and Eros in terms of the Christian concept of the God who is Love. Luckily for me, the way is still clear to discuss what *Till We Have Faces* is not about. It is not about evil, or at least, of all his works of fantasy, it is the one that possesses no specific character—and especially no supernatural character—who embodies evil. Because this is, as I think, true, there is a major character in *Till We Have Faces* who has been, for the most part, misunderstood. That character is Ungit. I think Orual has been misunderstood too, but I'll get to that later.

In Peter J. Schakel's *Reason and Imagination in C.S. Lewis: A Study of Till We Have Faces* (1984) Ungit's name does not appear in the Index. It does, however, appear early in his book, as he relates "the pouring of human blood over the stone statue of the goddess Ungit" to "the crudity and cruelty of that world," that is, of Glome, which Lewis himself called "a little barbarous state."[1] Schakel has accepted at face value what Lewis reportedly told Clyde Kilby about the realism of the setting, concluding with the statement that

1) this is a story where "things simply are themselves,"[2] and
2) "the imagined location of the setting is not very important."[3]

The implication here is that Ungit merely signifies the benighted state of Glome's religion and culture. In fact, the unimportance of Glome is an important symbol in the novel, and the dark religion of Ungit is at least as symbolic as it is realistic.

The naturalistic interpretation disappears when Schakel discusses what he calls "a central issue of the story, the problem of how Ungit on the one hand and her son on the other can be expressions of the same divine nature."[4] Noting Thomas Howard's comment (1988) that Ungit is "a much darker, more bloody, more earthy deity" than the Greek Aphrodite,[5] he also cites W.D. Norwood Jr. (1970), who says that "Ungit—Aphrodite, as she is identified by the Fox, or Venus—is one 'face' of the true God; i.e. she is God in his [sic] aspect of Love."[6] According to Schakel, Ungit is a "'numinous' god, not a god of the rationalists."[7] This dichotomous characterization accords with Schakel's major thesis that *Till We Have Faces* expresses a dichotomy in the writings of Lewis between reason and imagination. Another writer, Robert Holyer (1988), has also discerned a dichotomy in *Till We Have Faces*, "between two variations of the theistic view: that ultimate reality is jealous and cruel, or that it is mysterious and marvelous."[8]

I do not find either/or characterizations fruitful, as I have said in another essay,[9] and neither do I accept that Lewis ever wrote from a stance of "mere" realism. His works are endlessly allusive, and in expressing the character of Ungit (she is, I maintain, a character in the story, an active divinity, efficacious and successful) he draws upon his encyclopedic knowledge, according to the period of his training, to build his characterization of her. The focus is a double one, of course; we see Ungit through the eyes of Orual, the central character of the novel, as well as the eye of our own expectations. So we have been warned!

The basic plot of *Till We Have Faces* is outlined by Orual:

> The god of the Grey Mountain, who hates me, is the son of Ungit. He does not, however, live in the house of Ungit, but Ungit sits there alone. In the furthest recess of her house where she sits it is so dark that you cannot see her well, but in summer enough light may come down from the smoke-holes in the roof to show her a little. She is a black stone without head or hands or face, and a very strong goddess. My old master, whom we called the Fox, said she was the same whom the Greeks call Aphrodite; but I write all names of people and places in our own language. (TWF 4; ch. 1)

This description includes two physical elements: Ungit, who is "a black stone," and "her house." In addition, we have the statements that "she sits," and that she is "Aphrodite," the mother of "the god of the Grey Mountain," who is consequently identifiable as Eros, Aphrodite's son. This last matter will be touched upon in my conclusion; here, I will begin by addressing the first four assertions.

Ungit: The Black Stone

Schakel refers to "the stone statue of the goddess Ungit," but in fact, in Lewis's narration, Orual says simply that "She is a black stone." A stone proper, that is, without parts or passions. We learn only that she is black, that she is a stone, and that she sits. Blackness is a category of feminine divinity in many parts of the world. In Rajasthan, India, the goddess Kali is embodied in an "archetypal goddess image, a blackstone,"[10] and a photograph of her—clearly and simply a black stone—is illustrated to prove it. While Aphrodite is, in most, but not all, cases associated with the concept "golden," there is nothing golden about Ungit. She is "a black stone," period. J.E. Cirlot (1962) says that a "stone is a symbol of being, of cohesion and harmonious reconciliation with self."[11]

An example from antiquity is "the Black Stone of Pessinis, an aniconic image of the Phrygian Great Mother taken to Rome during the last of the Punic wars,"[12] but this was a meteorite, like the black stone housed in the Kaaba at Mecca, the *al hadjar alaswad*. And Orual writes explicitly that Ungit "had not, like most sacred stones, fallen from the sky," but instead "had pushed her way up out of the earth" (TWF 270; II, ch. 2). She is a stone of earthly rather than extra-terrestrial origin, like the Bethel, of which we read in the Bible: "And this stone which I have set for a pillar, shall be God's House" (Genesis 28.22). References to this motif recur throughout the Bible. Phrases using the word "rock" include "the Rock of his salvation" (Deuteronomy 32.15); "The Lord is my Rock" (I Samuel 22.33); "The Rock of Israel" (I Samuel 23.13); "my strong rock" (Psalm 31.2); "set my feet upon a rock" (Psalm 40.2); "the rock that is higher than I" (Psalm 61.2); "my rock and my salvation" (Psalm 62.6); and "my God and the Rock of my salvation" (Psalm 89.26). In Matthew 7.25 we read of what was "founded upon a rock," and of what was "upon this rock" (16.18); and in I Corinthians 10.4, that the "Rock was Christ."

The word "stone" is equally evocative: in Italy, Great Britain, and elsewhere standing stones as images of the goddess were set up;[13] and in Greece, Artemis was called "the stony one"; while in Mesopotamia, "Ninhursag was called the lady of the stony ground."[14] Psalm 118.22 refers to the "stone which the builders refused," a motif reiterated in the New Testament in references to Christ as the Cornerstone. The New Testament also refers especially to an association of stone with bread, both in Matthew 7.9 when Jesus asks if a father "will give him a stone" (instead of bread); and in Luke 4.9, where Satan tempts the fasting Jesus to "command this stone, that it be made bread." In the same passage as that cited above where Orual says that Ungit is a stone which came up out of the earth, she also states that the stone's surface forms "a face such as you might see in a loaf, swollen, brooding, infinitely female" (TWF 270; II, ch. 2). That is, she looks like a loaf in the way that a stone looks like a loaf. I would note in this context that in coal mines, the surface of the coal deposit that is to be addressed by the miners is called the "coal face," a very black stone indeed.

The two categories—stone versus bread and stone into bread—express duality as a matched set of contraries, and as a transformation from one category to another. Both stones and bread can be transformed; stones from the quarry become stones in the temple, and grain that is ground, mixed with moisture, and exposed to leaven, becomes bread in the oven. Marija Gimbutas (1989) says that "Bread prepared in a temple was sacred bread, dedicated to a Goddess and used in her rituals."[15] Such bread was still made in Europe in rural areas into the twentieth century, as in the "Bread Maria,"[16] which, like ancient bread ovens and curved hills, including human-made hills such as Silbury Hill, and curved stones, might be made in imitation of the goddess's pregnant belly. Whether occurring in nature or shaped by humankind, it had the same significance,[17] partly because of having the same curved surface as a woman's pregnant belly, partly because a loaf indeed rises into a smooth curved shape resembling the belly, and partly because in most places, bread was set to rise and then baked upon a hot stone. All of these allusions are present in Lewis's image of Ungit as expressed by Orual. If you ask why a doughy face can also be a belly, you can refer to the bawdy little Baubo who entertained the distraught goddess Demeter when she searched for her lost daughter Persephone, the goddess of the grain seed in the ground, who had been rapt away to the underworld. And if you ask why this symbolism has inspired me to write in such detail, I answer that the first religious symbol I can consciously recall is a Hot-Cross Bun presented to me on Good Friday by my mother when I was about three years old; she told me that it symbolized Jesus and was only available on that one day of the year!

The symbol of the stone also incorporated the union of opposites and the metamorphosis/transformation of stone and water. Numbers 20.10 refers to "water out of this rock," and I Corinthians states, "they drank from a spiritual rock." Both references are to Moses bringing water out of rock; in the Apocrypha, we read in Wisdom

11.4 that "When they were thirsty, they called upon you, and water was given them out of a flinty rock." The "you" in this passage is Holy Wisdom; the translation is from the New Revised Standard Version. The King James Version states that "their thirst was quenched out of a hard stone." Here again we have water versus stone and stone becoming water. There may be a similar transformational motif in the New Testament in the motif of both Jesus and Peter (the Rock) walking on water.

Wisdom offers one final, and perhaps most apposite element. Using its language, we can say that Ungit is not "a useless stone, the work of an ancient hand" (Wisdom 13.10 NRSV), or as the King James version says, in its characteristically salty way, "a stone good for nothing, the work of an ancient hand." She is not, that is, a stone formed "in the likeness of a human being" (Sirach 6.21). Sirach (Ecclesiasticus) gets in one last sense in which the stone can function: stating of Holy Wisdom that "She will be like a heavy stone to test them," or as the King James version of Ecclesiastes says, in words still more potent, "She will lie upon him as a mighty stone of trial." In the Old Testament, even in the Wisdom passages, the rock or stone signifies God; in the Apocrypha, it ("she") signifies Holy Wisdom. Blackness (as in "a black stone") does not constitute a negative feature in a goddess (or elsewhere, I should think!) In the first place, the terms "black" and (by implication) "white" do not mean in this context absolutely black and absolutely white, but "dark" and "light" as categories of contrast rather than of polarity. The language of color qua color (as opposed, for instance, to concepts intended to be taken as negative as regards race or states of enlightenment, both of which I regard as entirely unsuitable forms of discourse) does, in fact, in certain languages, divide all colors into these two categories alone. A photograph in black-and-white of the spectrum would show you which colors would fall into which category.

All of us, I dare say, have seen, and perhaps collected as a notable object, a black stone. A notable example of images in this category is available in the many European "black virgins," discussed by Ian Begg in *The Cult of the Black Virgin* (1985). These figures, which echo and may even perpetuate the appearance of the goddesses Kali, Lilith, Neith, Anath, Hathor, Sekhmet, Artemis, Hecate, Cybele, Isis, Ceres, Demeter, Fortuna, Juno, and Vesta in certain of their manifestations (as well as figures such as the queen of Sheba, the Shulamite, and St. Melania) also echo Aphrodite in that she is "sometimes represented as black, as [in] a small votive statue of her in Cyprus."[18] Begg says that "The first glimpse of an ancient statue of the Black Virgin shocks and surprises. Five minutes of contemplation of her suffice to convince that one is in the presence not of some antique doll, but of a great power, the mana of the age-old goddess of life, death, and rebirth."[19] North American readers who wish to test this hypothesis, or perhaps I should say, share in this experience, are invited to look at any of the many replicas of Our Lady of Guadeloupe (the guardian of the Americas) or of Our Lady of Czestochowa, whose veneration has been much promulgated by Pope John Paul II. Some North American Anglicans may be familiar with Our Lady of Walsingham, whose shrine in England is still a great center of pilgrimage.

In the Song of Solomon we read of the lady who says of herself, "I am black but comely, O ye daughters of Jerusalem, as the tents of Kedar, as the curtains of Solomon" (Song of Solomon 1.15), comparing herself to the color of certain textiles. In Buddhism, the dark lady is the black Tara, whose color represents "emptiness,"[20] interpreted as "the radiant black" of the "vast direct experience of being."[21] With this symbol of "being" as black, I have brought this sequence of symbols full circle to the definition offered by Cirlot of stone as a "symbol of being."

Ungit: The Seated Aphrodite

I now turn to the second set of categories applied to Ungit— that "she sits" and that she is "Aphrodite." In many ancient cultures, a seated goddess was a goddess undergoing childbirth;[22] the seated posture was, and is in many places even today, the posture of childbirth. This accords with, and probably signifies, what Orual says in her opening statement that "The god of the Grey Mountain [...] is the son of Ungit" (TWF 4; ch. 1). Ungit is thus by definition the mother of that "god." This association of Ungit with childbearing is poignantly evoked in a passage in which Orual encounters a woman at Ungit's shrine where she is seated to preside over "the morning of the Birth," a woman who "had not come for the Birth feast, but on some more pressing matter of her own" (TWF 271; II, ch. 2). She tells Orual that "There's no goddess like Ungit" (TWF 272; II, ch. 2); I will refer to this episode below. Ungit is in fact associated early on with fecundity; when the King's female slaves produce babies, he exclaims "Anybody'd think this was Ungit's house" (TWF 20; ch. 2). Of the girls so produced (no doubt in many cases through couplings with the King himself), some are kept and some are sold, and "some were given to the house of Ungit" (TWF 20; ch. 2).

As we have seen, Ungit is defined as Aphrodite in the first passage describing her. Orual's teacher, the Athenian slave Orual calls the "Fox," so defines her. Aphrodite was the mother of Eros, and it is their myth, or rather, the myth of their concourse with Psyche, that is being "retold" in *Till We Have Faces*, which Lewis subtitled, "A Myth Retold." Aphrodite is often defined as the "goddess of love"; Eros, too, is "the god of love." As mother and son they embody not only erotic love, a term based upon the name of Eros and not intended, needless to say, to define their love for each other, but the love of a mother for her son and the love of a son for his mother, and, I have no doubt, certain of the loves that Lewis himself discussed in *The Four Loves*, not least that love called caritas and agape. A daring thought! But Lewis dares it. Such loves—agape not least are sometimes harsh indeed, as in the case of the God who is love, who showed that love by dying on Calvary.

Ungit is the goddess of Glome, a little kingdom which Doris T. Myers (1994) situates in time between 310 BCE and 280 BCE[23] and in space either "in the Balkans, perhaps not too far from the Danube," or "in the Caucasus Mountains, looking east to the Caspian sea."[24] I might care to opt for the first of these locations because that area had been the heart of goddess country circa 6500–3500, as described in Marija Gimbutas in *The Goddesses and Gods of Old Europe* (1982), a work which Lewis cannot have done more than anticipate! It is in Glome, Myers says, that "The story of Psyche, a real person, becomes a myth which is to be authenticated by the Incarnation of the real God of Love."[25]

In the novel, whatever its larger meaning, Orual is the central character. She tells her own story both in her complaint which opens as we have seen with a reference to "the god of the Grey Mountain [Myers's "God of Love"], who hates me " (TWF 4; ch. 1), and in her report of the result of presenting the volume containing that complaint, to that God. From Orual we learn, in enormous detail, about

Ungit. We also learn all we are to discover about Glome. Two major structures dominate in Glome. One of these is the palace with its Pillar Room. The other is the House of Ungit.

The palace of Glome is one whose back is "wooden" (TWF 5; ch. 1)—this represents the older parts—and possesses a "byre-door" and a "big dunghill" (TWF 6; ch. 1); in other words, the palace combines within itself, as do/did many archaic dwellings, a living quarter for animals with one for humans. Arrangements like this are common in cold countries, especially those with mountainous regions, or those whose immigrants come from such places, because the heat generated by the animals helps to keep the section of the dwelling reserved for humans, warm. The palace is thus a house that also functions as a barn. The "new parts" (TWF 6; ch. 1) of the palace are not wooden, but constructed "of painted brick," with "the skins and heads of animals hung up on the walls" (like those decorating a hunting lodge, for instance), and most particularly, a "Pillar Room" with "the "hearth" (TWF 6; ch. 1)—only one, so far as we can tell, so the Pillar Room must be small enough to require only one source of heat. The Palace would obviously be a very archaic and humble structure to Greek eyes. However that may be, Orual's father, the King, acquires a slave to tutor his daughter.

As Orual's confidence in her new teacher grows, she "came to tell him all about Ungit, about the girls who are kept in her house, and the presents that brides have to make to her, and how we sometimes, in a bad year, have to cut someone's throat and pour the blood over her" (TWF 7; ch. 1). Blood, girls, and brides are thus associated with Ungit. Hearing this, the Fox comments learnedly, "Yes, she is undoubtedly Aphrodite, though more like the Babylonian than the Greek" (TWF 8; ch. 1). In other words, he identifies Ungit with the goddess worshipped in his own culture, a characteristic gesture in classical culture, and then distances himself from her by identifying her with what he regards as "the Babylonian [Aphrodite]." He tells Orual the story of Prince Anchises's encounter with Aphrodite: she "came down the grassy slopes toward his shepherd's hut, lions and lynxes and bears and all sorts of beasts came about her fawning like dogs" (TWF 8; ch. 1), reminding us of the green lady of Perelandra who first appears to Ransom surrounded by the Perelandrian population of beasts, including an elegant little dragon. Readers who want to

know the reach and accuracy of Lewis's knowledge of ancient goddesses can consult Buffie Johnson's study, *Lady of the Beasts: Ancient
Images of the Goddess and Her Sacred Animals* (1981), with both
benefit and pleasure. In fact, only a very few animals are associated
with Ungit in *Till We Have Faces*, and I will discuss them in due
course.

The meeting of prince and goddess in the story of Anchises
and Aphrodite, one very unsuitable for any schoolgirl but Orual, ends
with the horror of Anchises when "he knew he had lain with a goddess," and exclaims, "Kill me at once" (TWF 8; ch. 1), reminding the
alert Lewis reader of what the mare Hwin says to Aslan when she encounters him in *The Horse and His Boy*. From this incident, Orual, the
apt pupil, concludes that "if the goddess was more beautiful in Greece
than in Glome she was equally terrible in each" (TWF 8; ch. 1). The
word "terrible" occurs in the Old Testament. God, for instance, is
called "terrible" in Deuteronomy 7.21: "for the LORD thy God is
among you, a mighty God and terrible"; in Job 37-22, we read that
"with God is terrible majesty"; in Psalm 47.2, we are told that "the
LORD most high is terrible"; and in Joel 2.11 that "the way of the
LORD is great and very terrible."

In a book Lewis is certain to have read, *Prolegomena to the
Study of Greek Religion* (1903), Jane Harrison writes of "the old radi-
ance of Aphrodite [...], sobered somehow, grave with the hauntings
of earlier godheads."[26] With the onset of science, Harrison says, "only
the mystery of life, and love that begets life, remained, intimately re-
alized and utterly unexplained; hence Aphrodite keeps her godhead to
the end."[27]

In regard to the Fox's association of Aphrodite with Babylon,
Paul Friedrich (1978) says that "both sources, the Semitic and the
Indo-European, gave substantial input into the great figures of Aphrodite that we find in Homer and Sappho."[28] The origins of Aphrodite,
he says, include Old Europe (7000–3500), "a pre-Hellenic stratum in
which women and goddesses supposedly played a preponderant and
dominant role";[29] Neolithic Crete, where Demeter and Persephone
were venerated; the "invading Indo-Europeans," much influenced by
Cretan imagery but male-dominated; the Sumerian Inanna; the Semitic Ishtar of the Phoenicians, where "Ishtar is attended by 'girl'
devotees";[30] and Egypt, the source of Hathor and Sekhmet, not to say

(and he does not say), Isis. The appearance of Ungit is very far indeed from the Aphrodite of Homer's hymn's "Revered, golden-crowned, and beautiful Aphrodite,"[31] she who in Cyprus still appears through Mary under her title "Panghia Aphroditessa."[32] Interestingly, Friedrich examines Aphrodite's associations, which include, for our purpose, "Mountain Peaks,"[33] and the "Aphrodite of the bridal chamber,"[34] relating her to the same lady (or at least an earthly avatar) who appears twice in *That Hideous Strength*, and who may be seen in *Till We Have Faces* (as Ungit) to have arranged the marriage of Psyche (Orual's sister Istra) to Ungit's son.

Christine Downing (1981), who agrees with Johann Jacob Bachofen's (1815–1887) *Myth, Religion, and Mother Right* (1967) in "seeing Psyche as an aspect of [Aphrodite] [...] (as those who worshipped her [Psyche] initially, simply because of her physical loveliness—recognized)."[35] She comments, "How right was C.S. Lewis's decision to retell the tale of Psyche from the perspective of the ugly, jealous, self-righteous older sister who only at the end of her life discovers, 'You, too, are Psyche!'"[36]

The Priest of Ungit

It is in the role of Ungit as mistress of the bridal chamber that we meet "the priest of Ungit," as preparations are made for a new bride for the King of Glome, the father of Orual (and of her sister Redival). Orual's description of this priest, though superficially interpretable as ironic, is, I hope to prove, accurate, appropriate, and to be taken seriously by the reader as offering both realism and symbolic resonance. Orual says:

> I think that what frightened me (in those early days) was the holiness of the smell that hung about him—a temple-smell of blood (mostly pigeons' blood, but he had sacrificed men, too) and burnt fat and singed hair and wine and stale incense. It was the Ungit smell. (TWF 11; ch. 1)

The similarity of this inventory of smells with that of a liturgical church's sanctuary is not, surely, unintentional. I was once told by a minister of the largest Protestant denomination in Canada, the United Church, that he preferred his church to the Anglican because his altar was like a kitchen table, while the Anglican's was like a slaughtering block, presumably basing these similes on the fact that the Anglican

Church of Canada's Book of Common Prayer refers to the bread and wine of the Eucharist as the Body and Blood of Christ.

The priest of Ungit is present at the girl queen's bed because she is there to conceive Psyche, whom Ungit has destined as a bride for her son, the Mountain God. This priest is dressed in authentic shamanic garb with "skins" and "dried bladders" and "the great mask shaped like a bird's head which hung on his chest" (TWF 11; ch. 1). Although at first glance these accouterments suggest Lewis's depiction of the god Tash as a great carrion bird in *The Last Battle*,[37] the presence of the bird's head mask may be given another reading. Buffie Johnson (1988) finds the human with a bird head one of the most revered of all images.[38] A male figure wearing a bird's head mask is painted at the Paleolithic caves of Peche Merle and Lascaux, each one representing a different bird. A "costume of beak, wings, and feathers endowed the wearer with the bird's powers" which include "wisdom."[39] The bird-masked figures of the Paleolithic culminated "in a great flowering of the bird cult of the Mother Goddess in the Neolithic era."[40] As usual, Lewis is precisely accurate in his depiction of the priest of Ungit.

The main concern of the priest in this scene is to ask, "Are the young women to be veiled or unveiled?" (TWF 11; ch. 1). This is no idle question, but an immediate presentation of the theme of *Till We Have Faces*, which is a play upon the donning and doffing of veils. The King's harsh response, which has led to an entire essay interpreting Orual as the victim of a dysfunctional family is:[41] "'Veils, of course. And good thick veils too.' One of the other girls tittered, and I think that was the first time I clearly understood that I am ugly" (TWF 11; ch. 1). In accordance with Glomish religion, the King may have been waxing coarse as well as cruel. The veil, a feature of some aspects of Aphrodite worship, "is analogous to the hymen, which symbolized feminine integrity."[42] The veil has become a very ambivalent subject, to me as to many others, as a symbol of the suppression of women. Some young Moslem women born in Canada have taken up wearing the *hijab*, not, they say, as a symbol of submission to men, but as a sign of their religious faith. They do this against a certain amount of external opposition and hence with a certain air of defiance (expressed in assorted Ontario newspapers in articles and letters to the editor). After re-reading in *Till We Have Faces* how Orual regards the

84

veil she deliberately takes up for her queenship, I began for the first time really to understand (I don't know why it took me so long; I'm the only woman in my parish who still wears a veil in church) why Queen Orual writes "My second strength lay in my veil" (TWF 228; ch. 20).

As Orual's father marries for this second time, she recounts that "we took off layer after layer of her finery," leaving the young bride naked in his bed; and comments that "He made great sacrifices to Ungit every month after that" (TWF 13; ch. 2). His prayers are answered; the child is born—"There must have been some sacrifice too," says Orual; "there was a smell of slaughtering, and blood on the floor, and the priest was cleaning his holy knife" (TWF 14; ch. 2). The little mother is the sacrifice; she has died giving birth. The King, disappointed because the newborn child is a daughter rather than the son he has desired, asks the priest, "what have you to say for Ungit now?" (TWF 15; ch. 2). He adds, "Tell me, prophet, what would happen if I hammered Ungit into powder?" and the Priest, unmoved, retorts, "Ungit hears, King, even at this moment" (TWF 15; ch. 2).

The King responds by throwing Orual to the ground as the nearest example of a girl, and condemns her teacher the Fox to hard labor in the mines. As the dejected pair slip away, Orual points "to the ridge of the Grey Mountain, now dark with a white daybreak behind it, seen through the slanting rain" (TWF 17; ch. 2). This is the first clear description of the mountain, which is to play a central role in the book. Obviously, it lies to the east of the royal palace of Glome, and the "white daybreak" suggests, to the alert reader (or at least one exposed as Lewis was to the Book of Common Prayer) to "the dayspring from on high" hailed through the Benedictus in Morning Prayer, who is to come from thence.

The Day-spring is the dawn, and even more the dawning Sun of Righteousness, the divine Son of God, and the son of Ungit in *Till We Have Faces*. Lewis's imagery of the Utter East in *The Voyage of the Dawn Treader* anticipates this. One could add that the West-wind, who meets Psyche when she goes to the Tree as a sacrifice, is the wind who would have blown the Dawn Treader steadily toward the east, and is the god who carries Psyche eastward to the mountain fastness where her husband Eros awaits (unless, as I suspect, West-wind and Eros are one and the same).

Psyche

The above-mentioned materials have presented the dyad House of Ungit/Grey Mountain, firmly established as a symbolic pair, and Orual's abusive context has clearly been indicated in various allusions to her miserable palace life. Now we meet the center of Orual's story, her sister Istra, or, as she says, when the Fox asks for that name in Greek, "It would be Psyche, Grandfather" (TWF 20; ch. 2). This name appears in the novel for the first time here: it is given by Orual herself. It is useful, perhaps, to note the two definitions of the name Psyche given in *Webster's Collegiate Dictionary* for 1947: "A beautiful princess of whom Venus became jealous. Cupid, Venus's son, fell in love with Psyche, and Venus imposed many hardships on her, but Psyche was finally reunited with Cupid and made immortal." The definition adds the second meaning: "The human soul, also, the mind; the mental life."

Psyche, like the Grey Mountain (and unlike the House of Ungit), is associated with light. "You would have thought she made bright all the corners of the room where she lay" (TWF 20; ch. 2). As the child grows, the Fox and Orual take her out to look toward the Grey Mountain, and Psyche explains prophetically, "When I'm big [...], I will be a great, great queen, married to the greatest king of all, and he will build me a castle of gold and amber up there on the very top" (TWF 23; ch. 2). The phrase "the greatest king of all" is, for Lewis, literally meant. He is thinking of the King of Kings (as celebrated, for instance, by Handel's *Messiah*). When the Fox praises Psyche's beauty, saying she is "prettier than Aphrodite" (TWF 23; ch. 2), Orual is afraid; the Fox replies, "The divine nature is not like that. It has no envy" (TWF 24; ch. 2).

This passage presents a complete set of viewpoints. First, there is the association of Ungit with "the divine nature." Second, we have the Fox's declaration that the divine nature "has no envy." Third, we have Ungit's contention that it is dangerous (perhaps even blasphemous) to say that Psyche is more beautiful than Aphrodite/Ungit. Who is right? Does the divine nature reside in Ungit? Is the divine nature free of jealousy? If my thesis is correct, the answer to both questions is "Yes," and Orual is right about the first and wrong about the second. Orual's mistake, which concludes Chapter Two, is the pivot of the book, for it is precisely here that her complaint against the gods is situated.

In Chapter Three, the point is reiterated, as Orual's other sister, Redival, now also forced to spend her time with the Fox, surprisingly bows down to Psyche and says to Orual and the Fox, "Why don't you honour the goddess?" (TWF 27; ch. 3). A woman has asked Psyche to kiss her child so it will be beautiful, and has "laid down a branch of myrtle [...] and bowed down and put dust on her head" (a symbolic act of humility). Ungit's fears of divine jealousy are again aroused, and Redival wonders slyly what Ungit "thinks of our new goddess" (TWF 28; ch. 3). When the Fox wryly replies, "It is not very easy to find out what Ungit thinks," Redival retorts that "it would be easy to find out what the Priest of Ungit thinks" (TWF 28-29; ch. 3). Orual says "All my old fear of the Priest [...] stabbed through me" (TWF 29; ch. 3). Priests, she thinks, can be jealous, whether or not jealousy is a trait of the divine nature.

The symbol of the myrtle, offered above to Psyche, is no casual motif. This evergreen plant was one of the flowers used for offerings in Ptolemaic Egypt,[43] and Theophrastus satirized "those superstitious Greeks who hung myrtle wreaths on their household gods."[44] Appropriately, "Myrtle was sacred to the Goddess Aphrodite." For the Feast of Booths, a very old Judaic festival, structures made of "cypress branches and myrtle" were erected, "symbolizing happiness and fertility" (see Nehemiah 8.15), and in Rome, "successful Roman generals were awarded the crown of myrtle."[45] The Hebrew name for myrtle is *hadas*, as in Hadassah, in Esther 2.7.[46] The myrtle's "aromatic branches [...] also figured in betrothal rites" in ancient Greece, where it was explicitly used "because of its association with Aphrodite, as well as for the crowns of initiates into the Eleusanian Mysteries."[47] Nothing is ever a throwaway with Lewis.

The Sacrifice of Psyche

Whatever may be said about the jealousy of gods, things now begin to go very wrong with the kingdom of Glome: insurrection, bad harvest, and famine. "Now mark the subtlety of the god who is against us" (TWF 30; ch. 3), says Orual, building her case. The Fox is taken with the fever and Psyche nurses him back to health. The people of Glome call out to her to deliver healing for their fevers, too, along with food to make up for their lost harvest, crying as she appears, "A goddess, a goddess," and hailing her, as does one woman: "It is Ungit herself in mortal shape" (TWF 32; ch. 3). Is this blasphemy? Can a goddess become a young woman? Can God become "man" [sic]?

After the healing, and after Psyche has herself recovered from the fever, the people offer "myrtle branches and garlands and soon honeycakes and then pigeons, which are specially sacred to Ungit" (TWF 33; ch. 3). Honey (and bees) and pigeons (or doves) are profoundly significant in the context Lewis uses here. Petronius said that "Mother Earth lies in the world's midst rounded like an egg [more of this below] and all blessings are there inside her as in a honeycomb."[48] Bees "were the souls of [...] priestesses who had been in the service of Aphrodite," at the temple of Eryx "where her symbol was a golden honeycomb,"[49] While bees could symbolize mortality[50] honey was also a symbol of resurrection,[51] Hence, it is not surprising that Gimbutas says that the Goddess is related to transformation and regeneration.[52]

As for the dove goddess (Webster defines "pigeon" as "a dove"), she had her sanctuary at Knossos.[53] Barbara Walker (1988) remarks that "Despite its later Christianized transformation into a symbol of the Holy Ghost, the dove formerly represented the specifically sexual aspect of the Goddess."[54] There is an element of this in the many images of the Annunciation to the Blessed Virgin Mary by the angel Gabriel that she is to be the mother of Jesus, in which a dove, surrounded by rays of light, descends on a trajectory suitably directed toward her abdomen, and a lovely symbol it is, too. Finally, the dove is a symbol of Hokmah–Sophia–Sapientia–Holy Wisdom— "the triumphant dove having been the most common symbol of the Goddess's spirit brooding over the waters of creation."[55]

Clearly the myrtle, honey cakes, and pigeons are gifts offered to the goddess, presumably Ungit, whose healing power (and perhaps embodiment) is perceived by the Glomish population to be associated with Psyche. As for the Priest of Ungit, he is sick with the fever in his turn, and can do nothing. Everything goes wrong. Illness continues, a second harvest fails (not necessarily implying a second year, since two harvests can be possible in a single year in some latitudes), and now Psyche is seen as the cause of this suffering, as the river dries, the fish die, the cattle and bees perish, the fever continues, lions begin to stalk nearby, and the king's enemies also start to prowl, alerted to Glome's weakness.

Now the Priest of Ungit recovers. "The bearers set down the litter and the Priest was lifted out of it […] he had two temple girls with him to lead him […] They looked strange under the sun, with their gilt paps and their huge flaxen wigs and their faces painted till they looked like wooden masks" (TWF 42; ch. 4). Led to the Pillar Room, the Priest confronts the King, and

> The girls stood stiffly at each side of his chair, their meaning-less eyes looking straight out of the mask of their painting. The smell of old age, and the smell of the oils and essences they put on those girls, and the Ungit smell, filled the room, It became very holy. (TWF 43; ch. 4)

Again, are these passages, so vivid and so potent, ironic? Is Orual's attributed holiness mistaken? Presumably, at least to judge by the references to painted faces, elaborate wigs, and heavy perfumes, as well as to "meaningless eyes." One could assume that Lewis is al-luding to the supposed temple prostitutes which Herodotus depicted in his account of the temple of Ishtar [Mytilla] in Babylon, which is in fact the only actual historic reference, true or not, to this idea. Tikva Frymer-Kensky (1992) concludes that "the whole idea of a sex cult—in Israel or in Canaan—is a chimera, the product of ancient and mod-ern sexual fantasies."[56] She states flatly that "The whole tradition of considering ancient pagan religion sexy and its women cultic func-tionaries as sex partners is a myth," based on the Western "inability to think of roles for women priestesses in any arena other than sexual."[57] In fact Lewis does not actually imply that these young priestesses are prostitutes, and I will discuss their symbolic role below, as they reap-pear much later in the novel.

The priest of Ungit, accompanied by the young women, comes to the King with dire news. Ungit, he says, wants "the Great Offering" (TWF 46; ch. 5): the offering of a human life. "The Brute" (TWF 47; ch. 5) has been seen walking abroad, and he is "very black and big, a terrible shape"—a shadow, in fact. The source of this particular motif may be the Shadow who pursues Anodos in George MacDonald's *Phantastes*, the book that Lewis said (with accuracy) had "baptized" his imagination.

For the Brute is, in a mystery, Ungit herself or Ungit's son, the god of the Mountain; or both. The victim is led up the mountain to the Holy Tree, and bound to the Tree and left. [...to become ...] the Brute's Supper. And when the Brute is Ungit it lies with the man, and when it is her son it lies with the woman. [...] The best in the land is not too good for this office. (TWF 48-49; ch. 5)

The resonance of these interlocking images is, of course, extraordinary, vibrating with hints of the Cross ("the Holy Tree,"), the Eucharist (the "Brute's Supper"), and even, in a quote not cited above, the vows of a religious who becomes the bride of Christ—"the bride of Ungit's Son" (TWF 49; ch. 5). No wonder Orual states that "The holiness and horror of divine things were continually thickening in that room" (TWF 49; ch. 5).

In corroboration, the Priest states coolly to the protesting King: "Holy places are dark places. [...] Holy Wisdom is not clear and thin like water, but thick and dark like blood" (TWF 50; ch. 5). This is the most explicit suggestion by Lewis that Ungit is in fact Holy Wisdom; recent commentators (as well as medieval ones) have specifically associated Christ with Holy Wisdom so that the divine nature appears in the Godhead as both feminine and masculine.

The element of darkness as a category of the divine appears in Deuteronomy 5.12: "The Lord spake with all your assembly in the mount out of the midst of the fire, of the cloud, and of thick darkness"; and in Psalms 18.11: "He made darkness his secret place." It has been pointed out that the Holy of Holies in the Temple of Solomon was "a dark windowless room in which the ark was placed."[58] One notes that the Ark of the Covenant, which was kept in this dark room, contained the stones which bore the Law; as Psalm 18, says: "The Lord is my rock," a motif appropriate to Ungit, who is a rock in a dark place.

At the conclusion of the encounter between the King of Glome and the Priest of Ungit, lots are cast, and Psyche is the chosen sacrifice. Orual, despairing, notices "some temple girls sitting in the hall. From the courtyard came the smell of incense, and sacrifice was going on. Ungit had taken the house; the reek of holiness was everywhere" (TWF 62; ch. 6). This passage resembles the "Descent of the Gods" upon St. Anne's Manor in *That Hideous Strength*, in which

Venus's descent is described: "a smell of burning cedar or of incense pervaded the room" (THS 319; ch. 15). Even as Orual goes to comfort the imprisoned Psyche, seeking her own solace from her doomed sister, she is forced to hear of Ungit:

> "But what's a city built on? There is earth beneath. And outside the wall? Doesn't all the food come from there as well as all the dangers? ... [...] more like, yes, even more like the House of—"
>
> "Yes, of Ungit," said I. "Doesn't the whole land smell of her?" (TWF 70-71; ch. 6)

Here too is a whiff of the descending Venus of *That Hideous Strength*, whose coming brings a scent of "ripe fields in August" (THS 319; ch. 15). These evocations of olfactory memory extend to Psyche's experience of Ungit's son, as she tells Orual, "Do you remember? The colour and the smell, and looking across at the Grey Mountain in the distance?" (TWF 74; ch. 7).

In the central scene of confrontation between Orual and Psyche, we indeed see jealousy, but it is not the jealousy of the god—Psyche says "All my life the god of the Mountain has been wooing me" (TWF 76; ch. 7)—but of Orual. A major element in this book, I think, is the jealousy of the unconverted for the converted, the parent who hates to see a daughter marry, the family of a prospective nun, family members for those who become Christian (or any other religion), even Janie Moore when her young companion, C.S. Lewis, turns toward God. Lewis describes the process in *The Screwtape Letters*. And this is not simple jealousy; it is by no means so ignoble as that. Accounts of early Christian martyrs contain passages where friends and family implore them to burn the necessary incense and escape the arena. The apostles themselves never understood beforehand their Lord's intention as he went to the cross.

In her anguish, Orual limps away to bed, wakened on the morning of the sacrifice to the sound of "temple music, Ungit's music, the drums and horns and rattles and castanets, all holy, deadly—dark, detestable, maddening noises" (TWF 79; ch. 8). Besides noting the role of the sistrum (a form of rattle) used in the worship of Isis and still used in Egyptian Coptic Christian worship, we can acknowledge that Orual here attributes malignant aural elements to the imagery of

Ungit, recalling the "sound of the cornet, flute, harp, sackbut, psaltery, dulcimer, and all kinds of music" required by Nebuchadnezzar's image (see Samuel 6.5 and Daniel 3.5). Worse still for Orual is the sight of Psyche: "they had painted and gilded and be-wigged her like a temple girl. I could not even tell whether she saw me or not" (TWF 80; ch. 8). Many a parent has felt the same as her or his daughter came up the aisle to her wedding, so garmented, veiled, coifed, and otherwise bedizened as to be almost unrecognizable, and so intent upon the face of her future husband that the parents cannot tell whether she sees them or not.

Orual's Quest

The bereft Orual falls into a long illness. When she recovers, she sets out to rescue at least the bones of the sacrificed Psyche. It is at this point that we finally read a detailed description of Ungit's house:

> We passed the house of Ungit on our right. Its fashion is thus: great, ancient stones twice the height of a man and four times the thickness of a man, set upright in an egg-shaped ring. They are very ancient, and no one knows who set them up or brought them to that place, or how. [...] This is a holy shape, and the priests say it resembles, or (in a mystery) that it really is, the egg from which the whole world was hatched or the womb in which the whole world once lay. [...] There was smoke going up from it as we passed, for the fire before Ungit is always alight. (TWF 94; ch. 9)

The primordial egg is an idea originating in the Paleolithic, and elaborately expanded in the very early Neolithic cultures.[59] Gimbutas says that "Cucuteni vases"—which were made by a culture in the Danubian area "reveal the formation of the world and beginning of life from an egg in the midst of which a germ resided."[60] The egg can comprise the central or fundamental germ from which being emerged, and/or the universe itself as fully formed.[61] It is also "a rich and very ancient symbol of life."[62]

The great stones, twice as tall as a man and four times thicker, of which Ungit's house is made, remind us not only of the great orthostatic stones arranged to create sacred sites in Britain including Stonehenge and New Grange, but of stones like the one of which Jacob says, "This stone which I have set up for a pillar, shall be God's house" (Genesis 28.22), and of the house of Holy Wisdom of which Proverbs 9.1 says, "Wisdom hath builded her house, she hath hewn out her seven pillars." The pillar motif recurs in the final chapter of *Till We Have Faces*, where in a dream, the Pillar Room of Glome proves to have three layers, each one deeper than the one before.

Orual's journey to reclaim her sister Psyche continues the stream of apparent ironies, which can be interpreted not only as reversals caused by her perceptions but images capable of alternative readings. Looking toward the Grey Mountain, she sees "a cursed black valley" (TWF 97; ch. 9), like the "valley of the shadow of death" in Psalm 23.4, or the "valley that was full of bones" in Ezekiel 37.7, or "the valley of decision," where "The sun and the moon shall be darkened and the stars shall withdraw their shining," in Joel 3.14-15. Looking upwards she sees "Against the sky [...], a single leafless tree" (TWF 98; ch. 9), perhaps the cross, often depicted in art as a tree, with its "iron girdle" by which its victims were clasped to it, both empty. Bardia, Orual's military commander and companion, continues the theme by announcing that "We are very near the bad part of the Mountain—I mean the holy part" (TWF 100; ch. 9).

Now the moment of enlightenment comes: "the sun—which had been overcast ever since we went down into the black valley—leaped out" (TWF 100; ch. 9). In this sequence, just as Orual has misread her experiences with holy darkness, she now misreads two vivid experiences of holy light. The first is a vision—both physical vision of an actual place and spiritual vision of its profound significance—which is pure Lewis, and pure Narnia:

> It was like looking down into a new world. At our feet, cradled amid a vast confusion of mountains, lay a small valley bright as a gem [...] I never saw greener turf. There was gorse in bloom, and wild vines, and many groves of flourishing trees, and great plenty of bright water [...] We were out of the wind now [...] soon we could hear the chattering of the streams and the sound of bees. (TWF 101; ch. 9)

This intense passage brings together every element of Lewis's personal experience of *Sehnsucht*. The phrase "new world" brings with it every concept of newness from Paradise, through the discovery by

Europe of the Americas—reflected when Miranda says, at the end of *The Tempest*, "O brave new world" (Act V, Scene I, line 185)—to the concept of "New heavens and new earth" (Isaiah 65.17) as expressed in *The Last Battle*, which concludes with the replacement of the extinguished Narnia by a new Narnia, better than before. We read in *Surprised by Joy* of the tiny garden in a tin prepared by Lewis's elder brother Warren in Lewis's childhood, which introduced him to supernal desire. The green turf, "bright as a gem" reminds us that in *The Great Divorce*, the dreaming narrator encounters heavenly grass so immutable that it is as hard as diamonds. The flowering gorse speaks of Lewis's many hillside walks in rural England; the "wild vines" remind us of the romp of Bacchus, Aslan, and the wild girls, which concludes with a miraculous proliferation of grapevines, in *Prince Caspian*; and the "groves of flourishing trees" also make us think of Narnia, where such trees can indeed dance. The phrase "we were out of the wind now" has its source in the paradisal visit to the back of the North Wind by Little Diamond in George MacDonald's *The Back of the North Wind*.

All these images resonate with the deepest roots of Lewis's spirituality. The passage concludes, in this supernal context, with "the sound of bees," that is, with an image of the divine feminine, of Aphrodite and the house of Ungit. Ungit, indeed, has a house; here we read of the house of her son, which contains "the most delicate pillared court open to the sky" (TWF 114; ch. 10)—a clear doublet for the bright watered, green-turfed valley which was also open to the sky. And of course, Orual responds, "We must go away at once. This is a terrible place" (TWF 117; ch. 11).

And well Orual might fear, since she is, as Psyche tells her, "standing on the stairs of the great gate" (TWF 116; ch. 10) of the god's house. Psyche makes this very clear. When asked her consort's name, she replies, "My god, of course," and adds, in a series of profound words which Lewis expected all Christians to echo: "My lover. My husband. The Master of my House" (TWF 122; ch. 11). Finally, when asked to describe her divine husband, Psyche reiterates the central theme of the book; she cannot see him, she says, because "He comes to me only in the holy darkness" (TWF 123; ch. 11).

At this, Orual rallies. She retorts: "Holy darkness, you call it [...] Faugh! Everything's dark about the gods" (TWF 124; ch. 11). As

Psyche continues in her efforts to explain, Orual continues with her theme—"Oh, you ought to have been one of Ungit's girls […] in the dark—all blood and incense and muttering and the reek of burnt fat […] dark and holy and horrible" (TWF 125; ch. 11).

This sequence concludes with the moment when Orual, who has already been unable to read the meaning of the bright valley, is now vouchsafed a vision of the god's "palace, grey—all things were grey in that hour and place—but solid and motionless, wall within wall, pillar and arch and architrave, acres of it, a labyrinthine beauty" (TWF 132; ch. 12). Lewis here invokes the great House of the Axe, the Labyrinth of Crete, which was sacred to the Goddess. Like the mountain, it too is grey, neither black nor white but both at once. Then, alluding to another great house dedicated to a Holy Lady, he evokes the cathedrals of medieval Europe: "it was like no house ever seen in our land and age. Pinnacles and buttresses leaped up […] unbelievably tall and slender, pointed and prickly as if stone were shooting out into branch and flower" (TWF 132; ch. 12). The house of Ungit, the house of Psyche's God, and the cathedrals of Notre Dame (Our Lady): all are related, all are one in this vision.

Then, out it goes; "the whole thing was vanished." Orual's quest is hopeless. In a heart-rending parody of the Holy Trinity, Orual imagines Psyche in the hands of "some holy and sickening thing, ghostly [the Holy Ghost] or demonlike [the Father] or bestial [Jesus, the Lamb of God]—or all three (there's no telling with gods)—enjoyed her at its will" (TWF 137; ch. 12). Making her sad way home, Orual passes "in sight of the house of Ungit" (TWF 138; ch. 12) and decides that "Psyche should not—least of all, contentedly—make sport for a demon." That has been the final "sin" committed by Psyche against Orual: that she is contented in her love for someone—anyone—else. With this specific fact—Orual cannot endure to see Psyche happy with anyone else—Book I of *Till We Have Faces* is almost exactly halfway through. From this point on to the end of Book I, we hear very little of Ungit. Orual returns to her father's little palace, then sets out again to the mountain valley and presses upon Psyche to light a lamp in the great palace's bedroom, with the result that Psyche is condemned to exile and Orual is condemned to take up Psyche's tasks. Orual leaves the blighted valley, now "all bare rock, raw earth, and foul water" (TWF 175; ch. 15), and goes back home to the rest of her life.

Her father dies; Ungit replaces him; the old priest of Ungit dies, and a new priest comes to replace him, too. In a brief reference to Ungit, we learn that she is "now weakened," that "her house was not so dark," that "it smelled cleaner and less holy," and that the new priest has set up "a woman-shaped image in Greek fashion—in front of the old shapeless stone" (TWF 234; ch. 20). Orual, having enacted all possible reforms, sets out to visit the neighboring kingdoms with which she has long since made peace. In the last chapter of Book I, Orual and her party of young travelers, seek to visit "a natural hot spring" (TWF 239; ch. 21), with its echoes of healing spas and underworld places, located, naturally, in "a warm green valley." Orual goes ahead alone toward the sound of "a temple bell" (TWF 240; ch. 21). There she finds "a mossy place free of trees" with a little temple, "no bigger than a peasant's hut but built of pure white stone"—white stone, mind you—with the "small thatched house" of its priest behind it (TWF 240; ch. 21). The temple is cool and silent, empty and clean, and "there was on the altar the image of a woman about two feet high carved in wood" with "no painting or gilding but only the natural pale color of the wood" (TWF 241; ch. 21). The face of this image is veiled.

In exchange for an offering of coins, the priest tells the story of this "very young goddess" (TWF 241; ch. 21), whose name, we discover, is Istra, Psyche's Glomish name. In this story, Ungit is jealous of Psyche and causes her to be sacrificed; Psyche is rescued by Ungit's son, "the most beautiful of the gods" (TWF 242; ch. 21), and taken to his palace, where she is forbidden to see his face. So far, so good, from Orual's viewpoint. But then she is told that Psyche's sisters had visited Psyche and "seen the beautiful palace" of the god (TWF 243; ch. 21). She exclaims, "They *saw* the palace?" and the priest retorts, "Of course they saw the palace! They weren't blind" (TWF 243; ch. 21). The sisters destroyed Psyche's happiness, he explains, "because they were jealous" (TWF 244; ch. 21). Orual rages, "Jealousy? I jealous of Psyche?" (TWF 245; ch. 21). On her way home she decides to write a condemnation of the gods and make her case against them; Book I has been that book. In it, she has asked the central question of

Lewis's novel: "Why must holy places be dark places?" (TWF 249; ch. 21).

Book II gives Orual's answer. As she sorts through her memories, fulfilling the task of Psyche, to sort through the mixed seeds, she learns that her love for the Fox and for Psyche has broken the heart of her sister Redival, and that her close advisor, the brave Bardia, has been worked to death by her demands upon him. In this descent to reality, Orual again encounters Ungit.

At the yearly ceremony of "the year's birth," despite all the new priest's liturgical reforms, "there had been censing and slaughtering, and pouring of wine and the pouring of blood, and dancing and feasting and towsing of girls, and burning of fat, all night long." Into this setting comes Orual, to seat herself "on the flat stone which is my place opposite the sacred stone which is Ungit herself" (TWF 269; II, ch. 2). She and the goddess are face to face. She continues: "I saw the terrible girls sitting in rows down both sides of the house, each cross-legged at the door of her cell" (TWF 269, II, ch. 2). The phrase "terrible girls" used here suggests the question asked about the Shulamite (whoever she is) in The Song of Solomon (6.10): "Who is she that looketh forth as the morning, fair as the moon, clear as the sun, and terrible as an army with banners?" The "terrible girls" are potential brides of the goddess's son; we recall that Psyche was dressed in their characteristic garb when she was presented to Him, and note that Psyche's mother, the little bride of the King of Glome, was arrayed in the same way. The cells of these formally garbed girls are thus to be compared with the cells of nuns, the Brides of Christ.

In this same passage we learn that Ungit "had not, like most sacred stones, fallen from the sky," but "had pushed her way up out of the earth," as I recounted above. The priest explains to Orual that Ungit "signifies the earth, which is the womb and mother of all living things" (TWF 270; II, ch. 2)—in clear concert with much contemporary environmentalist symbolism. He also answers Orual's question as to whether Ungit is "the mother of the God of the Mountain" in the affirmative.

These teachings gradually become clear to Orual when a peasant woman, weeping, enters with an offering of "a live pigeon" (TWF 271: II, ch. 2), and, after the sacrifice, rises "calm, patient, able for whatever she had to do" (TWF 272; II, ch. 2). One thinks of the

Blessed Virgin Mary offering two pigeons at the Temple of Jerusalem, so that she may take her Son home with her. "There's no goddess like Ungit," the peasant woman assures Orual, and when asked why she has made her offering to the stone instead of to the new statue, she explains simply of the latter that "There's no comfort in her" (TWF 272; II, ch. 2).

Orual goes home, trembling on the brink of enlightenment. As she first meditates, and then drifts into sleep after her long night, her father stands before her and orders her to come with him "to the Pillar Room" (TWF 274; II, ch. 2). There was a Pillar Room in the brick portion of the palace of Glome. But the reference is to something deeper, literally deeper; when Orual accompanies him to that Pillar Room, he commands her to break through the floor, no doubt also composed of brick. Beneath, they encounter "another Pillar Room, exactly like the one we had left, except that it was smaller and all made (floor, walls, and pillars) of raw earth" (TWF 274; II, ch. 2). The phrase "raw earth" has already been used in Ungit's experience of the mountainside valley after Psyche has gone into exile, above. This earthen level (bricks are made of earth, too) is surely under the sway of Earth herself. Then they dig still deeper, to "another pillar room, but this was of living rock." The expression "living rock" besides partially echoing the term "raw rock" also used above in regard to the abandoned valley, resonates powerfully in this setting. At the literal level, it is the actual rock of which the earth is made, rather than a rock hewn or worn away and thus free-standing. At the allegorical level it can be compared to the many rocks set up upon the earth in the Old Testament, each of which seems in their narrative settings to have been unhewn rock, rock detached from "living rock" but still maintaining its properties. As this is the third pillar room, it can be associated with the "house of God, which is the Church of the living God, the Pillar and ground of the house" (I Timothy 3.15) and to Revelation 7.2 in which we read that of "Him that overcometh I will make a pillar in the temple of my God." I have already referred above to the house that Wisdom built, for which she hewed out seven pillars. As the pillar rooms descend, level by level, they become more and more like the House of Ungit with its great pillars.

The King of Glome asks Orual the question she has, all this time, herself been asking: "Who is Ungit?" (TWF 276; II, ch. 2).

Looking into a mirror, she sees her own face, "the face of Ungit as I had seen it that day in her house," and answers, "I am Ungit" (TWF 276; II, ch. 2). This "Ungit" is not the Ungit of the devout peasant woman who went away justified. It is the face of Orual herself, and thus of Ungit as Orual has known her: "I was that [...] all devouring, womblike, yet barren thing." Orual has been barren, but Ungit has been fruitful; she is the mother of the Mountain God. Orual, gazing all the while at her own face, presses on: "Glome was like a web—I the swollen spider, squat in its center, gorged with men's stolen lives" (TWF 276; II, ch. 2).

Exactly. This image, most probably borrowed from Tolkien's evil Shelob in *The Lord of the Rings*, is not Ungit, but Orual herself, who has, indeed, done the evils she now recognizes in the mirror image of herself. She now determines to take off her veil and "go bareface" (TWF 278; II, ch. 2). Still in error, she thinks that, as she supposes to be true of Ungit, she has "become what the people called holy" (TWF 278; II, ch. 2). Indeed, she thinks she may even "be the Shadowbrute also" (TWF 278; II, ch. 2). Bowed down by these grossly mistaken projections, she goes to the river to drown herself. A god bars her way: "Die before you die. There is no chance after," he commands her. Protesting, she replies, "Lord, I am Ungit" (TWF 279; II, ch. 2). But there is no spoken answer. How could there be? What she has said is nonsense. Mara E. Donaldson, in her little known but significant study, *Holy Places are Dark Places*: *C.S. Lewis and Paul Ricoeur* (1988), superbly interprets Orual's sin as being

> not the Augustinian one of pride, which is what a naive first reading would suggest. Rather it is closer to those recent proposals concerning sin as self-negation proffered by such theologians as Judith Plaskow. We must distinguish Orual's manifest prideful, possessive craving for Psyche, which indeed is destructive rather than constructive, from its "sinful" presupposition of being allowed to have no-self at all (i.e., she is veiled and hidden from herself and others), rather than too much self.[63]

Alone, Orual is left to discover the answer to her own conundrum. Now she is offered another dream, not yet knowing that these dreams are in fact the god's answers. In this dream she carries out the tasks assigned to Psyche as penance for trying to see her divine husband's face before the time was ripe. Seeing a flock of sheep with "fleeces such bright gold that I could not look steadily at them" (TWF 283; II, ch. 3), she is trampled by "their gladness" but lives to see "another mortal woman" gleaning the strands of their wool (TWF 284; II, ch. 3). This woman, Orual says, has "won without effort what utmost effort would not win for me" (TWF 284; II, ch. 3).

Still thinking she must try not to be Ungit, she passes the spring season at her queenly tasks, continuing to believe that she "had at least loved Psyche truly" (TWF 285; II, ch. 3). Again, she has a vision: she walks "over burning sands, carrying an empty bowl" (TWF 285; II, ch. 3), which she must fill with "the water of death, and bring it back without spilling a drop and give it to Ungit" (TWF 286; II, ch. 3). These burning sands suggest Canto XIV of Dante's Inferno, which Dorothy L. Sayers describes as "a desert of Burning Sand, under a rain of perpetual fire,"[64] where, in 11.28-30;

> And slowly, slowly dropping over all
> The sand, there drifted down huge flakes of fire,
> As Alpine snows in windless weather fall.

This is the place of "the Violent against God, Nature, and Art," according to Sayers.

In the seeming "hundred years" of these labors, Orual is approached by "an eagle from the gods," which is appropriate to the eagle as a symbol "of the spiritual principle."[65] Asked who she is, she now answers correctly: "Queen of Glome," and realizes she is carrying "not a bowl but a book," indeed, her own "complaint against the gods." In the myth of Psyche and Eros, the bowl contains a "magical beauty ointment,"[66] that is, Beauty, the trait which Orual does not believe herself to possess. This is the last of the three tasks of Psyche, which have included "sorting over night a roomful of seeds, catching the sun-sheep's fleece," and "traveling to the underworld to ask for […] Persephone's ointment."[67]

Orual is flown once again to a vast cave, filled with "a great assembly" (TWF 288-89; II, ch. 3). This time she stands upon a single pillar, confronted by the ghosts of Batta, the King, the Fox, and many others. There, the judge orders her to be uncovered, of veil and all else, and commanded to read her complaint.

"I know what you'll say," she says, "You will say the real gods are not at all like Ungit, and that I was shown a real god and the house of a real god and ought to know it" (TWF 290; II, ch. 3). Of course, it is not true that the real gods are not like Ungit. And, still in her delusion, Orual comes to the nugget of her complaint. The gods are terrible, she declares, because "we want to be our own." This is in fact her final error. Her situation is not that she wants to belong to herself, or even that she wants Psyche to belong to her. It is her deepest, most desperate plight that she belongs to nobody, that she has been unable to accept all efforts to love and befriend her.

There is an immense silence, as this final untruth rings in her ears. And she recognizes what her complaint has actually been, and how false it is in the face of reality. "There was given to me a certainty that this, at last, was my real voice," that is, this was the false substance of her complaint, as the gods had always heard it. The judge asks, "Are you answered?" and we see that the answer has in fact been silence. She replies, having at last perceived the emptiness of her complaint, "Yes" (TWF 293; II, ch. 3), the beginning of the affirmation that makes love possible.

Following this silent enlightenment, she encounters the Fox. He leads her to "a cool chamber, walls on three sides of us, but on the fourth side only pillars and arches […] Beyond and between the light pillars and soft leaves I saw level grass and shining water" (TWF 297; II, ch. 4), in a reiteration of all Lewis has used in this book as symbols of mystical illumination. Shown a series of painted images on the three walls, she is led to recognize that she has borne all the pains of Psyche's tasks, just as Psyche has endured so much from her before. Now they "stood in a fair, grassy court, with blue, fresh sky above us; mountain sky" (TWF 305; II, ch. 4). This court is obviously a part of the great House of the God of Love, Psyche's husband. That god now arrives. "The pillars on the far side of the pool flushed with his approach" (TWF 307; II, ch. 4). And in the pool, Orual sees the reflection of herself and Psyche, both beautiful and both individual. "You also are Psyche," the "great voice" intones (TWF 308; II, ch. 4). Orual was never Ungit; how could she be? She and Psyche are both the brides of Ungit's Son, the God who is Love.

In her last words of Book II, Orual tells us, "I know, now, Lord, why you utter no answer. You are yourself the answer" (TWF

308; II, ch. 4). In the Note which concludes *Till We Have Faces*, Lewis claims that "The central alteration in my own version consists in making Psyche's palace invisible to normal mortal eyes," and that "Nothing was farther from my aim than to recapture the peculiar quality of the *Metamorphoses*—that strange compound of picaresque novel, horror comic, mystagogue's tract, pornography, and stylistic experiment" (TWF 313; note). Even at this last, he engages in misdirection! For *Till We Have Faces* has been all five of these, turning each element—picaresque novel, horror comic, mystagogue's tract, pornography (think of what you thought about Ungit's girls) and stylistic experiment upon its head in turn.

The complexly interlocked meanings of *Till We Have Faces* and of its central metaphor, in which Orual is asked, "Are you answered?" and concludes in the end by telling her Lord, "You are yourself the answer," have been discussed by many authors. Two of these who address the meanings and metaphors most successfully are Doris Myers and Mara Donaldson, as I have already demonstrated.

Myers says that Lewis is proof that "language [is] a relationship, manifesting itself through metaphor, between the human mind and the universe."[68] Mara Donaldson adds that "Narrative needs to be understood as an interplay between temporality, which gives sequential specificity to the logic of metaphor, and the logic of metaphor, which gives significance to that temporality."[69] At what Christians regard as the watershed of history, Pontius Pilate asks "What is truth?" Truth stands before him, bound and silent.

Notes

[1] Peter J. Schakel's *Reason and Imagination in C.S. Lewis: A Study of Till We Have Faces* (Grand Rapids, MI: William B. Eerdrnans, 1984) 11.

[2] Schakel 11.

[3] Schakel 184, chapter 1-2, note 1.

[4] Schakel 20.

[5] Thomas Howard, *The Achievement of C.S. Lewis* (Wheaton, IL, Harold Shaw, 1988) 166; cited in Schakel 186, note 1.

[6] W.D. Norwood Jr., "C.S. Lewis's Portrait of Aphrodite," *The Southern Quarterly* 8 (1970) 255, cited in Schakel 186, note 1.

Notes

[7] Schakel 21.

[8] Robert Holyer. "The Epistemology of C.S. Lewis's *Till We Have Faces*," *Anglican Theological Review* 70.3 (July 1988): 251.

[9] Nancy-Lou Patterson, "Thesis, Antithesis, and Synthesis: The Interplanetary Trilogy of C.S. Lewis" (1985), *Ransoming the Waste Land* (Clifford, ON: Valleyhome Books, 2015) 3-12.

[10] Ajit Mookerjee, *Kali: The Feminine Force* (New York: Destiny Books, 1988) 72.

[11] J.E. Cirlot, *A Dictionary of Symbols* (New York: Philosophical Library, 1962) 299.

[12] Cirlot 299.

[13] Marija Gimbutas, *The Language of the Goddess* (San Francisco, CA: Harper and Row, 1989) 40.

[14] Gimbutas, *The Language of the Goddess* 31, 110.

[15] Gimbutas, *The Language of the Goddess* 147.

[16] Gimbutas, *The Language of the Goddess* 147.

[17] Gimbutas, *The Language of the Goddess* 148-49.

[18] Ean Begg, *The Cult of the Black Virgin* (London: Routledge and Kegan Paul, 1985) 69.

[19] Begg 130-31.

[20] China Galland, *Longing for Darkness: Tara and the Black Madonna* (New York: Penguin, 1990) 341.

[21] Galland 342.

[22] Gimbutas, *The Language of the Goddess* 105-106.

[23] Doris T. Myers, *C.S. Lewis in Context* (Kent, OH: Kent State UP, 1994) 193-94.

[24] Myers 195.

[25] Myers 190.

[26] Jane Harrison, *Prolegomena the Study of Greek Religion* (1903; London: Merlin Press, 1962) 314.

[27] Harrison 314.

[28] Paul Friedrich, *The Meaning of Aphrodite* (Chicago, IL: University of Chicago Press, 1978) 4.

[29] Friedrich 9-10.

[30] Friedrich 16.

[31] Friedrich 78.

Notes

[32] Friedrich 71.

[33] Friedrich 73.

[34] Friedrich 85.

[35] Christine Downing, *The Goddess: Mythological Images of the Feminine* (New York: Crossroads, 1981) 205.

[36] Downing 188.

[37] Nancy-Lou Patterson, "'The Bolt of Tash': The Figure of Satan in C.S. Lewis's *The Horse and His Boy* and *The Last Battle*" (1990), in this volume.

[38] Buffie Johnson, *Lady of the Beasts: Ancient Images of the Goddess and Her Sacred Animals* (New York: Harper & Row, 1988) 11.

[39] Johnson 8.

[40] Johnson 9.

[41] Georgiana L. Williams, "*Till We Have Faces*: a Journey of Recovery," *The Lamp-Post* 18.4 (December 1994): 5-15.

[42] Friedrich 208.

[43] Jack Goody, *The Culture of Flowers* (Cambridge: Cambridge UP, 1993) 42-43.

[44] Goody 67 note 158.

[45] Barbara G. Walker, *The Woman's Dictionary of Symbols and Sacred Objects* (San Francisco, CA: Harper and Row: 1988) 449.

[46] Michael Zohary, *Plants of the Bible* (Cambridge: Cambridge UP, 1982) 119.

[47] Dorothy Burr Thompson and Ralph E. Griswold, *Garden Lore of Ancient Athens* (Princeton, NJ: American School of Classical Studies at Athens, 1963) n.p.

[48] Walker, *The Woman's Dictionary* 5.

[49] Walker, *The Woman's Dictionary* 414.

[50] Walker, *The Woman's Dictionary* 415.

[51] Walker, *The Woman's Dictionary* 488.

[52] Marija Gimbutas, *The Goddesses and Gods of Old Europe 6500-3500 BC* (Berkeley, CA: University of California Press, 1982) 181-83.

[53] Gimbutas, *The Goddesses and Gods of Old Europe* 146.

[54] Walker, *The Woman's Dictionary* 100.

[55] Walker, *The Woman's Dictionary* 206.

Notes

[56] Tikva Prymer-Kensky, *In the Wake of the Goddess: Women, Culture and the Biblical Transformation of Pagan Myth* (New York: Fawcett Columbine, 1992) 199.

[57] Prymer-Kensky 202.

[58] Simon Coleman and John Elsner, *Pilgrimage Past and Present: Sacred Travel and Sacred Space in the World Religions* (Cambridge, MA: Harvard UP, 1995) 42.

[59] Gimbutas, *The Goddesses and Gods of Old Europe* 101.

[60] Gimbutas, *The Goddesses and Gods of Old Europe* 101.

[61] Venetia Newall, *An Egg at Easter: a Folklore Study* (London: Routledge and Kegan Paul, 1971) 35.

[62] Newall 45.

[63] Mara E. Donaldson, *Holy Places are Dark Places: C.S. Lewis and Paul Ricoeur on Narrative Transformation* (Lanham, MD: University Press of America, 1988) 80.

[64] Dante Alighieri. *The Comedy of Dante Alighieri, The Florentine.* Trans. Dorothy L. Sayers (Harmondsworth, UK: Penguin Books, 1950) 156.

[65] Cirlot 87.

[66] Patricia Monaghan, *The Book of Goddesses and Heroines* (New York: E.P. Dutton, 1981) 247.

[67] Monaghan, *The Book of Goddesses and Heroines* 247.

[68] Myers 87.

[69] Donaldson 99.

Other Places, Other Beings, and Other Futures

I too acquired a long, lustrous, iridescent mane. I looked at the dog and his mane was like mine. A supreme happiness filled my whole body, and we ran together toward a sort of yellow warmth that came from some indefinite place. And there we played. We played and wrestled until I knew his wishes and he knew mine.

———Carlos Castaneda, *The Teachings of Don Juan,*
a Yaqui Way of Knowledge

Nancy-Lou Patterson. "Lucy of Narnia." First reproduced on the back cover of *Mythlore* 18.4 (Autumn 1992). Further reproduction prohibited.

5. The "Jasper-Lucent Landscapes" of C.S. Lewis

> It is nature—the character of shifting light and shade, of trees and running water and a gentle breeze, and their effect on the human nerves and emotion—that caused the locus to be amoenus [...]

> ——C.S. Lewis, *The Discarded Image* (1964)

Patterson begins "The 'Jasper-Lucent' Landscapes of C.S. Lewis" with reviewer Charles Brady's reference to the "jasper-lucent" quality of Lewis's landscapes, and examines the significance of both "jasper" and "lucent" with reference to biblical precedent and visionary experiences outside Christian contexts. She then turns to such landscapes in Lewis's writing, first in Spirits in Bondage *(1919),* The Pilgrim's Regress *(1933), and letters and diaries together; then* The Space Trilogy *(1938, 1943, 1945),* The Screwtape Letters *(1942), and* The Great Divorce *(1946); then the Chronicles of Narnia; and finally* Till We Have Faces *(1957). In her conclusions, Patterson expands the range of sources and parallels for Lewis's "green" symbolism with reference to grass; to forests, orchards, and flowers; and to other aspects of his landscapes. Patterson also addresses the import of the color green in "'Halfe Like a Serpent': The Green Witch in* The Silver Chair" *and "The Green Lewis: Inklings of Environmentalism in the Writing of C.S. Lewis." Both papers are included in this volume.*

"The 'Jasper-Lucent Landscapes' of C.S. Lewis" was first published in the Lamp-Post of the Southern California C.S. Lewis Society *22.1 (1999): 6-24; 23.2 (1999): 16-32; 23.4 (1999): 7-16*

When Charles A. Brady reviewed the last of the seven Chronicles of Narnia in *America* (1956), he wrote: "Narnia now takes its place forever beside the jasper-lucent landscapes of Carroll, Andersen, MacDonald and Kipling."[1] A child, Brady says, "will respond immediately [...] to the constant eliciting of the numinous." Lewis, he continues, "touches the nerve of religious awe on almost every page."[2] My essay explores the meaning of "jasper-lucent landscapes," and the central role they play in the fantasies of C.S. Lewis: he used them self-consciously and intentionally in an ever-mounting crescendo from the first of his Narnia works to the last.

I begin with the specificity and aptness of Brady's evocative phrase itself: "jasper-lucent landscapes." Jasper is defined by *The New Shorter Oxford English Dictionary* as "Formerly, any bright-coloured chalcedony other than carnelian, the most valued being of a green colour." In the Hebrew Bible the word "jasper" appears in Exodus and Ezekiel; in the New Testament, it appears in Revelation. Its setting in these books is no accident; jasper is clearly associated with sacrality and visionary imagery. Exodus 28.17 describes the breastplate of Aaron, the priest appointed by Moses, in a design prescribed, according to the narrative, by God: "Thou shalt set it in settings of stone," which include, among others of the twelve commanded gems, in "the fourth row a beryl, and an onyx, and a jasper" (Exodus 28.19). Again, the prophet Ezekiel addresses "the prince of Tyrus" in Ezekiel 28.13: "Thou hast been in Eden the garden of God: every precious stone was my covering." Among the stones designated is "the jasper."

In Revelation 4.3 the visionary—who is generally identified as St. John the Divine—sees a figure seated upon a throne "set in heaven," upon which "he that sat was to look upon like a jasper." Again, the visionary is shown: "The holy Jerusalem, descending out of heaven from God, having the glory of God; and her light was like unto a stone most precious, even like a jasper stone, clear as crystal" (Revelation 21.10-11). Finally, he says of the Heavenly Jerusalem that "the building of the wall of it was jasper" (Revelation 21.18), and "the foundations of the wall of the city were garnished with all manner of precious stones. The first foundation was jasper" (Revelation 21.19).

Aldous Huxley's "Heaven and Hell" (1956) provides an overview of visionary experience and forms that is not situated inside a specifically Christian setting. He describes the visionary experience: "Everything seen by those who visit the mind's antipodes is brilliantly illuminated and seems to shine from within."[3] This accords precisely with *The New Shorter Oxford Dictionary*'s definition of "lucent" as "shining, bright, luminous," as well as "translucent, clear." Huxley includes not only spontaneous but chemically-induced visions, such as those associated with peyote in the New World and whatever may have been ingested at Eleusis in the Old, as well as dreams, and adds the effects of works of art intended to be visionary, particularly religious art and the decor of sacred structures and environments, along with religious writings and visionary literature.

"It is worth remarking that, in most people's experience, the most brightly coloured dreams are those of landscapes,"[4] he says, and notes that George Russell spoke of "landscapes as lovely as a lost Eden."[5] Huxley cites the "similarity between induced or spontaneous visionary experience and the heavens and fairylands of folklore and religion," which include a "praeternaturally significant light that shines on, or shines out of, a landscape of such surpassing beauty that words cannot express it."[6] Associated with these luminous landscapes are "jewels and precious stones" to such an extent that "every paradise abounds in gems."[7] Finally, and perhaps most importantly for my argument, Huxley concludes that "the best vision inducing art is produced by men and women who have themselves had the visionary experience."[8]

Lewis, of course, was thoroughly aware of his own sources and fully comprehended the historic origins and meanings of the symbols he used. Perhaps the most valuable source for understanding what Lewis meant to express in his jasper-lucent landscapes is also the most recently published; Jeffrey Burton Russell, long associated with studies of hell and the devil, has published *A History of Heaven* (1996), in which he explains that "Traditionally, heaven is a place, a sacred space."[9] Tracing the sequence of historic images, Russell addresses the concept of the *locus amoenus*:

> The garden is the most common metaphor. Its origin is in the Hebrew Bible: the garden of the earthly Paradise at the beginning of the world. It was linked through the "garden enclosed" of the Hebrew Bible to the Greco-Roman images of the *locus amoenus*, the "lovely place." [...] The imagery closest to that of Genesis is orchard or wood.[10]

Here is an explicit reference to central and indeed climactic motifs in the writings of Lewis, where "Paradise [...] was the shady and fruitful orchard at the beginning of the world"[11] as, for instance, and indeed, most particularly, in *The Magician's Nephew*. Echoing Huxley's conclusions, Russell says that "To see and 'know' a vision of the other world and to make it intelligible to others, the prophet must be a poet and the poet a prophet, speaking of the ineffable in metaphors that are true."[12]

Historically, the paradisal motifs discussed above were made concrete in the physical world through the "geometrically laid out, enclosed water gardens" which in Mesopotamia expressed "the concept of Paradise as a Garden."[13] The word *Pairidaeza*—"walled garden"—used in Old Persian, and based perhaps on the paradise myth of the land of Dilmun, envisaged as "a divine garden by providing fresh water from beneath the earth [...] with fruit trees, green fields, and meadows,"[14] first appeared in biblical usage in Middle English. The Hebrew word *Pardes* was "used to mean garden" in Genesis.[15] Most importantly for my study of Lewis's usage of these motifs, especially in the Narnian Chronicles, Elizabeth Moynihan (1979) says that "In the Paradise myth, the Garden of Paradise—the primaeval beginning—is [also] the final reward."[16]

C.S. Lewis was fully aware of these historic origins—a point fully demonstrated in *That Hideous Strength* by Jane Studdock as she walks uphill through the garden of St. Anne's Manor. He was fully conscious, too, of the use of such mythological motifs in literature. In *The Allegory of Love* (1936), his first major work of literary criticism, he points out that "For poetry to spread its wings fully, there must be, besides the believed religion, the marvellous that knows itself as myth."[17] He specifically observes the use of these metaphoric and allegorical elements in medieval poetry. Considering Bernardus Sylvestris's *Di Mundi sive Megacosmos et Microcosmus*, he notes that "at the coming of Natura, the turf swells and the groves drop new odours,"[18] just as happens in Perelandra. Again, he gives a passage from Bernardus's description of *The Earthly Paradise*, describing it as "A land of streams and flowers,"[19] a land, that is, like Narnia. On that note, when Bernardus discusses the "grassy ridge or flowery mountain top [...] brightened with streams or robed in woodland greenery [and] Sylvans, Pans, and Nereias,"[20] it is, again, a world of which Narnia is an image. Bernardus teaches, as Lewis notes, that "the material world is the image of eternal ideas [... even though] it is only an image."[21]

In his study, *Spenser's Images of Life* (1967), in the chapter, "The Image of Good," Lewis comments that these images are generally "veiled, mysterious, even hidden," but adds that when, in *The Faerie Queene*, Una pulls aside her veil, her visage, in Spenser's words, "made a sunshine in that shadie place."[22] This, "the first image of good" in *The Faerie Queene*, according to Lewis, "thus reveals itself with brilliant effect."[23] The word "brilliant" in this context may have a double meaning, referring not only to mental brilliance, but to the brilliance of sunshine in the context of shade. The motif of sunlight also appears in Lewis's comments on Dante's *Commedia Divina* in *Studies in Medieval and Renaissance Literature* (1966). "The sunlight coming through a rift of clouds onto a flowerbed,"[24] is, he says, one of the three allegorical "images [in Dante] that might roughly be said to involve landscape."[25] This sudden light in a shady place accords with many passages in Lewis's fiction, as will be seen below.

A related motif pointed out by Lewis as characteristic of Spenser is the hidden chapel or hermitage, like the hermitages in the Narnian Chronicles and the chapel in *Till We Have Faces*. Writing of a hermit's lodging in *The Faerie Queene*, Spenser says:

> Small was his house, and like a little cage,
> For his own turne, yet—inly neate and clene,
> Dekt with greene boughs, and flowers gay beseene.[26]

I will return to the meaning of this eremetical motif for Lewis in my conclusion.

Summing up, in what could be an analysis of his own metaphorical usages, Lewis says that in Spenser, "Evil means starvation, good glows […]. Evil imprisons, good sets free. Evil is tired, good is full of vigour."[27] Narnia's joyous woodland romps and the luminous green lawns of its hermitages, alike reflect the Spenserian images of good in Lewis's fantasies. So far I have cited only Lewis's comments upon such motifs in his literary studies. He had long since become conscious of these elements of natural beauty in his own life, as his diaries, poetry, and other early writings reveal. But before discussing these, it is necessary to make my point of view upon them clear. The scholarly writings of C.S. Lewis show that he was fully aware of the history of paradisal symbolism and of its usage in works of literature including the greatest of the Christian fantasies. Those scholars who find in Lewis a dichotomy between his intellect and his imagination are, I think, quite mistaken.

When, as below, I refer to his youthful experiences of gardens, forest, and mountainsides, it is not to suggest that these experiences—

of which, after all, we know only through Lewis's writings—were ever, at least after he began to read for himself, separate from his analytical capabilities. All of his writings are remarkably self-conscious and aware: his letters and diaries and memoirs are all alike written for others to read, and we learn of him and his world what he chooses, with his vast capabilities as an experienced and scholarly writer, to tell. When he was an atheist, he wrote as a conscious atheist, and when he recovered his Christian faith he wrote as a conscious Christian. Indeed, nothing he ever wrote was free of a didactic intention, whether to instruct his closest friend, his own brother, or his vast list of other correspondents; to amuse his self-adopted "mother"; to inform his students and fellow scholars; to teach the truths of Christianity; to present, in supernal imagery, the profound wonder, beauty, splendor, and numinosity of the cosmos and its creator.

I.   "The Hidden Country": *Spirits in Bondage* (1919), *The Pilgrim's Regress* (1933), and associated letters and diaries

The letters of C.S. Lewis to Arthur Greeves provide a rich survey of his personal experiences of landscape, perhaps because he and his lifelong friend shared an appreciation of Nature, both in its vistas and in its enclosed green spaces, and because Arthur, as an adult, actually became a landscape artist whose paintings were accepted by the academy of his place and period. Lewis encapsulated their relationship with this beautiful couplet in a poem he dedicated to Greeves in 1919:

> Roaming without a name—without a chart—
> The unknown garden of another's heart.[28]

This passage, which moves from the concept of the chartless landscape to the garden within the heart, combines the two aspects of visionary landscape, which Huxley describes as "bright gardens with distant prospects of plain and mountain";[29] that is to say, in Huxley's words, "The most transporting landscapes" where one may wander chartless through both "natural objects a very long way off," and "the close-up landscape,"[30] most often a glimpse of a garden with its narrow paths and complex beddings. Both extremes feature in Lewis's writings from the beginning.

Nostalgic for home, the young scholar wrote from England to Arthur in Ireland in midsummer of 1914: "makes me furious to think of you being able to walk about your house and ours and all the beautiful places we know in the country, while I am cooped up in this hot, ugly country of England."[31] His early complaint is gradually supplanted by lyrical reports of English landscape: on the 17th of November, 1914, he wrote that "the pine wood near [here], with the white masses on ground and trees, forms a beautiful sight. One almost expects a 'march of dwarfs' to come dashing past!"[32] Here, surely, is a prefiguration of the entry into Narnia by the Pevensie children in *The Lion, the Witch and the Wardrobe*. The march of dwarfs, as well, prefigures certain members of the Narnian population, though for Lewis at the time of writing, this was a reference to his love of Wagnerian motifs, shared with Arthur from the beginning of their friendship.

The particular motif of snow is reiterated on the 28th of February, 1916: "'When you walk through the woods every branch is laden like a Christmas tree, and the mass of white arranged in every fantastic shape and grouping on the trees is really wonderful."[33] The reference to Christmas trees prefigures a third, and as I believe, especially significant motif which appears in Narnia: the entirely appropriate presence there of Father Christmas in *The Lion, the Witch and the Wardrobe*. Spring and Fall of 1916 brought further delicate vignettes of landscapes, including dwellings: Lewis's letter of the 16th of May, 1916, records "the sunny fields full of buttercups and nice clean cows, the giant century old shady trees, and the quiet steeples and tiled roofs of the villages popping up in their little valleys,"[34] and that of the 4th of October, 1916, says "You are walking in the middle of a wood when all of a sudden you go downwards and come to a little open hollow just big enough for a little lake and some old, old red-tiled houses."[35] Lewis was a long way from his first impressions of "hot, ugly [...] England" when he wrote these sweet evocations of its countryside's beauty and humane scale.

Lewis, like so many of his generation, went to war. Even as a conscript, he continues his letters in a poetic tone, writing from his posting in Plymouth (28 October 1917) of "cosy little bits of green country with cottages & water & trees, then woodier hills rising at last into big, open moors that make up the horizon."[36] After he is wounded in France, he still writes regularly, reporting on the 21st of February, 1918, of "a very pretty little village" in France with "pigeons" and "dovecotes."[37] A poem sent on the 23rd of May, 1918, from France presents a motif that will become a central theme in the Narnian Chronicles:

> Where eternal gardens smile
> And golden globes of fruit are seen
> Twinkling thro' the orchards green [...][38]

The poem ends as he describes

> [...] spirits that have trod
> Where the bright foot-prints of God
> Lie fresh upon the heavenly sod.[39]

Foot-prints, perhaps, like those that Aslan left for Shasta when he first entered Narnia.

The experience of war, and of thoughts like those expressed above, culminated in Lewis's first and most passionately desired publication, his volume of poems, *Spirits in Bondage* (1919). In the poem "Prologue," he openly broaches his subject and presents his vision: "Sing about the Hidden Country fresh and full of quiet green."[40] That this green country is "Hidden" is significant. One only encounters it in the countryside, in isolation, whether physical or in the mind.

The "green" motif recurs in "The Satyr" in a couplet that suggests the environment of Narnia:

> From the mountain and the moor,
> Forest green and ocean shore [...][41]

A contrasting but also recurring motif, the evocation of autumn, which features in a pivotal event in *That Hideous Strength*, appears in the last verse of "The Autumn Morning":

> Wherefore I will not fear
> To walk the woodland sere
> Into this autumn day
> Far, far away.[42]

The garden as an image makes its appearance in "Song of the Pilgrim," along with the theme of northernness which was to be a central symbol in *The Horse and His Boy*:

> —The red-rose and the white-rose gardens blow
> In the green Northern world to which we go [...][43]

Again and again, elements that will recur are broached here, in passages that parallel what Lewis had written to Greeves. In "How He Saw Angus the God," Lewis describes

—That little wood of hazel and tall pine
And youngling fir, where oft we have loved to see
The level beams of early morning shine
Freshly, from tree to tree.[44]

Such little woods receive the light in Lewis's letters as well as in his books, just as many far off mountains in the novels share their color with "the far horizon line,/ Where the blue hills border the misty west" in his poem "The Roads."[45] The note of "green" is sounded again in "The World's Desire": "[...] above the green / Of the wet and waving forest."[46]

The finest and most potent passage, not, perhaps, matched until the vision of the high valley of the mountain in *Till We Have Faces*, his last novel, is this, Lewis's most open expression of the pain in battle contrasted with the world of imagination, "Death in Battle":

At, to be ever alone,
In flowery valleys among the mountains and
        silent wastes untrod
In the dewy upland places; in the garden of God,
This would atone![47]

When Lewis returned to Oxford, he not only published his first book, but began his long relationship with Mrs. Moore. Now employed at Oxford University, he tells Arthur Greeves on the 19th of June, 1920, "I walk into Oxford down a green land and across the bridges and islands of the Cherwell; they are all white with may [...]."[48] May is hawthorne blossom, a flower associated with traditional May Day ceremonies, as both correspondents knew.

Between 1921 and 1929, Lewis wrote only six letters to Arthur. During this hiatus, he instead expressed his thought in the diaries he kept between 1922 and 1927. These diaries, which he regularly read aloud to his companion, Mrs. Janie Moore, contain descriptions of landscape which are appealing but seldom, except toward the last, touch upon the supernal, and, interestingly, very seldom use the word "green." On the 14th of April, 1922, for instance, he remarks upon "Another beautiful day" and "a very fine sunset."[49] Again, he notes that during the "very warm evening with a silver mackerel sky" of the 20th of May, 1922, "we had supper in the garden."[50] In contrast with these laconic observations, a walk taken on a Saturday, the 14th of October, 1922, is recorded in lyrical terms:

> The wood was glorious [...] in places there are open glades of green trunked oaks and brown bracken, elsewhere the intensest thickets [...] It was at once so lonely, so wild, so luxurious, that we both thought of Acrasia's bower of bliss.[51]

One notes the association of "green ... oaks" with Spenser. In a similar associative context, on the 7th of July, 1923, he writes of "Another exquisite day [...] there was a delicious cool and freshness reminding one of the appropriate passage in *The Ancient Mariner*,"[52] thus calling Coleridge to witness.

A visit to Arthur evokes another passage of landscape description; on the 20th of October, 1923, he writes, "we were in an absolutely deserted open rolling country full of bracken, standing pools and all kinds of woods and groves under a splendid grey autumn sky." And, on the same day, "the sun broke out; the grass [...] the trees, the swans, and one little stag that did not run away, took on glorious colours [...] It was all just like one of those luminous dreams I have so seldom dreamed."[53] In a similar mood, on the 16th of March, 1924, he touches again upon the supernal: "The High in all its early emptiness, cleanness, light and space was a thing to make a man shout."[54] The green image returns between the 19th and 26th of April, 1924, as Lewis notes "exceedingly beautiful, green hedges and flat blue distances."[55] Such passages are rare in the diaries, which genuinely reflect the domestic interests of Mrs. Moore, interests, I would add, which Lewis clearly shared and appreciated.

The correspondence between Lewis and Greeves recovers something of its frequency in 1929 and continues for the rest of Lewis's life. Landscape continues to play a role in these letters as he enters his thirties, and on the 29th of April, 1930, he told Arthur that the Ireland he "shared with [his brother Warren Lewis] seemed to be a strictly limited and rather thirsty land; yours was like dewy hills and woods fading into a mist where I felt that one could wander forever."[56] Here a contrast is made between the "limited" and "thirsty" actualities of Belfast life and the "'dewy" landscape of the imagination, where "one could wander forever." The phrase "thirsty land" is a reference to Psalm 63.1—"my flesh longeth in a thirsty land."

Probably the single most powerful passage in all these letters, and the origin, one may suppose, of Lewis's most potent passages in his many references to green places in his fiction, is this, written on the 10th of January, 1931, in which he reports to Arthur that

> Tintern [...] is an abbey practically intact except that the roof is gone, and the glass out of the windows, and the floor, instead of a pavement, is a trim green lawn. Anything like the sweetness and peace of the long drifts of sunlight falling through the windows on this grass cannot be imagined. All churches should be roofless. A holier place I never saw.[57]

Here is Lewis in full voice, far beyond, in its intensity, all he had written previously, speaking in his own true style, never afterwards abandoned or diminished.

In 1933 he published his first attempt to express the experience that had brought him to recovered faith, as a person for whom the Garden of God was an image not of escape but of hope, the hope which, along with charity, his recovered faith offered and embodied. In *The Pilgrim's Regress* (1933) the word "green" begins to recur like the delicate tolling of a sweet and single note. As the story opens, "On the other side of the road there was a deep wood, but not thick, full of primroses and soft green moss" (PR 3). Peering into a hole in the wall, "Through it he saw a green wood," and beyond that, "an island, where the smooth green turf slopes down unbroken to the bays," where "Oreads and enchanters" are seated upon "green chairs among the forests" (PR 8). The "green chairs" probably refer to the medieval custom of providing formal walled gardens with turf benches or seats overlain with sod[58] such as those depicted in medieval miniatures. The use of green as a motif of contrast also appears: "All this side of the brook was green and cultivated: on the other side of the brook a great black moor sloped upward, and beyond that were crags and chasms" (PR 10). Finally, in an intense evocation of what Lewis in his biography called "Joy," "John looked aside and saw a crocus in the grass. For the first time in many days the old sweetness pierced through John's heart" (PR 58). This image exactly parallels what Huxley says about "the close-up landscape," which, along with the distant view, most powerfully embodies the ineffable.

In *Surprised by Joy* (1955) Lewis describes "a toy garden or a toy forest"[59] of which so many commentators have rightly made much. It formed the first of his remembered experiences of the numinous, and, he says, "it made me aware of nature [...] as something cool, dewy, fresh, exuberant."[60] This he associated with "the Green Hills," that is, "the low line of the Castlereagh Hills which we saw from the nursery window, which were, to children, unattainable."[61] Later, "a flowering currant bush" brought him back his memory of this miniature garden, arousing in him what he calls Milton's "'enormous bliss' of Eden."[62] For Lewis, something green was something that reminded him of his first, holiest encounter with greenness. His use of the word "sweetness" in his letter to Arthur—"anything like the sweetness and peace of the long shafts of sunlight [...] on this grass"[63]—accords with John's reaction to the "crocus in the grass" which enabled him to experience "the old sweetness."

Such intimations of immortality in Lewis's childhood, shattered by the death of his mother, were followed by the long waste land of his schooling, only to be recovered after he went to be tutored for Oxford, where, traveling toward Great Bookham, he "saw steep little hills, watered valleys, and wooded commons [...] a world of red and russet and yellow greens."[64] The motif of a village in a landscape, reflected in his letters to Arthur Greeves, recurs here as "so many villages concealed in woods or hollows, so many field paths, such lanes, copses [...that] to walk in it daily gave one the same sort of pleasure that there is" in "the labyrinthine complexity of Malory or the *Faerie Queene*."[65]

Surprised by Joy, though not fictional, is a mature work, and in it Lewis enriches his narrative, a carefully constructed, subtly nuanced, exquisitely crafted, and richly artistic artifact. That is why he has placed the evocative passages not, as in his letters—themselves by no means unselfconscious wherever they may occur in recounting experiences contemporary with those letters—but in places in his autobiographical narrative where they mark periods of happiness. The toy garden and the flowering bush (like the Garden of Eden and the Burning Bush) represent the paradise of his childhood, before his mother's death, while the autumnal trip to Great Bookham marks a return of the possibility of happiness.

Still using landscape imagery, Lewis explains the effect of reading George MacDonald's *Phantasies*: "I did not break away from the woods and cottages [...] to seek some bodiless light shining beyond them, but gradually [...] I found the light shining on those woods and cottages."[66] From this first approach of his adversary, God, Lewis moves to the final surrender, at Whipsnade Zoo, with "the birds singing overhead and the bluebells underfoot [...] almost Eden come again."[67] Exactly.

II.   "A Green Sunlit Island": The Space Trilogy (1938, 1943, 1945); *The Screwtape Letters* (1942); and *The Great Divorce* (1946)

Lewis wrote two fantasies as didactic works addressing the great themes of hell, purgatory, and heaven. These, *The Screwtape Letters* (1942) and *The Great Divorce* (1946), interrelate with the three volumes of interplanetary travel and conflict between good and evil, published in 1990 as the Space Trilogy: *Out of the Silent Planet* (1938), *Perelandra* (1943), and *That Hideous Strength* (1945). All five of these works explicitly touch the nerve of the numinous through the evocation, however delicately, of landscape and seascape. The trilogy, published as it was between 1938 and 1945, encompasses the period of World War II. *Out of the Silent Planet* is set in a prewar world (as, indeed, 1938 must be said to have been); *Perelandra*, judging from its gloomy opening on Earth, may occur during the war, but its action takes place almost entirely in Perelandra, on a planet distinctly off-world, and in a conflict more lasting than any particular war. The third volume, *That Hideous Strength*, is specifically set after World War II, and accurately predicts many elements of the second half of the twentieth century, becoming more and more prophetic as its years have gone by.

Out of the Silent Planet (1938) begins like a thirties thriller or espionage novel, with an intriguing outdoors scene:

> The last drops of the thunderstorm had hardly ceased falling when the Pedestrian [...] stepped out from the shelter of a large chestnut tree into the middle of the road. [...] Every tree

and blade of grass was dripping, and the road shone like a river. (OSP 1; ch. 1)

The "blade of grass" is, even here, a hint of the supernal, and such references do not end when Ransom (the "Pedestrian," that is, the walking man) is kidnapped by the evil scientist Weston and his cohort, a former (and odious) schoolmate of Ransom's. From the spaceship in which he rides along with his captors, Ransom sees "the stars, thick as daisies on an uncut lawn" (OSP 33; ch. 5), a delicate touch not only of imputed goodness, but a suggestion that daisies are in the divine economy as significant as stars. Lewis never used any metaphor lightly or for mere effect. Outer space is not, in this novel, an alien place, and this exquisite image makes his point in the deftest, sweetest, most poignant of ways.

Landed on Malacandra (Mars), Ransom continues to see things in Earthly terms, viewing "a mass of something purple, so huge that he took it for a heather-covered mountain" (OSP 49; ch. 7). Such Earthly comparisons gradually fade as Ransom begins to see the Malacandran landscape in its own terms. In a hint of reversal, he speaks of "a world of naked, faintly greenish rock" (OSP 125; ch. 16), and notes that "the familiar green rock rose against the dark blue sky" (OSP 131; ch. 17). The reversal now full blown, the vegetation of Mars is red; Ransom sees "an island of pale red," with trees like "the noblest beech trees" surmounted by "golden flower bright as tulip" (OSP 132; ch. 17).

In this setting, he meets the eldil (angel/divinity) of the planet, and, reunited with his captors, is returned to "a patch of his native planet where grass grew" (OSP 194; ch. 21). In *Out of the Silent Planet*, clearly, grass signifies Earth, and is, as it were, a shorthand for its characteristic greenness, and a figure for life and intrinsic goodness.

The immediate successor to *Out of the Silent Planet*, published in 1938, is *The Screwtape Letters*, published in 1942. It is not part of the Space Trilogy, but it is a direct predecessor to *Perelandra* in terms of its theme, which is temptation. It takes place specifically on Earth and specifically during World War II (despite a misguided effort of one publisher to postdate it), and directly concerns hell, expressed in a potent inversion where what is good for God is bad for the two devils, senior and junior, whose one-sided correspondence is recorded. At the center of this discourse is a direct statement of the role of delight and pleasure in human life.

Screwtape explains to Wormwood that for one "who truly and disinterestedly enjoys one thing in the world for its own sake"—the categories mentioned are "country cricket or collecting stamps or drinking cocoa"—"there is a sort of innocence and humility and self-forgetfulness" (ST 69; Ltr. 13), which Screwtape distrusts and which he instructs his pupil to discourage in the young man he has been assigned to tempt. "Out at sea, out in *His* sea," he says with evident distaste, "there is pleasure, and more pleasure" (ST 112; Ltr. 22).

The motif of the sea, "His sea," as Screwtape's phrase so numinously puts it, recurs as a major symbol in *Perelandra* (1943). As in *Out of the Silent Planet*, the narration begins on earth, as Lewis (acting as narrator) walks through an Autumnal landscape—"clumps of red or yellowish trees" (PER 9; ch. 1)—and comes under demonic attack, perceiving a gloomy vista on "one of those still, dead evenings when no twig stirs, and beginning to be a little foggy" (PER 11; ch. 1). The phrase "no twig stirs" is an echo, perhaps, of Keats's poem in which "no bird sings." Even the garden of the house he finally reaches is dangerous: "Perhaps he *was* in the garden, waiting for me, hiding," he worries, "almost shrieking as a harmless spray of the hedge touched my face" (PER 14; ch. 1).

When the narrator Lewis meets Ransom, he helps him begin his second interplanetary voyage, this time to Venus (Perelandra). A year later, and still inside the Prologue, Lewis is present when the traveler returns, this time to "clear early sunlight in the little wilderness which Ransom's garden had now become" (PER 26; ch. 2), a vivid vignette of the passage of time and the symbolic importance of gardens. Moreover, Perelandrian flowers have returned with Ransom, which, again using an earthly floral simile, make "an English violet seem like a coarse weed!" (PER 27; ch. 2)—strong words!

The novel proceeds through long and rapturous descriptions of the Perelandrian environment, a Paradise where "the prevailing colour [...] was golden or coppery" (PER 30; ch. 3). "The sky was pure, flat gold like the background of a medieval picture. The ocean was gold too" (PER 32; ch. 3), but the waves "were green on their slopes: first emerald, and lower down a lustrous bottle-green, deepening to blue" (PER 32; ch. 3). On this peacock-colored ocean, beneath this golden sky, islands float freely, covered with fantastic vegetation and astonishing animals which, unlike the inhabitants of Malacandra, cannot speak. When a speaker arrives, she is a beautiful, naked woman, whose skin is like that of "a goddess carved [...] out of green stone, yet alive" (PER 48; ch. 4). She is the Green Lady, the Eve of her planet, who speaks to the philologist Ransom in Old Solar, the original language of the solar system. It would be hard to find a clearer meaning for the color green—it means not only life, but life unfallen, life everlasting.

Sadly, this idyll of innocence is interrupted by the arrival of Weston, the man who had kidnapped Ransom and taken him to Malacandra. He is to play the role assigned by many interpreters to the serpent in Eden, and occupies himself, between bouts of tempting, by torturing the colorful Perelandrian frogs. The temptation continues, as "all the time the little jewel-coloured land went soaring up into the yellow firmament [...] racing down into the warm lustrous depths between the waves" (PER 106; ch. 9): a jewel, perhaps, like jasper.

At last, Ransom realizes his only resort is to kill the body occupied by his demonic rival; a long sequence leads across the Perelandrian sea and into the planet's underworld, where he kills his adversary. Deep in the cave, he finds a region "lit with a cold green light" (PER 157; ch. 15). At last, Ransom passes from stone to water, and finds himself beside "a cliff mantled with streamers of bright vegetation" beneath "rich clusters of a grape-like fruit" (PER 159; ch. 15) whence he is breast-fed by the planet Venus herself in a "long Sabbath" full of "song" (PER 159; ch. 15). Restored, he makes his way to the site from which he is to depart to Earth.

The third novel of the trilogy, *That Hideous Strength* (1945) takes place entirely on the planet Earth, and, instead of containing comparisons to, or contrasts with, Earth, uses earthly images entirely to represent themselves; here the level of numinosity in such references rises powerfully. Within a few pages of the beginning, the narrator Lewis describes the immensely evocative Bragdon Wood, part of the property of Bracton College. Passing through a series of more and more enclosed and private spaces, "one became aware of the sound of running water and the cooing of wood pigeons" (THS 18; ch. 1). Soon after, "you caught a glimpse of sunlit green and deep shadow" (THS 18; ch. 1). Inside the "walled in" wood at last, the narrator Lewis "went forward over the quiet turf," walking between widely spaced trees in "mild sunshine" accompanied by sheep "whose nibbling kept the grass so short" (THS 19; ch. 1). This perfect place, this enclosed wood with its quiet, green, and sunlit turf, is doomed.

At a meeting held in the College, a plan is set afoot to sell this paradisal woodland, where, as we learn, Merlin lies buried in his magical sleep. The diabolically controlled conspirators intend to bulldoze the wood and strip away its turf in order to disinter the magician, who will, they think, side with their evil intentions to obtain control of humankind. A major element in the novel is the discovery that these infernal competitors are mistaken. In due time, Merlin awakens without their aid, rising in order to defeat them, though the wood is in fact destroyed, as so many woodlands have been, over many centuries, not least in the twentieth century.

In this sequence Lewis makes most explicit the contrast between the green tree and the dry. As Jesus says to the women of Jerusalem on his way to Calvary, "If they do these things in a green tree, what shall be done in the dry" (Luke 23.3 1)? *The New Oxford Annotated Bible* paraphrases this passage: "If the innocent Jesus meets such a fate, what will be the fate of the guilty Jerusalem?" Jesus is who or whatever is innocent. Jerusalem is all the rest of us. The ancient woodland, soon to be destroyed, is innocent; Bracton College, alas, is not. And indeed its fate is to perish too.

Many commentators have noticed the contrast between the sterile Belbury, with its artificial ornamental gardens, and St. Anne's Manor, with its wonderful vegetable garden, earthy pigpens, and wintering rosebushes. Belbury advances the plot with the aid of certain members of Bracton College, some of whom know not what they do. St. Anne's is where the company, of which Ransom has become the leader, gathers. Mark Studdock, a member of Bracton College who is being tempted to join the N.I.C.E. (a diabolical institute disguised as a think-tank) is riding to Belbury with Lord Feverstone—the other man who helped kidnap Ransom and carry him to Malacandra—in a speedy automobile in whose wake "villages streamed backward to join the country already devoured" (THS 47; ch. 2), while his wife Jane is "progressing slowly toward the Village of St. Anne's" (THS 48; ch. 2). Lewis disliked rapid travel and especially automobile travel; he was the very opposite of Kenneth Grahame's automobile-obsessed Toad, but he approved of trains, which were, in his time, many and leisurely.

Arriving at her destination, Jane walks uphill to the Manor of St. Anne's, to "a high wall" (THS 49; ch. 2) equipped with a door and a bellpull; in other words, to the archetypal walled garden. Mark's destination is "a florid Edwardian mansion which had been built for a millionaire who admired Versailles" (THS 49; ch. 2). Lewis passed the bitterest years of his childhood in the late Edwardian period, so his comparison of Belbury to Versailles is not a compliment. Jane is met by Camilla, and escorted "along a brick path beside a wall on which fruit trees were growing, and then to the left along a mossy path" to "a little lawn, [...] and beyond that a greenhouse." There are "a barn and a stable" (THS 59; ch. 3), "a second greenhouse, and a potting shed and a pigstye [...] narrow paths across a vegetable garden [...] and then, rose bushes, all stiff and prickly in their winter garb" (THS 60; ch. 4). Lewis describes this delicious and, as he would say, "homely" setting with an extraordinary number of precise literary references, almost as if he feared that some readers might fail to catch this extremely detailed set of allusions. "It was like the garden in *Peter Rabbit*," Jane thinks. "Or was it like the garden in *The Romance of the Rose*? [...] Or like Klingsor's garden? Or the garden in *Alice*? Or like the garden on top of some Mesopotamian ziggurat which had probably given rise to the whole legend of Paradise?" (THS 60; ch. 3).

These evocative motifs have provided Lewis scholars, including myself, with years of delighted contemplation, research, and commentary, and make clear in a single sequence his entire symbolic strategy and expressive technique. One could rest the thesis that Lewis used these motifs with complete self-consciousness, upon this passage alone.

The little community of people gathered around Ransom at St. Anne's produce more results from growing vegetables than all the malign endeavors of the N.I.C.E., despite the worst efforts of its demonic masters. Mark, having been drawn to Belbury by his need for recognition and inclusion, finds himself traveling through "brown fields [that] looked as if they would be good to eat [a motif to be repeated in the Narnian Chronicles], and those in grass set off the curves of the little hills as close-clipped hair sets off the body of a horse" (THS 84; ch. 4), a beautiful simile showing that Mark is in fact not yet far gone in depravity, and may well (indeed, will) be saved by exactly such tastes for rural beauty and capacity to appreciate what is fundamentally good. In the meantime, however, a village in this life-filled setting where the very hills are horses, is slated by the N.I.C.E. for destruction, and Mark has been sent to help advance the process.

Jane, who has returned home from St. Anne's, is again approached by Camilla, who with her husband Arthur takes her on a picnic "in a sort of little grassy bay with a fir thicket on one side and a group of beeches on the other" (THS 111; ch. 5), Lewis's ideal setting for goodness and virtue. Here the couple try to persuade her to join them at St. Anne's, hoping to use her gift of clairvoyance to counteract the N.I.C.E. Jane, not altogether unreasonably, refuses to yield; though Lewis uses her as an example of the reluctant convert that he himself had been, she is in the end driven to shelter at St. Anne's through sheer brutality (at the hands of the N.I.C.E.), a rather different route than the one Lewis himself followed. There is perhaps a touch of moral dilemma here, since it is her gifts that appear to be wanted, rather than herself.

Most of Jane's experiences take place out of doors, but Mark is almost entirely confined inside of Belbury after his single foray to the threatened village. The combination of oppressively rich surroundings, insecurity, and intensely claustrophobic settings which he endures, expressed in the halls he wanders, and the over-decorated rooms where he lingers like an anxious exile, are contrasted with the long views enjoyed by Jane as, after she travels again by train to St. Anne's, she

> saw that she was standing on the shore of a little green sunlit island looking down on a sea of fog [...] the wooded hills above Sandown where she had picknicked with the Dennistons; and the bigger and brighter one to the north was the many-caverned hills [...] in which the Wynd had its source. (THS 135; ch. 6)

To the woman previously confined to her house while her husband goes out to work, this broad vista offers more attractions than the cozy picnic in the autumnal dell.

Later, after visiting with Ransom, she "saw from the windows of the train the outlined beams of sunlight pouring over stubble or burnished woods and felt that they were like the notes of a trumpet" (THS 149; ch. 7). This intense, almost hallucinatory vision, even to the synaesthetic element of light which is also sound, exactly presents the kind of supernal experience that Huxley wrote about. In great contrast to this rich, vibrant, and life-filled vision, Filostrato, a member of the N.I.C.E., explains to Mark that he wants "cleanness, purity. Thousands of square miles of polished rock with not one blade of grass." Mark can see that this would be "A dead world" (THS 173; ch. 8). But Filostrato continues to rhapsodize: he wants everything to be cleansed of living matter, in the name of "hygiene." What he truly wants is "the art tree," with "the art birds singing when you press a switch inside the house" (THS 170; ch. 8). If Lewis could have seen the millions of people sitting indoors watching nature programs (usually about endangered species) on television today he would find that he had prophesied more truly than he could have desired. While Mark is being introduced to the claustrophobic horrors of the innermost N.I.C.E., Camilla takes Jane outdoors at St. Anne's Manor, and they walk "steeply uphill to the very summit of the garden" (THS 191; ch. 9). Looking up at the sky, she tells Jane of Ransom's visit to Perelandra, and explains that "Paradise is still going on there" (THS 192; ch. 9). In the imagery of this passage, the top of St. Anne's garden borders on Paradise, and it will be to this house (and this garden) that the planetary divinities of the fields of Arbol (the solar system) descend.

The inhabitants of St. Anne's go downhill in search of Merlin, "into a phantasmal world" with "tufts of grass, ruts filled with water, draggled yellow leaves," and "the two greenish-yellow fires in the eyes of some small animal," powerfully evoking the season, the autumnal landscape, and its non-human inhabitants. The searchers miss Merlin's passage, but he has indeed risen. "As they reached the lip of the hollow, mud changed into grass" (THS 247; ch. 12), and the track is lost, but they do see when, too sudden to be understood, "the shape of the horse [with Merlin astride it] appeared as it leaped a hedge some twenty yards away" (THS 251; ch. 12).

Soon we learn that for Merlin, "every operation on nature is a kind of personal contact, like coaxing a child or stroking one's horse" (THS 282; ch. 13). He has the ability to "set a sword in every blade of grass"—potent words indeed—against the N.I.C.E." But that, Ransom declares, "is in this age utterly unlawful" (THS 286; ch. 13). Animals, on the other hand, licitly continue this intimate relationship between forms of being; the bear Mr. Bultitude's consciousness is described as "a warm, trembling, iridescent pool" (THS 303; ch. 14). And, at the other end of the sequence (animal–human–divinity) Venus announces her presence with "a smell of burning cedar" (THS 319; ch. 15), "laden with ponderous fragrance of night-scented flowers" (THS 320; ch. 15).

In these passages Lewis, writing a work of fantasy, presents or at least suggests a world like that of many of Earth's aboriginal peoples (including some alive today) in which all forms of being, from stone and earth to animal and plant to human to supernatural (angels and/or spirits) have consciousness and can to some degree interact. He is very careful to suggest, in this novel, which is set upon our own planet, that there are matters of lawfulness in such intercourse between forms of being. Magic, as a form of coercion or intervention, he presents as strictly forbidden. On the other hand, a sort of grave courtesy is, at least in the fantasies, recommended. In this context, the arrival of the planetary presences continues. Mars, reminding Merlin of "the wintry grass of Badon hill" (THS 321; ch. 15); Saturn, making Dr. Dimble think "of stiff grass, hen-roosts, dark places in the middle of woods" (THS 321; ch. 15); and Jupiter, "like a long sunlit wave, creamy-crested and arched with emerald" (THS 324; ch. 15) continue this catalogue of these "five excellent natures" (THS 324; ch. 15), as Lewis plucks from Nature his exquisite metaphors for each. And, concluding this passage, which ripples with references to grass and green seas, "Merlin received the power into him" (THS 324; ch. 15).

The novel's climax, "Banquet at Belbury," follows, with its confusion of languages and failure of communication, and its revenging beasts, including Mr. Bultitude, engaged in terrible acts of licit reciprocity. Those banqueters who escape die elsewhere; the last to die is Lord Feverstone, killed by the Earth herself, who swallows him whole, maybe because of the way he drove his automobile upon her skin. The stately supper enjoyed at St. Anne's is also interrupted by the arrival of animals, but here they are welcomed, even rewarded, with junket and gooseberry jam (THS 375; ch. 17) for Mr. Bultitude and "a bunch of bananas" (THS 376; ch. 17) for the elephants.

That Hideous Strength concludes as Jane, descending through the "supernatural warmth of the garden and across the wet lawn (birds were everywhere) and past the see-saw and the greenhouses and the piggeries" (THS 380; ch. 17), a landscape green and sweet to the last, goes to meet her rescued husband. This masterpiece of Lewis's fiction is followed by the very last of his three didactic fantasies, which begin with *The Pilgrim's Regress* and also include *The Screwtape Letters*: I refer to *The Great Divorce* (1946). It continues the rich catalogue of all that is beautiful and green, seen from the point in its narrative when an omnibus brings souls from hell to visit heaven. The passengers see "a level, grassy country through which there ran a wide river," a clear allusion to Dante and MacDonald. To the narrator (Lewis, again) it seems "as if the sky were further off—and the extent of the green plain wider than they could be on this little ball of earth."[68] The river "was smooth as the Thames but flowed swiftly like a mountain stream; pale green where the trees overhung it but so clear that I could count the pebbles at the bottom."[69]

He finds that with effort, he can walk on this water: "The cool smooth skin of the bright water was delicious to [his] feet."[70] These images of the supernal continue, as the visitor to Paradise sees "a tree [which …] rose in many shapes of billowy foliage" and observes that "From every point apples of gold gleamed through the leaves."[71] In this perfect countryside, "There was water everywhere and tiny flowers quivering in the early breeze."[72] Passing from meadow to woodland, "All down one long aisle of the forest the undersides of the leafy branches had begun to tremble with dancing light."[73] Perhaps the central motif not only of this particular book, but of Lewis's whole oeuvre is found in this book, where, for the ghosts of the lost, "the grass did not bend under their feet; even the dew drops were not disturbed."[74] In an image both beautiful and terrible, the narrator Lewis says, "I bent down and tried to pluck a daisy which was growing at my feet. The stalk wouldn't break. [...] The little flower was hard, not like wood or even like iron, but like diamond."[75] This flower as hard as a gem embodies the heavenly jewels of Ezekiel and Revelation.

When Lewis published this book, he was forty-eight years old, and was, though he did not know it, soon to begin the series of children's books for which he is likely to be most remembered. Brady's beautiful metaphor of the "jasper-lucent landscapes" is reserved, one notes, only for works written to be read by and to children. And just as the works of "Carroll, Andersen, MacDonald and Kipling" are now read not only by children but avidly and with huge outpourings of literary criticism by adults, so I believe that the Narnian Chronicles will survive longest not only for children, but for the adults they are, if they live, inevitably to become.

III. "Green Slopes and Sweet Orchards": The Chronicles of Narnia

As the first of the Narnian Chronicles, *The Lion, the Witch and the Wardrobe* (1950) opens (and it must be read first, in order to allow its green magic to work its paradisal wonders), the Pevensie children are exploring the house "in the heart of the country" (LWW 3; ch. 1) where they have been sent to live in order to escape bombardment during World War II. "You might find anything in a place like this. Did you see those mountains as we came along? And the woods?" (LWW 5; ch. 1). These sights prefigure the all but preternatural mountains and woods they will soon see in Narnia. Afterward, Lucy—who is, like Jane, a visionary—is exploring; she enters a wardrobe, and "a moment later she found that she was standing in the middle of a wood at night-time with snow under her feet and snowflakes falling through the air" (LWW 5; ch 1). A moment after that, she meets a Faun, and the intercourse between the worlds has truly begun.

The second visit to Narnia takes a different turn. Edmund, too, enters the wardrobe and finds himself "stepping out from the shadow of some thick dark fir trees into an open place in the middle of a wood" where he stands "in crisp, dry snow" under a "pale blue sky," just as the sun is "rising, very red and clear" (LWW 29; ch. 3). "Everything," the narrator says, "was perfectly still" (LWW 29; ch. 3). Edmund is met not by a local inhabitant native to Narnia, but by an alien presence, the White Witch. Immediately all mention of woodland and weather ceases, and is not renewed until the second chapter afterwards, with its apt title, "Into the Forest" (LWW 54; ch. 6).

Even then, the landscape offers no hint of wonder almost until this chapter's last page, when Lucy exclaims, "Look! There's a robin, with such a red breast" (LWW 60; ch. 6). With this appearance, "the clouds parted overhead and the winter sun came out and the snow around them grew dazzlingly bright" (LWW 61; ch. 6). Enlightened, Peter adds his judgment: "They're good birds in all the stories I've ever read. I'm sure a robin wouldn't be on the wrong side" (LWW 62;

ch. 6). In Narnia, the very snow has meaning, as what at first seems a delightful early snowfall becomes an exhausting barrier when the children struggle through it, not least Edmund, who has been a prisoner on the Witch's sleigh.

"The snow was really melting in earnest and patches of green grass were beginning to appear in every direction" (LWW 119; ch. 11). In my world, that is, in southern Ontario, where I live, the grass that emerges from long lying snow is brown and sere, and becomes green with maddening slowness, sometimes in late May. My grandchildren think they are lucky if their Easter-egg hunt occurs on dead leaves instead of snowdrifts. But it is not so in Narnia: there, the magically prolonged winter melts at the breath of Aslan, and "Every moment the patches of green grew bigger and the patches of snow grew smaller" (LWW 120; ch. 11). Indeed, "Edmund saw the ground covered in all directions with little flowers—celandines. The noise of the water grew louder. Presently they actually crossed a stream. Beyond it they found snowdrops growing" (LWW 121; ch. 11). Narnia is once more the *locus amoenus* it was intended to be. As the chapter ends, the witch and Edmund pass through beech trees in full leaf, and "As [they] walked under them the light also became green" (LWW 122; ch. 11).

But these sweet passages are only foretastes, spring promises, like those that (somewhere south of Ontario) accompany Holy Week. There must be a Good Friday before there can be an Easter, before Aslan rises. Lewis expresses this contrast by the use of night for the Passion of Aslan, and morning for his rising:

> The sky in the east was whitish by now and the stars were getting fainter—all except one very big one low down on the eastern horizon. (LWW 160; ch. 15)

Suddenly, birds began to sing, and "red turned to gold along the line where the sea and the sky met" (LWW 161; ch. 15). The Stone Table cracks and Aslan is "There, shining in the sunrise, larger than they had seen him before, shaking his mane" (LWW 162; ch. 15).

He carries the two Pevensie girls (who, like the women at the tomb, have watched and waited) across Narnia on a supernal romp:

> [...] down solemn avenues of beech and across sunny glades of oak, through wild orchards of snow-white cherry trees, past

roaring waterfalls and mossy rocks and echoing caverns, up windy slopes alight with gorse bushes and across the shoulders of heathery mountains and along giddy ridges and down, down again into wild valleys, and out into acres of blue flowers. (LWW 165; ch. 15)

These blue flowers are, I am sure, those of whom Lewis became a devotee in his infancy.

In *Prince Caspian* (1951), the Pevensie children return to Narnia, literally "dragged" into "such a woody place that branches were sticking into them and there was hardly room to move" (PC 5; ch. 1). At the edge of these woods they find "a very calm sea was falling on the sand" beneath "a cloudless sky" (PC 5; ch. 1). After an exploration of what proves to be an island, they discover, beyond a "steep bank," "an old tree that was heavy with large yellowish-golden apples as firm and juicy as you could wish to see" (PC 13; ch. 1). The motif of the apple tree, broached first here, will become profoundly significant as the Narnian Chronicles draw toward their close. Now, after an exploration, they discover a place of "level grass and daisies, and ivy, and gray walls. It was a bright, secret, quiet place, and rather sad," sad because it has been deserted for "ages" (PC 14; ch. 1), and in fact it is the overgrown floor of the castle of Cair Paravel, whose walls have broken and roofs long since fallen. This motif, surely, grew in the mind of Lewis from his visit to Tintern Abbey, many years before. But despite the hint of poignancy—"rather sad"—this apparent image of abandonment and desolation is characterized by the key word, "bright," suggesting that the sadness is temporary, and will, in due season, turn into joy.

The children now encounter a dwarf, who tells them the story of Prince Caspian, the rightful Prince of Narnia who has been usurped by his uncle Miraz, but rejoices in a tutor who is half-dwarf and who secretly informs him of his Narnian heritage. This knowledge has led Caspian to a wonderful discovery. He and his tutor "entered a dark and seemingly endless pine forest" (PC 63; ch. 5) and are rescued by the badger Trufflehunter and two dwarfs, Trumpkin (who is recounting these events), and Nikabrik.

Trumpkin's narrative continues: "On a fine summer morning when the dew lay on the grass he set off [...] through the forest to a high saddle in the mountains and down onto their sunny slopes where

133

one looked across the green wolds [grassy uplands] of Archenland" (PC 72; ch. 6). The dewy grass, the forest, and the green wolds, all signify the *locus amoenus*, making visible the world of the Old Narnians who are now reduced to "living to themselves in woods and caves" (PC 78; ch. 6). This is why the valiant Mouse Reepicheep appears "at the mouth of a little hole in a green bank" (PC 79; ch. 6), assuring the attentive reader that the occupant of a green place (read "good place") will himself be good. That night, Prince Caspian first sees the old Narnians dancing, including the Fauns; in the morning, "the grass was covered with little cloven hoofmarks" (PC 83; ch. 6). In the next chapter we learn that this is "The Dancing Lawn" (PC 79; ch. 6). All the Old Narnians come out to meet Prince Caspian, and Master Cornelius, his tutor, at a sacred place which now covers the Stone Table where Aslan was once sacrificed.

At the end of the Dwarf's narrative, the Pevensies begin making their way toward Old Narnia: "soon the green, wooded coast of the island was falling away behind them [...] close round the boat [the water] was green and bubbly" (PC 112; ch. 8). In this green sea they travel safely, landing where "the little streams [...] poured down from the forest into Glasswater" (PC 115; ch. 9) the estuary that leads the travelers to a place of rest. Everybody goes to sleep but Lucy, whose visionary gifts lead her into the woods, where she calls: "Trees, Trees, Trees," hoping to awaken the dryads within. Her power recurs the next day, when she cries out, "Look! Look! Look!" (PC 125; ch. 9) and declares that she has seen Aslan showing the true path.

When her siblings refuse to follow, she yields and follows them, "crying bitterly" (PC 128; ch. 9). The downward way they have chosen is beautiful—"rumbling waterfalls, silver cascades, deep, amber-colored pools, mossy rocks, and deep moss on the banks in which you sank over your ankles, every kind of fern"—but in the end they are forced to return the way they have come (PC 130; ch. 10). As they sleep, Aslan calls again: "Lucy" (PC 137; ch. 10). She is led to "a circle of grass, smooth as a lawn [...], with dark trees dancing all around it." And, "*he* was there; the huge Lion" (PC 141; ch. 10).

The party starts out again next morning, following the true path, and the rest of the children encounter Aslan too. The conclusion of this meeting is in some ways the most memorable event in all the story of Narnia—the moment when "Aslan shook his mane and roared," and the trees take their true forms as "Pale birch-girls [...] tossing their heads," "willowwomen [who] pushed their hair from their brooding faces to gaze at Aslan," and "queenly birches stood still and adored him" (PC 157; ch. 11). One is reminded of Chronicles 16.33: "Then shall the trees of the wood sing out at the presence of the LORD, because he cometh to judge the earth."

Having become High King again, Caspian goes to fight the usurper Miraz, and wins, with the help of "the Awakened Trees" (PC 196; ch. 14). The narrator asks, "Have you ever stood at the edge of a great wood on a high ridge when a wild southwester broke over it in full fury on an autumn's evening?" (PC 196; ch. 14). This may be a memory from one of Lewis's walking tours, but it will remind many readers of the line, "On Wenlock Edge the wood's in trouble," from the poem "Wenlock Edge" in A.E. Housman's *A Shropshire Lad*, while others will think of Birnam Wood advancing to overcome Macbeth, or of the march of Treebeard's Ents, in Tolkien's *The Lord of the Rings*, or all three.

As all things in Narnia are restored to their proper order and place, the followers of Miraz, humans called Telmarines, are returned to "the glaring green and blue of an island in the Pacific," and the children go back to "the English sky and the summer term before them" (PC 222; ch. 15). Obviously, Aslan's power extends beyond the little world where these children have met him.

Although *The Voyage of the Dawn Treader* (1952) begins with an unflattering description of Eustace Scrubb's likes and dislikes, the Narnian part of the story opens with a ship sailing through "water [...] full of greens and purples" (VDT 5; ch. 1). Within moments the Pevensie children, along with their cousin Eustace, find themselves swimming in this green water and then taken aboard this ship, scenting "the wild, briny smell" (VDT 8; ch. 1) of the Narnian sea. Their first landing, at the Lone Islands, begins with "downy turf" and "a lark singing" (VDT 41; ch. 3). Unfortunately, the local inhabitants include slavers who capture the children, along with Caspian, now King in his own right, Reepicheep the mouse, and their shipmates. Rescued, they are "royally feasted in a low, pillared house overlooking the bay" (VDT 52; ch. 3). Dwellings of this design are symbols of goodness for Lewis, especially when associated with downy turf, though the latter did not prevent the practice of slavery. Caspian sets right the affairs of this island, and the voyage continues.

The next landfall finds them in dragon country: Eustace notices "how very silent and warm and dark green the wood became" (VDT 82; ch. 5). In due course, he encounters a dying dragon, falls asleep on its abandoned horde, and wakens to find himself—he has been behaving rather badly—endragoned. In this form he returns to his comrades, who offer sympathy and accept him despite his previous misdeeds. This mishap is corrected in an exquisite passage involving a motif which recurs in the later Chronicles: "on top of this mountain there was a garden—trees and fruit and everything. In the middle of it there was a well" (VDT 114; ch. 7). In this place, the universal *locus amoenus* with its suggestion of baptism, Eustace is undragoned in the waters of the wide, marble-stepped well.

Sailing onward, the voyagers visit a "low green island" (VDT 121; ch. 8) and, soon afterwards, encounter a sea serpent. In this volume Lewis opens the possibility that what is green is not always and everywhere good: the "dark green [...] wood" of the dragon's island, and the "green island" with its dangerous sea creature, introduce green as a negative motif, a notion that becomes fullblown (if only briefly) in *The Silver Chair*, to be discussed below. A third island now appears, where the voyagers find "a deep little mountain lake" (VDT 130; ch. 8) whose waters turn everything, including human flesh, into gold. These touches of green danger are, perhaps, necessary correctives for a symbolic system that might otherwise become too glib. Certainly they accord with human life as actually lived.

The heart of *The Voyage of the Dawn Treader* is reached on "The Island of the Voices," where the voyagers find "level lawns" of smooth grass and numerous trees, where "Pigeons sometimes cooed" (VDT 140; ch. 9). In the distance, "they now caught sight of a house—very long and grey and quiet-looking in the afternoon sun" (VDT 140; ch. 9). This evocation of the perfect English country house with its "level lawns" fulfills its promise of goodness; Lucy is to meet the resident magician, Coriakin, here. Her visit upstairs into the vast indoor silence of the house offers her opportunities and temptations (both taken up) and eventually brings her to Aslan, through pronouncing "*A Spell to make hidden things visible*" (VDT 168; ch. 10). I would say that all of Lewis's fantasies are devoted to precisely this task.

As is so often the case, this experience of illumination is followed by a loss of light. The next "adventure" concerns "what looked like a great dark mountain" (VDT 189; ch. 12) and is in fact "a darkness." Here it is the absence of things seen that provides the horror, as each voyager undergoes a private nightmare. Rescued by Aslan, they come "into the sunlight and were in the warm, blue world again" (VDT 201; ch. 12). This visual expression of the contrast between depression and happiness is probably based on Lewis's own close observation of psychological, perhaps even spiritual—if the two are not the same—experiences, not necessarily his own if one considers the dreadful psychotic ordeal of Mrs. Moore's brother described in *All My Road Before Me*.

In very great contrast, "On an evening of startling beauty, when the sunset behind them was [...] crimson and purple" (VDT 206; ch. 13) the voyagers come to the island where Aslan's Table is located and they meet a Star and his daughter (who will become King Caspian's wife). This episode begins with "fine springy turf dotted here and there with a low bushy growth" (VDT 207; ch. 13), clearly a place of promise in Lewisian terms. At this table, where Reepicheep dares to dine, the Star's daughter and her "mild and grave" father receive a visit of birds who fly from the Sun to bring the "Old Man" nourishment (VDT 221 ff; ch. 14).

At this point, all the lost Lords of Narnia (for whom the voyagers have been seeking) have been found and their fates discovered. But the voyage of the *Dawn Treader* is not yet ended. It sails on into "The Last Sea" (VDT 237; ch. 15), which has its own underworld, an under-water world with "shafts of sunlight falling through the deep water onto the wooded valley—and, in the extreme distance, everything melting away into a dim greenness" (VDT 240; ch. 15). Soon after, the water is discovered to be "sweet" (not salty) and the travelers encounter at last "The Very End of the World" (VDT 253; ch. 16). Now, the sea becomes filled with lilies; Lucy lifts up "wet arms full of white petals and broad flat leaves" (VDT 257; ch. 16).

At last, this sea comes to an end, in a "greenish-grey, trembling, shimmering wall" of water (VDT 264; ch. 16). Beyond, to the East, "beyond the sun," there are mountains:

these were warm and green and full of forests and waterfalls however high you looked. And suddenly there came a breeze from the east [...] it lasted only a second or so but what it brought them in that second none of those three children will ever forget." (VDT 265; ch. 16)

Asked "afterward," "Lucy could only say, 'It would break your heart.' 'Why,' said I; 'was it so sad?' 'Sad! No,' said Lucy" (VDT 265; ch. 16). In this passage, the narrator Lewis himself speaks, as if he had interviewed Lucy in the way he had, in the Space Trilogy, interviewed Ransom. This open expression of a joy so intense that it approaches pain is a precise statement of the experience that all his profoundest works are meant to invoke.

By this time we cannot be surprised that this shore leads to "a huge plain of very fine short grass," to which "the sky really did come down" in "a blue wall" (VDT 267; ch. 16). Here the children meet a Lamb: "There was a fire lit on the grass, and fish roasting on it" (VDT 268; ch. 16). No fire can burn this supernal grass, just as death could not harm this Lamb. The children are, for this brief preview, in Aslan's country, visitors, as visionaries sometimes are, in Heaven.

In *The Silver Chair* (1953), the reformed Eustace and a new character, Jill Pole, escape persecution from their schoolmates by calling upon the name of Aslan: they enter a world where "a blaze of sunshine [...] made the drops of water on the grass glitter like beads. [...] They saw smooth turf, smoother and brighter than Jill had ever seen before" (SC 12; ch. 1). This paradisal imagery introduces the children (and the reader) to Aslan's Country, high above Narnia. After quarreling with Eustace so that he falls off the edge of this high place, Jill encounters Aslan. He is standing "just on this side" of a "stream, bright as glass, running across the turf" (SC 21; ch. 2).

Clearly, this is that stream of which George MacDonald wrote in *At the Back of the North Wind*: "He [Diamond] said the river—for all agree that there is a river there—flowed not only through, but over grass: its channel [...] was of pure meadow grass, not overlong."[76] As MacDonald says, all—that is, Diamond, Dante, and Kilmeny[77]— agree that there is a river, but only MacDonald actually describes it as flowing over grass. This unforgettable image, which I first heard at the age of seven in my second grade class as my teacher read it aloud, delicately raises the level of numinosity in Jill's encounter with Aslan.

138

In order to quench her desperate thirst, Jill must pass the lion and, with the greatest effort, she does pass, and does drink: "It was the coldest, most refreshing water she had ever tasted" (SC 23; ch. 2).

Aslan now assigns her a task based upon "the four signs" (SC 26; ch. 2) which he makes her memorize, and sends her safely down upon his own breath, to Narnia, to "a smooth, green lawn" (SC 31; ch. 2), where the Narnians are gathered to see the now-aged Caspian depart on his way back to the east. This is the first sign, but as Jill has not told Eustace of her assignment, the sign is missed.

That night, the children are called to "a parliament of owls" (a play upon Chaucer's *The Parlement of Fowles*) and learn of the serpent, "green as poison," that killed King Caspian's wife, the mother of Prince Rilian. As J.R.R. Tolkien has remarked, on the work that immediately comes to mind—*Sir Gawain and the Green Knight*—in encountering this sudden appearance of what is very clearly a malignant rather than supernal form of green, "If we are introduced to a green man, with green hair and face, on a green horse, at the Court of King Arthur, we expect 'magic'."[78] And, as Tolkien continues, in the poem the assembled banqueters indeed thought this vision to be "a phantom and fay-magic." In this case, as in that, one is right to think so; clearly, green is not always and in every place a sign of goodness. Rilian, in fact, has been tempted away by a woman "tall and great, shining, and wrapped in a thin garment as green as poison" (SC 60; ch. 4). The phrase "green as poison," having already been used to describe the murderous serpent, is a major revelation of what in the end proves to be the identity of woman and serpent: "This shining green woman," we learn, and not to our surprise, "was evil" (SC 60; ch. 4). She in fact, is the serpent, and the Prince has become her deluded captive.

The two children and the owl Glimfeather travel to "a place without trees" to find Puddleglum, in his marsh, which is "bordered with reeds and rushes" (SC 66; ch. 5). He tells his visitors in his gloomy way that they will encounter giants in their search for the lost prince, at which news, "Scrubb's face [...] turned rather green" (SC 74; ch. 5). This sequence of green serpent, green lady, and green face represents a series of reversals; the whole book warns against judging by appearances, and presents the four signs of Aslan in unexpected forms not easily detected by a glance or a stereotype.

Traveling through the giants' country, the children encounter a "lady, who [...] wore a long, fluttering dress of dazzling green" (SC 88; ch. 6), and her companion, a knight in black armor riding a black horse. The lady's horse, on the other hand, is white and "so lovely that you wanted to kiss its nose and give it a lump of sugar at once" (SC 87; ch. 6). Quite forgetting what they have been told about the green witch and the lost prince, the children listen to her cheerful lies about the "mild, civil, prudent, and courteous" giants who dwell at Harfang, where the children are expected for the Autumn Feast (literally, as it happens, since they and the Marsh-wiggle are actually intended to form part of the menu). Only after a dream of Aslan does Jill realize that a ruined city below Harfang is the next clue, and that the city's very form spells out "UNDER ME." In due time the children recognize their danger and make their escape, dashing underground just in time.

The underworld is illumined by "a cold light" (SC 140; ch. 10) borne by "pale" gnomes. Its trees are "flabby like mushrooms" (SC 143; ch. 10), and there is "deep moss" (SC 145; ch. 10). A vast lake of "smooth dark water" is crossed, and the party arrives at "a great castle," illuminated by what the travelers take to be "honest, yellowish, warm light" (SC 150; ch. 10). In the room so lighted, the travelers find the Black Knight, who does not know who he truly is—Prince Rilian—except in those moments when he is bound in a silver chair. So bound, he recalls himself and calls upon Aslan, another sign. As the children release him, the "Lady of the Green Kirtle" (SC 171; ch. 12) arrives. With "a handful of a green powder" (SC 173; ch. 12), she attempts to continue her reversal of reality. Then Puddleglum ends the spell by burning his own foot in the fire:

> "Suppose we *have* only dreamed [...] trees and grass and sun and moon and stars and Aslan himself. Suppose we have. Then all I can say is that, in that case, the made-up things seem a great deal more important than the real ones." (SC 182; ch. 12)

This manifesto or confessio or credo of Puddleglum's is notable for the inclusion of "trees and grass," earthly things, along with "sun and moon and stars" in the context of the divine Aslan. In this novel, many of the green things have been costumes and smoke—

outward, and in fact, false—appearances. But "trees and grass" are real, really green, and really good. The last we hear of evil green is when "the long green train of [the witch's] skirt thickened and grew solid," and becomes "a writhing green pillar" (SC 183; ch. 12), as she resumes her serpent form and is killed by Rilian, Eustace, and Puddleglum.

A long trek through the Underworld brings its gnomes to a deeper, lovelier place, Bism, which is filled with jewels (including jasper perhaps?) and the rescue party and the Prince follow a series of "pale lamps" to an ever smaller place, "strange and ghastly in the green glow" (SC 212; ch. 14). Here, the reversal changes direction; the enclosure leads to "a cold blue sort of light" (SC 213; ch. 14) which is in fact the night sky above Narnia, and the party emerges into a merry moonlit night where "trim little Fauns and Dryads with leaf-crowned hair" are playing snowballs with Dwarfs in "scarlet with fur-lined hoods and golden tassels" (SC 217; ch. 15). The escape party is dug out (opening a convenient concourse between Narnia's surface and its perfectly innocent Underworld). Next day the Prince and his rescuers are welcomed by Aslan, who calls the children back to his "Mountain," where he revives the now dead Caspian with a drop of his own blood.

The Horse and His Boy (1954) records events that occurred when the Pevensie children were Kings and Queens in Narnia, during the period briefly described near the end of *The Lion, the Witch and the Wardrobe*. It "is the story of an adventure that happened in Narnia and Calormen and the lands between" (HB 1; ch. 1). In Calormen, a boy named Shasta lives with his "father," a fisherman. He often looks to the north, but sees "nothing but a grassy slope rising up to a level ridge and beyond the sky," like Lewis gazing at the unreachable green hills above Belfast. The visit of a Tarkaan (a Calormene lord) brings a Talking Horse, who tells Shasta, significantly, of

> "The happy land of Narnia—Narnia of the heathery mountains and the thymy downs, Narnia of the many rivers, the plashing glens, the mossy caverns and deep forests ringing with the hammers of the Dwarfs." (HB 11; ch. 1)

This is the green Narnia, the perfect northland based on Lewis's deepest longings, even to the presence of the dwarfs. Drawn,

Shasta dares to accompany the Horse (whose name is Bree) in his escape. Narnia, of course, is a long way away, but already there are hints of it; as the escapees rest on the way, "Before them the turf, dotted with white flowers, sloped down to the brow of a cliff" (HB 20; ch. 2). Shasta breathes in—"this new air was so delicious" (HB 20; ch. 2)—while Bree rolls rapturously on the grass. Unknown to them, Aslan is near; the escapees hear "a long snarling roar" (HB 26; ch. 2) and are driven into the company of a Calormene girl, Aravis, and her own Talking Horse, Hwin, who are also trying to escape to Narnia. While "the horses had a little grass […] Aravis produced rather nice things to eat from her saddlebag" (HB 34; ch. 2).

The two young people share their stories as well as these "nice things," and travel along together toward Tashbaan, the principal city of Calormen. The city, huge and crowded, teems with people, all of them looking and behaving in accord with Lewis's Orientalizing vision of a city out of the Arabian Nights, with one significant exception: "half a dozen men" wearing "tunics of fine, bright, hardy colors" of which "woodland green" (HB 57; ch. 4) is first on the list. These are Narnians, and to Shasta's astonishment, he is mistaken for a prince of Archenland (Narnia's allianced neighbor kingdom) and rushed away in their company. Taken to their lodgings, he is called Corin, and meets not only the Kings and Queens of Narnia, but Tumnus the Faun. These persons are trying to escape from the efforts of the Calormenes to capture Queen Susan and force her to marry a Calormene prince. (The problem is not that he is a Calormene prince as such, but that he is Prince Rabadash, a man who, literally, makes an ass of himself at the end of the story.)

Shasta finally understands why they so trustingly tell him all this, when the true Corin enters through a window; they meet face to face and recognize each other as twins. Corin tells Shasta how to escape, and Shasta makes his way beyond the city to the tombs at the edge of the desert where "all the grass stopped quite suddenly" (HB 83; ch. 6). Here he waits, but not quite alone; a miraculous cat with "big, green, unblinking eyes" sleeps at his back all night long.

Meanwhile Aravis, too, arrives in Tashbaan, and visits her friend Lasaraleen, who lives in a dwelling with "a courtyard-garden" and "a beautiful pillared room" (HB 98-99; ch. 7), both motifs beloved by Lewis but used here ironically, since such loveliness is wasted on Lasaraleen, whose main interest is directed toward the Calormene palace, where she takes Aravis to hide while the Tisroc (the ruler of Calormen) speaks with Lasaraleen's betrothed, the Grand Vizier (an obsequious toady) and his own son, the self-approving Prince. The two girls hear of the plot to kidnap the Narnians and detain Queen Susan. Escaping, they pass through the palace gardens, where "grey lawns, quietly bubbling fountains, and the long black shadows of cypress trees" (HB 124; ch. 9) form a perfect vision of benighted Calormen as opposed to the green Narnia described by the Horse Bree.

Aravis says "Good-bye" to the foolish Lasaraleen, and puts out upon the river in a punt (delightful thought; perhaps this river was a branch of the Isis which runs through Oxford). After crossing, she finds "the same road that Shasta had found, and came just as he had done to the end of the grass," and "the beginning of the sand" (HB 126; ch. 9), and the awaiting tombs. Together, Bree and Hwin, carrying Shasta and Aravis, gallop across the night desert, until, suddenly, "the grey sand turned yellow and twinkled as if it was strewn with diamonds," a flashing hint of the supernal, though the travel through sunlit sand becomes more and more terrible, until, at last, "They came to [...] a tiny trickle of water through softer and better grass" (HB 133; ch. 9), a sure sign that Narnia is near. Soon they reach a valley: "The whole glade was full of the coolest, and most delicious smells. And out of the darkest recess among the trees there came a sound Shasta had never heard before—a nightingale" (HB 134; ch. 9). As they move along,

> The valley itself, with its brown, cool river, and grass and moss and wild flowers and rhododendrons, was such a pleasant place that it made you want to ride slowly. (HB 137; ch. 9)

"A pleasant place" is a direct translation of "*locus amoenus*." But Shasta is not allowed to rest. On he must go, driven by necessity in the form of "a huge tawny creature" (HB 142; ch. 10) who pursues both riders and their horses into an enclosure "barred by a smooth green wall about ten feet high" (HB 142; ch. 10).

> They were in a wide and perfectly circular enclosure, protected by a high wall of green turf. A pool of perfectly still water, so full that the water was almost exactly level with the

ground, lay before him. At one end of the pool, completely overshadowing it with its branches, there grew the highest and most beautiful tree that Shasta had ever seen. Beyond the pool was a little low house of stone roofed with deep and ancient thatch […] The level ground was completely covered with the finest grass. (HB 145; ch. 10)

This paradisal setting contains the whole vision of the good place, the edenic source and goal of the created world. It is the dwelling of the Hermit of the Southern March, who takes in the travelers and, after offering them food and shelter and rest, sends Shasta on yet another errand: "When Shasta went through the gate he found a slope of grass and a little heather running up before him to some trees" (HB 153; ch. 11). Here, he meets "the jolliest, fat, apple-cheeked, twinkling-eyed King you could imagine" (HB 154; ch. 11). He is King Lune, Shasta's and Corin's father. Off they ride together, but the Horse tires, slows, and slips behind. Then Shasta discovers that there are Calormenes, led by Rabadash, secretly invading and headed for Narnia.

Terrified, Shasta rides away in desperation, and discovers that he has an "invisible companion" (HB 162; ch. 11): Aslan, who had been all the lions (and even the green-eyed cat). "After one glance at the Lion's face he slipped out of the saddle and fell at its feet" (HB 166; ch. 11). Then, as the vision disappears, "He was alone with the horse on a grassy hillside under a blue sky" (HB 166; ch. 11). The Lion has left a great footprint in the grass: "Soon it was full to the brim, and then overflowing, and a little stream was running downhill, past him, over the grass" (HB 167; ch. 12). Here again, the sacred stream flows over the turf, just as it does in Paradise.

In fact, Shasta is in Narnia: "It was a green valleyland dotted with trees" (HB 168; ch. 12). Quietly, Narnians gather to his aid—a Hedgehog, a Dwarf, a Rabbit, a Stag—and within hours he is reunited with his twin and off to battle in defense of Narnia. The battle itself is described as the Hermit sees it in the magic pool into which he "looked when he wanted to know what was going on in the world outside the green walls of his hermitage" (HB 187; ch. 13). Narnia is victorious, and the villainous Rabadash is left dangling by his hauberk from "a hook in the wall" (HB 194; ch. 13), unharmed and harmless.

Shasta, now called by his true name of Cor, becomes the crown prince of his father's country (much to the relief of his twin brother Corin). Rabadash (after a brief sojourn as a donkey) goes home to stay, and Aravis and Cor get married. Charmingly, Narnia as a place of delight is last suggested when Cor promises Bree, who will never be ridden again, that "you'll be galloping and rolling on the hills of Narnia" (HB 209; ch. 14).

The Magician's Nephew (1955), which explores "how all the comings and goings between our own world and the land of Narnia" (MN 3; ch. 1) came about, begins in a garden. Two children, Polly and Digory, meet there, and become friends. This garden is no idle motif, as will be seen in the last chapter, in a sequence of events which are in many ways the climax of the entire Chronicles in their use of supernal imagery as expressed in terms of the garden of Paradise; the little backyard garden in Edwardian London is revealed as playing its own central role in the history of Narnia.

Exploring the connected attics of the row-houses where the two children live, they find themselves in the clutches of Digory's uncle, a would-be magician. The kind of magic in which he engages exactly fits Dorothy L. Sayers's dictum: "Irresponsible power, producing effects without cause or consequence, is the very definition of magic."[79] As a result of his illicit and fruitless magic, he sends Polly into another world without knowing how to get her back and without the slightest concern for her welfare, and Digory follows her; they find themselves in "The Wood Between the Worlds" (MN 31; ch. 3) where "all the light was green light that came through the leaves" (MN 32; ch. 3). It is a place of potentiality: "This wood was very much alive" (MN 32; ch. 3). Pools are scattered everywhere, and each leads to a different world. To mark their choice, Digory "cut out a long strip of turf on the bank of the pool." The soil (which smells nice) "was of a rich reddish brown and showed up well against the green" (MN 41; ch. 3), an aesthetic remark which may have its origins in Lewis's long acquaintance with Arthur Greeves.

It is perhaps no coincidence that the magic rings that "would take you out of the wood into a world" (MN 42; ch. 3) are themselves green. At the very least, green in this context signifies both potency and potentiality. But, grasping their rings, the children find that the world they enter by this means, Charn, is no green place, but a silent and blasted desert of ruined buildings, in which, "where the dry earth showed between the broken flagstones there was no grass or moss" (MN 50; ch. 4). In this deadly place, devoid of all that is green, the children encounter a terrible and beautiful woman seated on a throne, frozen in a magic sleep. In her malign presence, they fall to quarreling over a little golden bell. Digory strikes a note from it, and the woman—the Empress Jadis—awakens, forcing the children to accompany her. When they finally make their escape from her, they go together into the "warm green light" (MN 71; ch. 5) of the wood between the worlds.

Finally, the children, Jadis, and Uncle Andrew all travel to Earth, where Digory's mother lies dying. "Suddenly it flashed upon his mind [...] that there might be a real Land of Youth somewhere," and "fruit in some other world that would really cure his mother" (MN 92; ch. 7). In a sense, perhaps, the entire creation of Narnia is based upon the need of a boy to find a place by which his mother could be healed; C.S. Lewis's mother died of cancer when he was nine years old, and his life thereafter, for many years, was very far indeed from paradise. Certainly, the creation of Narnia by Aslan may be said to have come about because of the events, apparently random, which carry Digory, Polly, Jadis, Uncle Andrew, a London cab, cab-horse, and cabby, to a place where the "shapes of hills" (MN 108; ch. 8) stand up against a sky grey with dawn.

There, the great Lion—Aslan—brings this new world, Narnia, into full being:

> And as he walked and sang the valley grew green with grass.
> It spread out from the Lion like a pool. It ran up the sides of
> the little hills like a wave." (MN 112; ch. 9)

Then "The higher slopes grew dark with heather," and "Patches of rougher and more bristling green appeared in the valley" (MN 112; ch. 9), soon to become trees; these trees "stood on cool, green grass, sprinkled with daisies and buttercups" (MN 114; ch. 9). Watching, Polly realizes that these delights are coming directly from the mind of the maker, Aslan. Presently, animal forms emerge from the "grassy land," and at last, as the stars sing overhead, Aslan calls upon the inhabitants of Narnia, vegetable, animal, and mineral, to "Be walking trees. Be talking beasts. Be divine waters" (MN 126; ch. 9).

146

This beautiful passage is followed by Uncle Andrew's predictably foolish response (he wants to exploit it), and culminates with the Cabby and his wife (miraculously called into Narnia) being named "the first King and Queen of Narnia," by Aslan (MN 150; ch. 11). Aslan has plans for the cabby horse Strawberry, too, and also for Digory and Polly: the horse grows wings and becomes "Fledge," and Digory and Polly fly upon his back to the mountain valley as Aslan commands. "All Narnia, many-colored with lawns and rocks and heather and different sorts of trees, lay spread out below them" (MN 159; ch. 12) as they travel to the place that Aslan had described:

> You must journey through those mountains till you find a green valley with a blue lake in it [...] At the end of the lake is a steep, green hill. On the top of that hill there is a garden. In the center of that garden is a tree. Pluck an apple from the tree and bring it to me." (MN 155; ch. 12)

From the height of their flight, "Aslan himself was only a bright yellow spot on the green grass" (MN 159; ch. 12). This litany of green valley, blue lake, green hill, garden, and tree, reads like an endless rosary of jasper and sapphire, images so ardent, so diamantine, that they can never fade nor stale, no matter how often repeated.

At last the goal is reached: "All round the very top of the hill ran a high wall of green turf. Inside the wall trees were growing. Their branches hung out over the wall; their leaves showed not only green but also blue and silver when the wind stirred them" (MN 170; ch. 13). Green turf, leaves of green, blue and silver; the reader who has followed the Narnian Chronicles in the order in which they were written is rewarded beyond measure by this paradisal scene, for this garden, hinted at and briefly glimpsed from book to book, now opens with all its promise of fulfillment, its foretaste of what Lewis and those who believe as he does, hope one day to see for themselves; if not this, then something unimaginably better.

Digory picks his permitted apple and brings it back uneaten, as he has been told to do. Still obeying, he proceeds to "sow the seed of the tree that is to be the protection of Narnia" (MN 180; ch. 14). Almost immediately, in the supernaturally speeded ecosystem of the newly created Narnia, the tree springs up; "Its spreading branches seemed to cast a light rather than a shade, and silver apples peeped out like stars from under every leaf" (MN 188; ch. 14), the narrator says, suggesting a model of the cosmos in the form of a tree. Then Aslan commands Digory to "Go. Pluck her an apple from the Tree" (MN 191; ch. 14). And he does, and, magically returned to Earth, he gives it to his mother, who is healed.

Lastly, "That evening he buried the core of the Apple in the back garden" (MN 198; ch. 15). It grows to be a great apple tree that proceeds to "bear apples more beautiful than any others in England" (MN 201; ch. 15), that is more beautiful than any apples anywhere! In the end, its wood is used to make "a wardrobe" which Digory, by now a Professor, places in his country home, with the result that it becomes "the beginning of all the comings and goings between Narnia and our world" (MN 202; ch. 15). Logically, Digory and Polly's visit to Narnia is, one would assume, chronologically the first, but here Lewis makes it clear that for him and for his readers, the visit through the wardrobe is "the beginning of all comings and goings," and thus, *The Lion, The Witch and the Wardrobe*, during which the sequence of visits commencing with the wardrobe actually starts, is to be read first.

Beginning with "the west beyond Lantern Waste" (LB 3; ch. 1), there is nothing green in the early chapters of *The Last Battle* (1956), the seventh and final volume of the Narnian Chronicles. The impeccable illustrator Pauline Baynes depicts the occasionally mentioned trees as being leafless. Therefore one cannot be surprised when a voice calls to the young King Tirian, "Woe for my brothers and sisters! Woe for the holy trees! The woods are laid to waste. The axe is loosed against us" (LB 20; ch. 2). A dryad is seen "lying dead in the grass," and the grass is given no color. The King comes upon "a hideous lane like a raw gash in the land, full of muddy ruts where felled trees had been dragged down to the river" (LB 26; ch. 2). And who is cutting down these Holy Trees? The Calormenes!

There is a false Aslan in this threatened Narnia; a donkey in a lion's skin, dominated by an ape. In the name of this falsity, King Tirian and his Unicorn are captured and imprisoned in a "little hut like a stable" where, "on the grass, there sat an ape" (LB 32; ch. 3). Again, grass; not green grass. The King is tied up where he can overlook the view of his subjects submitting helplessly to this false leadership. As he waits, he is aided (as Aslan was after his death in *The Lion, the*

Witch and the Wardrobe) by Mice, along with a Rabbit and two Moles, who offer him food and drink. Refreshed, he calls upon the "Friends of Narnia," and the children of the previous novels arrive. Now, in their company, we read of a valley "where they [the King and his rescuers!] found a mossy cliff with a little fountain bubbling out of it" (LB 56; ch. 5). Entering a small tower, they arm themselves and eat the iron rations provided. Traveling across the sere landscape, they encounter disloyal Dwarfs, and are reduced to eating "a Narnian weed called wild Fresney, which looks rather like our wood-sorrel" (LB 87; ch. 7), according to the helpful narrator.

Soon they learn that the Calormene divinity Tash has arrived, a creature with a "deathly smell" so dire that "the grass seemed to wither beneath it" (LB 92; ch. 8). He has arrived to seek and claim his lawful prey; soon after, the young King recognizes that "Narnia is no more" (LB 103; ch. 8). As the characters in the story assemble at Stable Hill, where a bonfire has been set alight, a certain cat dares to enter the stable door and is thrown out, no longer able to speak. Then a young Calormene, Emeth, volunteers to enter. "He is worthy of a better god than Tash," the Unicorn (a close advisor and friend of the King) says (LB 127; ch. 10). Finally, the last battle is fought, and, outnumbered, the Narnians and their friends enter the stable too, pursued by a Tarkaan, a leader of the Calormenes who soon becomes the prey of Tash; both Tash and Tarkaan are banished by the real Aslan.

Now fully adult, the Kings and Queens of Narnia rejoice: "Look!" says Peter. "Here are lovely fruit-trees. Let us taste them" (LB 155; ch. 12). This is indeed their entry into Paradise, where they will be able to feast forever. "In reality they stood on grass [...] not far away from them rose a grove of trees, thickly leaved, but under every leaf there peeped out [...] fruits such as no one has seen in our world" (LB 156; ch. 13). The sequence, "grass," "trees," "leaves," and "fruit," is precisely that which has been reiterated again and again, briefly or occasionally in the previous books, then, in a rising crescendo, becoming the climactic theme of *The Magician's Nephew*.

From here to the end of *The Last Battle* it is the central, though endlessly varied, melody, one of which its hearers will never tire. In this sublime context, Tirian sees "blue sky overhead, and grassy country spreading as far as he could see in every direction" (LB 161; ch. 13). Only certain of the dwarfs are able to see these verdant wonders. Even Aslan, who now greets the young Narnian ruler, cannot make all the dwarfs see. It is a warning which Lewis derived from a passage in George MacDonald's masterpiece, *The Princess and the Goblin*, also expressed in Lewis's other work, *The Great Divorce* (where MacDonald is a character in the narrative): not everybody is capable of being happy in Heaven. This is the end of Narnia, the end of that green little world, a world even smaller and more fragile than our own green Earth. Aslan calls down the stars: "They made a hissing noise as they landed and burnt the grass" (LB 173; ch. 14)—the grass which is the most frequently cited element of the Narnian environment. Now, "Every bush and almost every blade of grass had its black shadow behind it" (LB 173; ch. 14). All the inhabitants pass through a great door that Aslan has provided. Then, as the narrator says, in a single terrible sentence, "The grass died." Trees, forests, all fall. "In that tree-less world" (LB 178; ch. 14), the waters gather together and rush "to the very threshold of the Doorway" (LB 179; ch. 14) and Time, a giant raised and commanded by Aslan, reaches up and puts out the Sun.

Those who have passed through the doorway, however, "look round and find themselves in warm daylight, the blue sky above them, flowers at their feet, and laughter in Aslan's eyes" (LB 181; ch. 14). Here, too, is a litany of motifs: daylight, blue sky, flowers, Aslan. As the survivors walk away, accompanied by joyous dogs who "sniff at smells in the grass"—endearingly reiterating the motif of grass—"till they made themselves sneeze" (LB 182; ch 14), the party meets Emeth. The "humans sat down on the grass. And [...] the dogs all had a very noisy drink out of the stream" (LB 184; ch. 14). The presence of the dogs accords with Lewis's concept that domesticated animals, at least, might make their way to Heaven. And we know from this tiny, perfectly phrased incident, that this stream from which they drink is the stream that flows over the grass in Paradise.

Emeth now tells what he faced when he entered the stable: "I said, By the Gods, this is a pleasant place" (LB 187; ch. 15); that is, he has come to the *locus amoenus*. "I went over much grass and many flowers and among all kinds of wholesome and delectable trees" (LB 188; ch. 15), he reports, reiterating the features—grass, flowers, and trees—to which Lewis has so often referred; and then he met Aslan, who assured this good Calormene (as in "good Samaritan") that all true service is service to himself.

In the "early and […] morning freshness" (LB 192; ch. 15) of this place where nothing is ever late or stale, the company looks up to see "hills, nice woody ones,"—another frequent motif—and recognizes that they are in a Narnia renewed. As Lucy says, "They have more colors on them and they look further away than I remembered" (LB 193; ch. 15). The narrator, making his point once again, explains that in this "new Narnia," "every rock and flower and blade of grass looked as if it meant more" (LB 196; ch. 15).

Now, off they run, untiring, up the great waterfall beyond the renewed Pool where this novel began, the water now "flashing like diamonds in some places and dark glassy green in others"—these others flashing like jasper, one may assume—(LB 198; ch. 16) a waterfall so miraculous that the whole party is able to swim up it, "with all kinds of reflected lights flashing at you from the water and all manner of colored stones flashing through it" (LB 200; ch. 16) in perfect accord with Aldous Huxley's finding that "every paradise abounds in gems."[80]

At the top of their sublimely jeweled waterfall, the climbers reach a long valley leading to a mountain range. There, at last, or as one might add, as always, "they saw a smooth green hill" of which "the grass was smooth as a bowling green" (LB 202; ch. 16). On arriving, they enter between "great golden gates" to find a "walled garden" (LB 167), where they meet Reepicheep, "walking on springy turf that was dotted with white flowers" (LB 205; ch. 16), which is, by this time, only to be expected, and yet always and everywhere most to be desired. Everybody is there; all the beloved Narnians join them; they find that "it was not really a garden but a whole world" (LB 207; ch. 16), which extends infinitely, even to England, where the Pevensies "saw their own father and mother" (LB 208; ch. 16) approaching. There was no snow on these mountains; there were forests and green slopes and flashing waterfalls, one above the other, going on forever. In this infinite green world, the most pleasant of places, the story, as the narrator tells us, truly begins, and never ends.

IV. "Valley Bright as a Gem": *Till We Have Faces* (1957)

Lewis's last work of fiction, *Till We Have Faces* (1957), is set not in heaven or purgatory or hell, or on Mars or Venus, or in England or Narnia, but in a small kingdom in the deep classical past. It tells the story of Psyche from the point of view of one of her sisters, Orual, Queen of Glome. The narrative is in the first person, and the narrator is Queen Orual. The novel abounds with numinous motifs, especially those surrounding the worship of the Goddess Ungit, but the element of green wonder is significantly present, and appears most particularly in association with the affairs of Psyche, both in her lifetime, and in the exquisite religion that arises from her life.

Queen Orual, writing in her old age, recalls her childhood and youth with the companionship of her sister Psyche:

> I think the almonds and the cherries blossomed earlier in those years and the blossoms lasted longer [...] I see the boughs always rocking and dancing against blue-and-white skies [...] (TWF 22-23; ch. 2)

The white blossoms and blue-and-white skies are associated with spring, and repeat both in the spring of a remembered year and in the springtime of two lives, a motif which delicately spangles all of Lewis's imaginative writing, including the letters he wrote to Arthur Greeves when he and his friend were also young.

Orual becomes a Queen, but Psyche, a beloved public figure adored by the populace and believed to be capable of aiding the harvest and healing the sick, becomes a human sacrifice and disappears. At this point, the color green comes into play, accompanied by the supernatural gleam of precious stones. Orual goes out in search of her lost sister, to find that "Heavy dew made the grass jewel-bright" (TWF 95; ch. 9). Then, climbing upward to the sacred mountain, she reaches her goal:

> It was like looking down into a new world. At our feet [...] lay a small valley bright as a gem [...] I never saw greener turf. There was gorse in bloom, and wild vines, and many groves of flourishing trees, and great plenty of bright water [...] soon we could hear the very chattering of the streams and the sound of bees [...] (TWF 100-101; ch. 9)

Nothing is lacking in this jasper-lucent landscape, this "new world," this "valley bright as a gem" (TWF 101; ch. 9). It possesses green turf, blooming gorse, wild vines, groves of trees, bright water, and chattering streams, all the elements of Paradise in one small valley. Indeed, at this numinous sight, Bardia, Orual's companion, declares: "This may be the secret valley of the God" (TWF 101; ch. 9). In this place, at the very end of his career as a novelist, Lewis evokes the motif with which he began. In *Spirits in Bondage*, his poem "Death in Battle," speaks of "flowery valleys among the mountains and silent wastes untrod / In the dewy upland places, in the garden of God."

Orual devotes enormous effort to denying the truth of what Bardia has said and of what she has seen, as well as the testimony of Psyche, not only surviving but thriving as that god's wife. Only long, long afterwards does she begin to understand, and when she does, the green glory returns. Her wars completed, she sets forth again, and encounters a shrine.

> [W]e went further down the warm, green valley [...] I rose and went slowly through the trees to find the temple [...] I came out into a mossy place free of trees, and there it was [...] (TWF 240; ch. 21)

The little temple or dwelling in the circle of green which so often recurs in Lewis's fantasies, reaches its apotheosis here.

Finally, Orual encounters the god (so long evaded) face to face. She goes, significantly, "by the little eastern doorway that opens on the herb-garden" (TWF 278; II, ch. 2) just as Jane went to the garden of St. Anne's where at length she too found her God. Then, wandering "a little way along the river" (TWF 278; II, ch. 2) still in a state of despair, seeking a place in which to commit suicide, Orual hears the divine voice: "Do not do it" (TWF 279; II, ch. 2). Not long after, she meets the god again in a final encounter:

> He was leading me somewhere and the light was strengthening as we went. It was a greenish, summery light. In the end it was sunshine falling through vine leaves. (TWF 297; II, ch. 4)

The light of summer is made green by the vine leaves of the god of ecstasy; in this setting she is meets Psyche again;

153

> He took my hand and led me out between the pillars (the vine leaves brushed my hair) into the warm sunlight. We stood in a fair, grassy court, with blue, fresh sky above us; mountain sky. (TWF 305; II, ch. 4)

This "summery light," falling on the "fair, grassy court" under the "blue, fresh sky," echoes, surely, Lewis's visit to Tintern Abbey.

As *Till We Have Faces* approaches its end, Orual recalls, "They found me lying on the grass" (TWF 308; II, ch. 4), like Ransom, returned from his first voyage to outer space. The word "grass," along with its occasional cognates, "lawn" and "turf," is the second most used in all of Lewis's landscapes; the first most used word, the omnipresent, most copiously invoked word, is "green."

Conclusion

In the evocations of green numinosity in his poems and fantasies, C.S. Lewis sought to reach the innermost responses of the human soul, or mind, or even body, since as Lewis says, in the quotation forming the epigraph of my essay: "It is Nature [...] and [its] effect on the human nerves and emotions which caused the locus to be *amoenus*."[81] The Bible, writings of which, along with classical literature, formed the basis of Western culture, resounds with evocations of greenness; from God's giving of "every green herb" in Genesis 1.30, through the "green pastures" of Psalm 23.2, to the command not to "hurt the grass of the earth, neither any green thing" in Revelation 9.4. For desert dwellers who first envisioned Paradise as a garden or grove (both evoked in *That Hideous Strength*), green hills, green pastures, and green grass were not only the symbols but the physical source of life itself to the ancient herding peoples of the Near East; all the cultures based upon these origins glitter with jasper-lucent images of the sacred, the holy, and the divine.

What, then, do we mean by the word "green?" *The New Shorter Oxford English Dictionary* begins its long sequence of definitions for "green" thus: green is "Of the colour of grass, foliage, an emerald, etc." There is a remarkable correlation between this short series and the frequency of such usages in Lewis's writing. The word "green" is indeed, and not surprisingly, the one he most frequently uses in evoking landscape as an image of the numinous, and, as I have said above, the frequency of the word "green" is closely matched by the word "grass."

What sorts of objects are green? A forest, a wood, wolds, hills, a little wood, slopes, and, most particularly and repeatedly, grass. Grass as the ubiquitous green thing is associated with such modifiers as dewy, sloping, level, wintry, patchy, downy, springy, fine, bright, and smooth. The negative usages of "green" are so few as to be cited in detail: "green as poison," "dazzling green," "green kirtle," "a long green train," "writhing green pillar," and, as a figure of negativity, "no green place." Other green things—woods, forest, and trees—are mentioned about half as often as "grass" or "green." Slightly fewer still are mentions of flowers, including crocuses, daisies, heather, buttercups, and flowers described as blue, white, tiny, or simply "flowery." Occasional references to moss, fern, and thyme also appear.

These many evocations of things green and growing are followed in frequency by three sets of images associated with luminosity; the "blue sky" is mentioned at least eight times; the word "bright" nearly as often; "light" appears here and there, and "shining" and "dazzling" at least once each. Mere mention, however, cannot convey the significance of the word "bright." A list of its usages makes the matter clear. Lewis writes of "bright water," a "bright, secret, quiet place," "bright turf," a "bright yellow spot," and, most potently, "bright as a gem." Related motifs include water, dew, lakes, and streams; green things flourish only where water is available, and the presence of water (the fundamental necessity of life) is combined in such images, with its reflective qualities, as the earliest, and long the only, mirror of all that is light or bright.

The meaning of these various images is made explicit in three profound adjectives used by Lewis: "holy trees," "divine waters," and "sacred space." All may be defined, according to Jeffrey Burton Russell, as "metaphors that are true." Human life, indeed, almost all life on Earth, is sustained by green things, water, and air. These sublime gifts of the creator make our planet the only place in our solar system that is comfortably inhabited by humans. In this sense, at the very least, all of Earth is sacred space. But Lewis meant more, as well as other, than this alone, He used green and its associated forms and functions, as a figure for the sacred in the unqualified sense, the sacred that abides whether we live or die. I will now consider the categories of "Green," "Grass," "Forest and Flowers," "Blue and Bright," along with an associated motif of human intervention, "A Low Pillared House," to discern what they tell us, in their metaphorical manner, about the divine, the sacred, and the holy.

1. Green

In a nutshell (Julian of Norwich saw "all that is" in a nutshell), a jasper-lucent landscape is one that is both green and bright. The term "jasper-lucent" combines precisely these concepts in an interlocked pair. One might say that Lewis associates "green" with immanence, and "bright" with transcendence, but to say so without qualification would create a dichotomy. In fact (that is, in actual spiritual experience), the concepts immanence and transcendence are not only linked but interdependent. There is nothing oppositional about them. It is the luminosity of greenness and the greenness of its luminosity that makes grass a figure of the sacred, as Lewis records in his description of sunlight falling on the grass that lies inside of Tintern Abbey.

Because Lewis uses the word "green" more than any other, to embody the sacred, he can and does use it—all true symbols are ambivalent, as Jung tells us—to embody evil as well. In accord with Lewis's teaching that heaven is huge and hell is tiny, the list of evil green is very short, and that of good green is very long. When Lewis most wishes to elicit the numinous, he is most inclined to speak of something green. In this, he is powerfully paralleled by William Blake's most potent landscape, in the poem which prefaces "Milton":

> And did those feet in ancient time
> Walk upon England's mountains green?
> And was the holy Lamb of God
> On England's pleasant pastures seen?
>
> And did the countenance Divine
> Shine forth upon our clouded hills?

England's green mountains, England's pleasant pastures, the light that shines on England's hills: these are the metaphors Blake associates with the divine presence, while his allusion to Jerusalem in the last lines of the poem—

Till we have built Jerusalem
In England's green & pleasant Land

implies the jasper lucence of the Heavenly City, which, with its be-
jeweled walls, Blake's Jerusalem will be.

2. Grass

The importance of grass as a symbol used by Lewis is clearly
based upon biblical sources. This image first appears in Genesis 1.1—
"Let the earth bring forth grass" is God's chief command on the third
day of Creation. The Bible mentions "grass" almost as many times as
Lewis mentions "green," and almost as many times as he mentions
"grass" as well. Phrases that echo from the Authorized Version include "He shall come down like rain upon the mown grass" (Psalm
72.6), the Dominical phrase, "If God so clothe the grass of the field
[…] shall he not more clothe you?" (Matthew 6.30) and the harsh
prophecy, "All green grass was burnt up" (Revelation 8.7), an event
which is paralleled in *The Last Battle*; all express the range and depth
of this potent image.

As a symbol of immanence, grass, always understood as
green, shows the power of God operating inside the context of matter.
It provides food for animals, which in turn provide food for humans,
and it clothes the earth as God clothes humans, both physically and
figuratively (Paul tells us to "put on Christ"); and it provides a figure
of human frailty: "All flesh is grass" (Isaiah 40.6). All these passages
combine a tenderness with a poignant awareness of the frailty of humankind and of the natural world. When Tintern Abbey is stripped of
its vaulted roof and its windows of their glass, the sunlight falls upon
a carpet of grass, and the earth and the worshippers who kneel upon it
are again in contact with the sky, in a meeting of immanence with
transcendence.

3. Forests, Orchards, and Flowers

The motifs of immanence and transcendence continue in the
matched lists of flowers and trees. Trees, because of their rootedness,
span the range from immanence to transcendence, by means of their
verticality and height. In Northern European mythology (upon which,
along with Near Eastern and Classical mythology, Western culture

stands) the World Tree ties together heaven and hell, with Earth (Middle-Earth) at the center. In the New Testament, Jesus meets his death on a tree, descends into the earth, and ascends into a cloud, in a series of images not lost upon missionaries to many cultures over the last two millennia. Forests and orchards are alike composed of trees, and Lewis repeatedly resorts to these motifs, most particularly in his descriptions of Narnia.

The Bible begins and ends with trees, from the Tree of Knowledge in Genesis 2.17 to the Tree of life in Revelation 22.2. The lovely passages describing the Narnian Trees contain echoes not only of Greco-Roman mythology, with its nymphs and dryads, but of the beautiful phrase in 1 Chronicles. The whole passage suggests the ambiance of Narnia:

> Let the sea roar, and the fullness thereof;
> let the fields rejoice and all that is therein.
> Then shall all the trees of the wood sing
> at the presence of the LORD
> (1 Chronicles 16.32-33)

The feminine trees of Narnia not only reflect Greek mythology (and some of Narnia's trees are masculine, as well), but hint at the presence of Holy Wisdom: "She is a tree of life," the author of Proverbs (3.18) tells us. Lucy's discovery of Aslan among the dancing trees in *Prince Caspian* makes explicit the role of trees, woods, and forests, as holy places. Again, Orual's "small valley bright as a gem" with its "many groves of flourishing trees" and "great plenty of bright water" brings the interplay between immanence and transcendence in Lewis's writings to the very last of his novels.

Flowers, too, carry a complex meaning. Lewis said that his childhood experience of a toy garden made him a devotee of the Blue Flower (a figure of the numinous). In the list of flowers he describes, there are indeed "blue flowers," as might be expected, but other flowers also appear. He writes of "flowery valleys," of "daisies and buttercups," of "a crocus in the grass," of "white flowers," "tiny flowers," "little flowers," and "petals in the wind." Most striking of these is his comparison of the starry sky with "daisies on an uncut lawn," as Ransom travels the heavens and finds these fields of Arbol to be filled with luminous life.

The Bible is based upon the experience of people for whom flowers appear infrequently and then, all but miraculously, with the onset of rain. Isaiah speaks of those moments when "the desert shall blossom as the rose" (Isaiah 35.1), and the author of The Song of Solomon celebrates "the flowers [...] that appear in the earth" (2.12), and allows his heroine to declare: "I am the rose of Sharon, the lily of the valleys" (2.1). The only lasting flowers are those on the great lamp stand standing before the Holy of Holies of the Temple of Israel, with its "knops" (flower-buds) and "flowers" which represent a flowering almond tree (Exodus 25.33).

Flowering trees in fact play a major role in Lewis's life-writings: he often describes the astonishment afforded by a tree in flower. Fleeting and fragile, present only for a moment in the process of turning buds into fruit, such trees are poignant images of divine lavishness and generosity. And, in his many Paradise gardens, Lewis shows us the fruit that grows from these blossoms, apples and other fruits of rainbow colors, silver and gold, supernatural fulfillments of every prophecy of eternal joy.

4. Blue and Bright

At the height of Lewis's many mountaintop gardens, based upon Dante and Milton—the garden of St. Anne's, the gardens with which Narnia (like the Bible) begins and ends—there is always trembling just out of reach the possibility of everlasting life, the life of transcendence and fulfillment. Here we touch upon the meaning of blue sky and boundless brightness. Lewis writes of a "blue-and-white sky," a "blue fresh sky," a "blue lake," "a blue sky," a "warm blue world," an "English sky" (blue, obviously), "a pale blue sky," and "blue hills."

He also writes of "light [...] rather than shade," "warm light," "bright water," "grass jewel bright,"—of course—snow [...] dazzling," things "shining in the sunrise," a bright, secret, quiet place," "bright turf," and most significantly, perhaps, a lake "bright as a gem." Both "light" and "bright" are found in the Bible. The word "Light" first appears in the creation narrative which opens Genesis (1.3): "and God said, Let there be light; and there was light." This is the very light of God, as Isaiah says, "The LORD shall be to thee an everlasting light." The apostles are told in Matthew 5.4: "Ye are the light of the world," and in John, the most mystical of the Gospels, Jesus says plainly, "I am the light of the world" (8.12), adding that his followers "shall have the light of life." As for the word "bright" in Revelation 22.16, He who says "I am the Alpha and Omega" also says "I am the root and offspring of David, and the bright and morning star." In Matthew 17.5, on the occasion of the transfiguration, God's presence is made known in "a bright cloud," a motif which also occurs in Job 37.11, where the translator of the edition I consulted adds that "the Hebrew is to be literally translated as 'the cloud of his light'." In the context of these elements, the allusion to "bright [...] gem" suggests Malachi 3.17, who, last of the prophets in the Hebrew Bible, causes the Lord of Hosts to declare of those that have feared him, "They shall be mine [...] in that day when I make up my jewels."

Beyond these biblical usages of "light" and "bright," the most numinous and mysterious passages in the Hebrew Bible are those which use the word "sapphire." A sapphire is defined by *The New Shorter Oxford English Dictionary* as "a transparent, blue precious stone." The image of blueness expressed as a sapphire appears most explicitly in Exodus 24.10 when the leaders of Israel "saw the God of Israel; and there was under his feet a paved work of sapphire stone, and as it were the body of heaven in his clearness." This amazing passage can be compared with Ezekiel 1.26—"And above the firmament [...] was the likeness of a throne, as the appearance of a sapphire throne," where sat "the likeness as the appearance of a man." God, the paving upon which God stands, and the throne where God is seated, are all imaged in these visionary passages as "a sapphire stone," that is, by the color blue, the color of the sun-filled sky.

There are no blue dyes, nor are there pigments, that can convey the luminosity of the blue sky in its fullness, let alone of the God who walks on sapphire, looks like sapphire, and is enthroned upon sapphire. In Lewis's many passages where brightness is a figure for the numinous, he resorts more than once to the jewel or gem, to "grass jewel bright," and a lake "bright as a gem." In these breathtaking images of transcendence, Lewis comes as close as anyone can to expressing that which is beyond all images, too bright to be perceived except by the eyes of the mind.

5. A Low Pillared House

A final motif, always associated with grass and greenery when it appears, is accorded only a few examples, which are none-the-less potent. Lewis writes of "a low pillared house," a "beautiful pillared room," "a little low house," a "tiny white temple" and, in many places in *Till We Have Faces*, he describes both the stone-pillared "House of Ungit" (the *bona dea* of Glome) and the pillared rooms one below the other, from Orual's father's little brick palace to the last and lowest pillar in the depths of the earth, where she sees, at last, herself as others see her. In Lewis's writings, pillared places are always sites of vision, places where people see. The Hermit of the Southern March watches a battle in the water of his sacred well inside his walled environs. Such enclosures and simple dwellings are the homes of hermits, magicians, priests, retired stars, and consecrated women. They imply contact with the Earth; even the "blue room" in St. Anne's Manor, which is provided with a pillared entrance and windows that look out upon the clouds, is situated in a house built upon earth that can support a complex series of gardens.

Pillar, house, and temple are closely associated in the Hebrew Bible; Jacob, after setting up a stone at the site of his dream at Bethel, declares, "This stone, which I have set up for a pillar, shall be God's house" (Genesis 28.22). And in the New Testament, John is commanded to write: "Him that overcometh will I make a pillar in the temple of my God" (Revelation 3.2). Clearly, both temple and house signify God's presence, as in Psalm 122: "Let us go unto the house of the LORD, "and Isaiah 2.3, "let us go up to the house of the God of Jacob." In all these passages, just as Lewis's pillared houses and temples imply, and as the proto-martyr Stephen says in Acts 7.48, "the most High dwelleth not in temples made with hands," but rather, in accordance with Revelation 11.19, "the temple of God is opened in heaven."

Lewis's profound symbol—the little pillared chapel or hermitage with its enclosed lawns and walled gardens and lavish trellises of grapevines, suggests that perfect combination of immanence (enclosure) and transcendence (openness to the sky) that Lewis sought all his life. In his early visit to Stonehenge, that pillared place on a green plain; in his visits to the "Ladies at Wantage" (an order of Anglican nuns); in his quiet walks along the green paths and among the quiet cloisters of Oxford; in his preference for simplicity and silence, as opposed to song, in worship; in his withdrawn house with its kilns and bathing pool in the woods; in his lack of travel (he went once only to France, to fight in the trenches of World War I, and once only to Greece, where he wandered the stony, sacred hills with his dying wife); in his preference for small villages, low hills, and small inns: in all these ways he was a man in touch with pillared, arcaded, walled places and green enclosures, small woods, little orchards, green lawns, and blue English skies. The green visions of C.S. Lewis embody for us his dearest and highest values. Through his images of jeweled intensity and vernal freshness, God, God's creatures, God's earth, and God's universe are embodied in ways that are, in all Lewis's writings, most lucent and most numinous.

Notes

[1] Charles A. Brady, *America* (27 October 1956), cited in Walter Hooper, *C.S. Lewis, A Companion and Guide* (London: Harper-Collins, 1996) 451.

[2] Brady cited in Hooper 451.

[3] Aldous Huxley, *The Doors of Perception and Heaven and Hell* (1955; Harmondsworth, UK: Penguin, 1959) 75.

[4] Huxley 77.

[5] Huxley 79.

[6] Huxley 82-83.

[7] Huxley 83.

[8] Huxley 88.

[9] Jeffrey Burton Russell, *A History of Heaven* (Princeton, NJ: Princeton UP, 1996) 13.

[10] Russell 13

[11] Russell 31.

[12] Russell 36-37.

[13] Elizabeth B. Moynihan, *Paradise as a Garden: In Persia and Mughal India* (New York: George Brazillier, 1979) vi.

[14] Moynihan 3.

[15] Moynihan 4.

[16] Moynihan 5.

Notes

[17] C.S. Lewis, *The Allegory of Love* (1936; New York: Oxford UP, 1958) 83.

[18] C.S. Lewis, *The Allegory of Love* 95.

[19] C.S. Lewis, *The Allegory of Love* 92.

[20] C.S. Lewis, *The Allegory of Love* 95.

[21] C.S. Lewis, *The Allegory of Love* 98.

[22] C.S. Lewis, *Spenser's Images of Life* (Cambridge: Cambridge UP, 1967) 79.

[23] C.S. Lewis, *Spenser's Images of Life* 79.

[24] C.S. Lewis, *Studies in Medieval and Renaissance Literature,* collected by Walter Hooper (Cambridge: Cambridge UP, 1966) 82.

[25] C.S. Lewis, *Studies in Medieval and Renaissance Literature* 82.

[26] C.S. Lewis, *Spenser's Images of Life* 87.

[27] C.S. Lewis, *Spenser's Images of Life* 95.

[28] C.S. Lewis, *They Stand Together: The Letters of C.S. Lewis to Arthur Greeves 1914-1963*, ed. Walter Hooper (London: Collins, 1979) 5.

[29] Huxley 99.

[30] Huxley 102.

[31] C.S. Lewis, *They Stand Together* 48.

[32] C.S. Lewis, *They Stand Together* 62.

[33] C.S. Lewis, *They Stand Together* 91.

[34] C.S. Lewis, *They Stand Together* 99.

[35] C.S. Lewis, *They Stand Together* 132.

[36] C.S. Lewis, *They Stand Together* 200.

[37] C.S. Lewis, *They Stand Together* 209.

[38] C.S. Lewis, *They Stand Together* 216.

[39] C.S. Lewis, *They Stand Together* 216.

[40] C.S. Lewis, *Spirits in Bondage: A Cycle of Lyrics* (1919; London: Harcourt Brace Jovanovich, 1984) xlii.

[41] C.S. Lewis, *Spirits in Bondage* 5.

[42] C.S. Lewis, *Spirits in Bondage* 35.

[43] C.S. Lewis, *Spirits in Bondage* 47.

[44] C.S. Lewis, *Spirits in Bondage* 47.

[45] C.S. Lewis, *Spirits in Bondage* 63.

[46] C.S. Lewis, *Spirits in Bondage* 72.

Notes

[47] C.S. Lewis, *Spirits in Bondage* 74.

[48] C.S. Lewis, *They Stand Together* 282.

[49] Walter Hooper, ed., *All My Road Before Me: The Diary of C.S. Lewis, 1922-1927* (London: HarperCollins, 1991) 20.

[50] Hooper, ed., *All My Road Before Me* 37-8.

[51] Hooper, ed., *All My Road Before Me* 118.

[52] Hooper, ed., *All My Road Before Me* 253.

[53] Hooper, ed., *All My Road Before Me* 276-77.

[54] Hooper, ed., *All My Road Before Me* 304.

[55] Hooper, ed., *All My Road Before Me* 317.

[56] C.S. Lewis, *They Stand Together* 349.

[57] C.S. Lewis, *They Stand Together* 401.

[58] See John Harvey, *Medieval Gardens* (Beaverton, OR: Timber Press, 1981).

[59] C.S. Lewis, *Surprised By Joy: The Shape of My Early Life* (1955; New York: Harcourt, Brace, Jovanovich, 1966) 7.

[60] C.S. Lewis, *Surprised By Joy* 7.

[61] C.S. Lewis, *Surprised By Joy* 7.

[62] C.S. Lewis, *Surprised By Joy* 16.

[63] C.S. Lewis, *They Stand Together* 401.

[64] C.S. Lewis, *Surprised By Joy* 132.

[65] C.S. Lewis, *Surprised By Joy* 146.

[66] C.S. Lewis, *Surprised By Joy* 180.

[67] C.S. Lewis, *Surprised By Joy* 238.

[68] C.S. Lewis, *The Great Divorce* (1946; HarperCollins, 1973) 19-20.

[69] C.S. Lewis, *The Great Divorce* 33.

[70] C.S. Lewis, *The Great Divorce* 45.

[71] C.S. Lewis, *The Great Divorce* 46.

[72] C.S. Lewis, *The Great Divorce* 78.

[73] C.S. Lewis, *The Great Divorce* 117.

[74] C.S. Lewis, *The Great Divorce* 21.

[75] C.S. Lewis, *The Great Divorce* 21.

[76] George MacDonald, *At the Back of the North Wind* (1868; Gutenberg ebook #225) ch. 10.

[77] Editor's note: "Kilmeny" is the main character in a ballad by the Scottish writer James Hogg (1770–1835). It is available on-line in *The*

Notes

Oxford Book of English Verse: 1250–1900 edited by Arthur Quiller-Couch. <http://www.bartleby.com/101/514.html>.

[78] J.R.R. Tolkien, *The Monsters and the Critics*, ed. Christopher Tolkien (London: George Allen and Unwin, 1983) 75.

[79] Dorothy L. Sayers, *The Letters of Dorothy L. Sayers*, vol. 2, ed. Barbara Reynolds (Cambridge: The Dorothy L. Sayers Society, 1997) 269.

[80] Huxley 82.

[81] C.S. Lewis, *The Discarded Image: An Introduction to Medieval and Renaissance Literature* (Cambridge: Cambridge UP, 1964) 200.

6. The Green Lewis: Inklings of Environmentalism in the Writing of C.S. Lewis

> Once in those very early days my brother brought into the nursery the lid of a biscuit tin which he had covered with moss and garnished with twigs and flowers so as to make it a toy garden or a toy forest. That was the first beauty I ever knew.

——C.S. Lewis, *Surprised by Joy*

In "The Green Lewis" Patterson reviews the influences on Lewis's representation of nature, including William Morris, the pleasure he took in picturesque environments, his distaste for cities, and his Christianity. She then contextualizes Lewis's literary treatment of nature, particularly in the Chronicles of Narnia and the Space Trilogy, and his other statements on the subject relative to Rev. Ian Bradley's God is Green *(1992), Rosemary Radford Ruether's* Gaia and God *(1992), and Anne Primavesi's* From Apocalypse to Genesis *(1991).*

Patterson analyzes Lewis's treatment of both the color green and landscape in "The 'Jasper-Lucent' Landscapes of C.S. Lewis" and the symbolic uses of green in "'Halfe Like a Serpent': The Green Witch in The Silver Chair.*" Both papers are included in this volume.*

"The Green Lewis: Inklings of Environmentalism in the Writing of C.S. Lewis" was first published in the Lamp-Post of the Southern California C. S. Lewis Society *18.1 (Mar. 1994): 4-14.*

As a nature mystic from early childhood, C.S. Lewis developed within a deep tradition of Western spirituality, one that had given rise in the Romantic movement to what he described as the "old indeterminate, half-Christian, half-Pantheistic, piety of the last century."[1] This mixed piety he pronounced to be "gone," but certain late twentieth-century theologians, under the pressure of environmental concerns, have proposed revised versions of Christianity that Lewis would have recognized as belonging in the same category. He addressed this subject while discussing William Morris, a writer who exemplifies the profound environmental concerns of the nineteenth century.

Morris expressed his ideas in terms of a dichotomy between the countryside with its forests, fields, villages, and towns, and the city, with its suburbs and industrial districts. He wrote of "London and our other great commercial cities" as "mere masses of sordidness, filth, and squalor,"[2] and of "wretched suburbs" which "spread all round our fairest and most ancient cities."[3] He reported that "a man was killed by being compelled to work in a place where white-lead was flying about, and that no precautions were taken to prevent his dying speedily,"[4] and urged efforts to "keep the air pure and the rivers clean."[5] And, in contrast, he wrote: "suppose people lived in little communities among gardens and green fields."[6]

Lewis expressed similar concerns throughout his life: he wrote of Belfast in his diary in 1922: "we walked in the black and lifeless park which lies between the slums and the shipyards, separated from the latter by an impure channel in which they are at work building an island of garbage,"[7] and in *The Four Loves* (1960) of one who "will be sorry when he hears that the garden past which his walk led him that day has now been swallowed up by cinemas, garages, and the new by-pass."[8] The same themes appear in his fiction: he says of the idealized village of Edgestow in *That Hideous Strength* (1945) "No maker of cars or sausages or marmalades has yet come to industrialise the country town" (THS 15; ch. 1). And in his poem "The Future of Forestry" (1938) he writes:

> How will the legend of the age of trees
> Feel, when the last tree falls in England?
> When the concrete spreads and the town conquers
> The country's heart; when contraceptive
> Tarmac's laid where farm has faded,
> Tramline flows where slept a hamlet,
> And shop-fronts, blazing without a stop from
> Dover to Wrath, have glazed us over?[9]

Unlike Morris, Lewis took no political stands in expressing these concerns for the violation of the natural world (including the living conditions of humans) by industrialization, but he was well aware of them. Indeed, he accurately (if ironically) predicted the dangers of the post-industrial era as well: when Mark Studdock, undergoing his infernal education, comes to the heart of the N.I.C.E.'s true program, he learns that "every advance in industry and agriculture reduces the number of work-people who are required. A large, unintelligent population is now becoming a deadweight" (THS 255; ch. 12).

Lewis used the dichotomy of polluted cities and unspoiled countryside to symbolize Hell and Heaven: in *The Great Divorce* (1946) he begins his journey in Hell by "standing in a bus queue by the side of a long, mean street."[10] Presently he finds himself walking:

> However far I went I found only dingy boarding houses, small tobacconists, hoardings from which posters hung in rags, windowless warehouses, goods stations without trains, and bookshops of the sort that sell *The Works of Aristotle*.[11]

When he finally does catch a bus, it takes him to Heaven; here, "There was water everywhere and tiny flowers quivering in the early breeze. Far off in the woods we saw the deer glancing past, and, once, a sleek panther came purring to my companion's side."[12]

Evidently, it is the spiritual dimension of these contrasts and the dilemmas they pose that are central to C.S. Lewis's environmental thought. To approach these I shall outline three recent attempts by environmentally concerned theologians to create an "Ecology for Christians," and then see how Lewis's writings agree and disagree with such efforts. The briefest of these is *God is Green* (1992), written by the Rev. Ian Bradley, a member of the British Green Party. It has the advantage, in the field of Lewis studies, at least, of being essentially orthodox. God, the author tells us, has "concern for all creation,"[13] and it is God who has set into motion "the dance of creation,"[14] a motif that will remind all Lewis readers of the "Great Dance" which forms the climax of *Perelandra*. Further, and still in agreement with Lewis, the author speaks of "the fall of nature,"[15] a broader vision than the fall of humankind alone. He then introduces a concept which, as will be seen below, is perfectly orthodox and part of Lewis's expression of Christian theology: "the Cosmic Christ,"[16] the Christ "through whom all things were made." Finally, he addresses "the role of human beings,"[17] a role he expresses succinctly by saying:

> It is certainly not just standing back and letting wild nature rule. We may have gone far too far in the West in objectifying

and taming nature but the whole Christian tradition is clear that man is not there simply to worship wild nature. We stand together with nature as fellow-sufferers in this world of pain and sorrow and we also stand together with God as co-operators in his plan to perfect and complete creation.[18]

With this, Lewis does not precisely agree. For him, the end of humankind lies beyond the fate of the earth, whatever responsibilities we undoubtedly share in its conservation in the meantime.

In a little-quoted essay, "On Living in an Atomic Age," first published in 1948—three years after the bombings of Hiroshima and Nagasaki—he pointed out that we "were already sentenced to death before the atomic bomb was invented."[19] As he explains, "The astronomers hold out no hope that this planet is going to be permanently inhabitable. The physicists hold out no hope that organic life is going to be a permanent possibility in any part of the material universe. Not only this earth, but the whole show, all the suns of space, are to run down."[20] Lewis feared, more than the careless or deliberate harming of Earth, the excesses of those determined to preserve it (and us): "We must resolutely train ourselves to feel that the survival of [humanity] on this Earth, much more of our own nation or culture or class, is not worth having unless it can be had by honourable and merciful means."[21]

Readers who find Lewis's fear of social manipulation to what seem to be good ends excessive, may object: did Lewis, they may ask, not recognize the problems we face? I think he did; in a related essay, published in the aptly titled collection, *The World's Last Night,* he associates the putative behaviors of planetary explorers with the actual behavior of humans on earth: humanity "destroys every species [it] can. Civilized man [sic] murders, enslaves, cheats, and corrupts savage man [sic]. Even inanimate nature" humankind "turns into dust bowls and slag-heaps."[22] Lewis equates the explorer and the pioneer with the "needy and greedy adventurer or the ruthless technical expert. What they will be if they meet things weaker than themselves, the black man and the red man can tell."[23] The "things" such explorers would meet are animate forms in outer space.

Our ecological efforts might also be carried out in the same spirit, or so Lewis seems to suggest. He recognized the dangers of single-issue concerns, having portrayed his animal rights advocate, Aunt Lily, thus:

> On the subject of pit ponies I mentioned the days when young children had crawled about pulling trolleys in the mines. She said she much preferred that: she had no sympathy with the children because they all grew up, and would grow up to be brutes themselves. She said it did not affect her as cruelty to animals did: humans were less helpless and also they were so vile that they deserved no sympathy.[24]

In all his writings Lewis counseled the taking of a long view, the one from eternity, that places him in sharp contrast with the apparent meaning of the idea that humans are to co-operate with God in bringing about a perfect and complete creation; if, that is, this means a perfection reached in the context of our present dispensation—"this world," as we say. If it means a new world, in the sense of the Dominical phrase from Revelation, "Behold, I make all things new," that is another matter.

A second, far more elaborately argued attempt at a Green theology, is Rosemary Radford Ruether's *Gaia and God* (1992), which, as above, shows strong parallels with orthodoxy, and hence with Lewis, for most of its argument, and then parts company with orthodoxy in its culmination. She begins by allowing that Christianity may not be fundamentally at war with the environment: "Although the cosmological tradition in Christianity needs reinterpretation to be adequate for ecological spirituality, nevertheless it has not been absent."[25] Hence, "cosmological understanding of Christ as both creator and redeemer of the cosmos [...] is central to much of New Testament thought," even though "Western Christianity since the late medieval and Reformation periods has ignored this holistic vision."[26]

Pursuing her argument, Ruether says that cosmological Christology has its roots in Hellenistic thought, but must be distinguished from "Gnostic anti-cosmic dualism."[27] By this she means the gnostic concept of a sharply antagonistic division between spirit and matter. In Hellenism, the cosmos is the creation of and the embodiment of the Logos, the Word of God, as, for instance, in the first chapter of John; in Jewish Wisdom literature, portions of which appear in the *Tanakh* (the Old Testament) and in the Apocrypha (used in the lectionaries of most liturgical churches), this immanent manifestation of the divine is identified with Wisdom, and hence with the feminine principle.[28] Ruether uses the Christological hymn in Colossians 1.15-20 as an example of the Christian incorporation and expression of "cosmological Christology":

> He is the image of the invisible God, the firstborn of all creation; for in him all things in heaven and on earth were created, things visible and invisible, whether thrones or dominions or rulers or powers—all things were created through him and for him. He himself is before all things, and in him all things hold together. He is the head of the body, the church; he is the beginning, the firstborn from the dead, so that he might come to have first place in everything. For in him all the fullness of God was pleased to dwell, and through him God was pleased to reconcile to himself all things, whether on earth or in heaven, by making peace through the blood of his cross. (NRSV)

This beautiful liturgical formulation, with which Lewis was in all his writings perfectly in accord, is now understood to be a "Christ-hymn," one of seven appearing in the New Testament, used by Paul and others as a quotation from liturgical usage, rather than as an original formulation by the writer. As such it played the role that quotes from well-known hymns and other poems do in sermons of our time. Its subject is always the same: "The content of the Christ-hymn is the Good News as it was preached to the peoples of first-century Asia Minor."[29] These hymns "celebrate a single story, the story of Christ's pre-existence; incarnation, humiliation, suffering, and death; and then his resurrection, ascension, and subjection of the Powers."[30] The Powers so-mentioned are "political, economic, religious, educational, and so forth."[31]

This pre-existing Christ figure appears in *The Magician's Nephew,* as Aslan brings Narnia to life by "singing his new song."[32] Grass springs up and spreads over the previously empty "earth, rock and water," followed by trees and flowers. Soon the earth brings forth animals too: moles, dogs, stags, frogs, panthers, leopards, birds, butterflies, bees, and an elephant. From them, Aslan selects particular pairs. Then, speaking in "the deepest, wildest voice they had ever heard," he commands representatives of the whole continuum of creation, chemical, vegetable, and animal, to become conscious: "Narnia, Narnia, Narnia, awake. Love. Think. Speak. Be walking trees. Be talking beasts. Be divine waters" (MN 126; ch. 9).

In the Colossians Christ-hymn, Ruether says, "Christ is seen as the power of the new creation, not severed from the cosmos created in the beginning, but the principle through which this cosmos was originally created and now is renewed and reconciled with God."[33] In this cosmology, as Ruether puts it, "The regions of earth [...] and the planetary spheres" are "ruled by angelic governors" of whom certain "angelic spirits [...] revolted against God, creating an alienated universe."[34] This cosmological conception appears in Lewis's Space Trilogy: Ransom learns in *Perelandra* that every planet has its planetary Intelligence or Oyarsa, an eldil (angel) of special authority, but Earth is "cut off from communication with the other planets," for our planet is "in a state of siege [...] in fact, an enemy-occupied territory, held down by *eldila* [...] at war both with us and with the *eldila* of 'Deep Heaven', or 'Space'" (PER 12; ch. 1).

Irenaeus (130–202 CE), Ruether tells us, taught that "In the incarnation divine power permeates bodily nature [...] so that the bodily becomes the sacramental bearer of the divine, and the divine deifies the bodily."[35] Of this, "The Christian sacraments are paradigmatic," Ruether says.[36] For Irenaeus, at the millenium "the whole creation shall [...] come and rejoice in Mount Zion,"[37] and all creation, not merely humankind, will be involved. The question is whether this event will occur in the context of the present dispensation, or has already occurred, or will, following various foretastes such as those offered to contemplatives and to any of us who partake of the sacraments, occur in a new dispensation. Ruether discusses several twentieth century efforts to retain or recover the vision of Ireneaus, citing Matthew Fox, Teilhard de Chardin, and Alfred North Whitehead,[38] and offers penetrating critiques of all three.

Fox, she says, fails by denying that the "deep questions of sin and death [...] are real questions."[39] For Teilhard, "all of nature is part of this salvation drama," but Ruether sees "disturbing elements" in the notion of "Eurocentric progress,[40] as well she might. She prefers his insight that "mind is the interiority of matter, and it is continuous from the simplest molecule to the most complex organism."[41] Finally, she discusses process theology, as suggested by Whitehead, holding that the cosmos interrelates with God and possesses the freedom to choose evil along with good.

In developing this idea, she maintains that "At the subatomic level, the classical distinction between matter and energy disappears. Matter is energy moving in defined patterns of rationality."[42] At this fundamental level, energy and order coincide. Having said all this, Ruether like many other Western commentators maintains that "humans alone, amid all the earth creatures and on all the planets of these vast galaxies, are capable of reflective consciousness. We are, in that sense, the 'mind' of the universe, the place where the universe becomes conscious of itself."[43] This might be seen as a reversal of her previous argument, and indeed, she goes on to reverse her position yet again: in this "web of life," she says, "consciousness is and must be where we recognize our kinship with all other beings [...] along a continuum of organized life energy."[44]

Lewis depicts a "web of life" in *Perelandra;* the interweaving of the culminating vision beheld by Ransom incorporates a catholic array of being: "peoples, institutions, climates of opinion, civilisations, arts, sciences [...] flowers and insects, a fruit or a storm of rain [...] a wave of the sea [...] crystals, rivers, mountains, or even stars" (PER 187; ch. 17). All these Ransom sees woven into the Great Dance of creation, and he sees these patterns form and reform, almost suggesting what Ruether, contemplating a similar vision, calls the "transience of selves."[45] But not quite. Ruether calls upon her readers to embrace what for her is the absence of immortality, and, with Eastern religions (as she interprets them) we are to "relinquish our small self back into the great Self."[46]

This, Lewis does not teach. In his essay, "The World's Last Night," he says, "I am convinced that those who find in Christ's apocalyptic the whole of his message are mistaken."[47] For him, "the modern conception of Progress or Evolution (as popularly imagined), is simply myth, supported by no evidence whatever, even though he accepts that "Darwinian biology is correct."[48] Indeed, "the idea of the world slowly ripening to perfection, is a myth, not a generalization from experience."[49] In this context, "the whole life of humanity in this world is also precarious, temporary, provisional."[50] He knows as well as Ruether that the end of human life is death. But all his Christian writings, that is, the works that post-date his conversion (circa 1929), declare that the goal of human life lies beyond the margins of this dispensation entirely. These words in his most famous sermon make this eminently clear: "Nature is mortal; we shall outlive her. When all the suns and nebulae have passed away, each one of you will still be alive."[51] And again, he says, "Nations, cultures, arts, civilisations—these are mortal, and their life is to ours as the life of a gnat."[52]

Perhaps I have misunderstood Ruether—perhaps she is only recommending, as Lewis does, the glad relinquishment of our lives as is practiced by the *hrossa* of Malacandra in *Out of the Silent Planet,* where this Martian species greets death and physical dissolution with equanimity. But I don't think so. Her plain words suggest that unless we are prepared to regard this world as all there is, we shall not cherish it as we should.

My third theologian is Anne Primavesi. In her study, *From Apocalypse to Genesis* (1991) she too attempts first to winnow and then to revise orthodox Christianity. She reminds us that Julian of Norwich "came to understand Creation as the self-giving love of God," and expressed an "appreciation that all created things are good in themselves."[53] Nothing, let alone another person, is a "thing" in a pejorative sense.[54] Moreover, all things enjoy equality; hence, for Primavesi, hierarchy must be rejected. Certainly this part of her argument will be regarded by many commentators as very much contrary to what Lewis believed. He expressed his apparently hierarchical vision in *That Hideous Strength,* where at the climax of the novel, all forms of being from planetary Intelligences, through human couples and animal couples, rejoice in the paradisal gardens of St. Anne's Manor. Ransom declares that humans are "no longer isolated. We are now as we ought to be—between the angels who are our elder brothers and the beasts who are our jesters, servants, and playfellows" (THS 376; ch. 17).

Here the words "elder" on the one hand, and "servants" on the other, may indeed seem to imply hierarchy, though an alternative reading might suggest that the angels are "elder" because they were created first, according to the mythological structure Lewis has borrowed, while the animals, also created before humankind according to scientific theory, might play, as servants, a role whereby humankind, made in the image of Christ, could choose to become the servants of these servants in a dance of reversal and reciprocity. John Laurent, in his study, "C.S. Lewis and Animal Rights" (1993), treats in admirable detail the interest Lewis showed in "evolutionary theory"[55] and in the consequent kinship between humans and other animals; an element requiring the application of the Golden Rule between the human species and all others.[56]

In the Space Trilogy, Lewis used, as we have already seen, many elements of the medieval synthesis, combining the concepts of that model of the universe with the model used in our present century. In the earlier model, "man is a rational animal," akin to angels and animals alike, in a "cross-section of being,"[57] possessed of a range of souls, in a psyche as complex as the one portrayed by Jung, and a body controlled by its "Humours," whether sanguine, choleric, melancholy, or phlegmatic. Humanity in this model "had a built-in significance," and was a structure of "admirable design," which manifested "the wisdom and goodness that created it."[58] Such a vision of humankind is precisely the one perceived by Lady Julian, as Primavesi says: "whoever lives mythically, she or he is expressing life as meaningful."[59]

"Christian ecological thought," Primavesi insists, must keep "intact the mystery of Jesus's humanity as well as his divinity," and the human Jesus behaved non-hierarchically, consorting with the outcasts of his society including women. Going still further, he is, she says, also "the saviour of the world," of *all* creation, as well as of humankind."[60] In his teachings he argues from "the beginning of creation," as in Mark 10.6, "But from the beginning of creation, 'God made them male and female'" (NRSV), and from "the processes of Nature," as in his many parables. This specifically nonexclusive viewpoint can be seen in Lewis: as he says in *Miracles* (1947), nature, like humankind, while "doomed [...] to run down and die," nevertheless, "like ourselves, is to be redeemed."[61] He depicts this eventuality in *The Last Battle,* using the imagery of unspoiled nature combined with an image of Paradise borrowed from Milton, as his characters leave the dying Narnia and pass through

> winding valley after winding valley and up the steep sides of hills [...], following the river [...] till at last at the end of one long lake which looked as blue as a turquoise, they saw a smooth green hill [...] round the very top of it ran a green

wall: but above the wall rose the branches of trees whose leaves looked like silver and their fruit like gold. (LB 201-202; ch. 16)

Presently, Lucy sees that what she has taken for a garden is "a whole world, with its own rivers and woods and sea and mountains" (LB 207; ch. 16). It is the renewed Narnia, which in its turn proves to be but one precinct of Aslan's Country.

Primavesi's study now turns from the Apocalypse of her title to the Genesis story, which she says we have been taught to see as a story of how "the interconnectedness established by God is shattered by woman, man, and Nature."[62] She points out that neither version of the creation story in Genesis contains the words "apple," "fall," or sin."[63] She proposes a new reading of these materials in which Adam lives happily with the world and with Eve, and in which Eve obtains wisdom from the serpent and shares it with Adam. Sin, in this reading, enters the story in the conflict between Cain and Abel over the validity and sacrality of animal versus vegetable products depicted in Genesis 4.2-5:

Now Abel was a keeper of sheep, and Cain a tiller of the ground. In the course of time Cain brought to the Lord an offering of the fruit of the ground, and Abel for his part brought the firstlings of his flock, their fat portions. And the Lord had regard for Abel and his offering, but for Cain and his offering he had no regard. (NRSV)

The commentator on this translation says that "The story reflects the tensions between farmers and semi-nomads, two different ways of life that are symbolized in the two types of offerings."[64]

Primavesi proposes that the Genesis stories are, in fact, about food, and that Jesus reversed the notion that one form of food is to be preferred over another, by eating everything, and eating it with everybody. Thus, she says, "Eve's decision to eat a particular food and share it with Adam, against religious prohibition, was the same kind of ethical choice made by Jesus." Primavesi in this interpretation equates Eve with Jesus. "In both cultures food was a symbol of life: of life shared and sustained at every level, including our relationship with God."[65] From this she concludes that "The basic criterion of Christian morality is to be found in what the heart bids a person to do in the face of the needs of our fellow human beings."[66] This accords with Genesis 4.7, which gives the Lord's definition of sin, using that word—"sin"—for the first time: "If you do well, will you not be accepted? And if you do not do well, sin is lurking at the door; its desire is for you, but you must master it" (NRSV). Cain promptly proceeds to murder Abel, and that murder, surely, represents the fallen condition of the world in the starkest of terms. A stringent application of this relationship between the use of food and morality is Primavesi's proposal that we should treat *all* crumbs of food (or material of any sort) the way we treat crumbs of Eucharistic bread, and that we should understand all creation as the incarnate body of God.[67]

At this point, Primavesi parts company most profoundly with orthodox Christian doctrine. She proposes that the Genesis story shows God as a "bad parent," who forbids as bad something that is actually good, and that the New Testament must be read to show that Jesus died for his own sins as well as for those of others. Certainly, a major difficulty for orthodox Christians—who believe that God as expressed in all three persons of the Trinity, is perfectly and absolutely good—is the conflict between a good God and an imperfect world. Evidently Primavesi hopes to solve the problem by declaring that God is not perfectly good and nor is Jesus. Lewis deals with this question differently. In *The Problem of Pain* he addresses the doctrine of the Fall: humankind "is now a horror to God" and to itself, "and a creature ill-adapted to the universe not because God made him so but because he has made himself so by the abuse of his free will." As he explains, "God is good," and "the free will of rational creatures, by its very nature included the possibility of evil; and [...] creatures, availing themselves of this possibility, have become evil."[68] Lewis observes that the church Fathers "Wisely, or foolishly [...] believed that we were *really*—and not simply by legal fiction—involved in Adam's action," and that we cannot "dismiss their way of talking as a mere 'idiom'."[69] Strikingly, he—like Primavesi, if not in so extensive a way—is willing to countenance alternative interpretations of Genesis. "I have the deepest respect for Pagan myths, still more for myths in Holy Scripture. I therefore do not doubt that the version which emphasizes the magic apple and brings together the tree of life and the tree of knowledge contains a deeper and subtler truth than the version which makes the apple simply and solely a pledge of obedience."[70]

He tries his hand at a retelling of his own, in which God chooses an animal to be "the vehicle of humanity and the image of Himself," and gives it "a new kind of consciousness,"[71] whereupon the creature denies its creaturely condition, falling into the "danger of self-idolatry," the very fate barely avoided by the Green Lady in *Perelandra,* where Lewis explored these ideas in great detail. Also in accord with that work is his conclusion that "The world is a dance in which good, descending from God, is disturbed by evil arising from the creatures, and the resulting conflict is resolved by God's own assumption of the suffering nature which evil produces."[72] He had meditated often in his life upon the role and meaning of nature and of the relationship between nature and humankind. In 1948 he wrote that "Mistaken for our mother, [nature] is terrifying and even abominable. But if she is only our sister—if she and we have a common Creator— if she is our sparring partner, then the situation is quite tolerable."[73] Again, in 1961, he wrote to his friend Dom Bede Griffiths, "Romantic Pantheism [...] has taught us to regard Nature as divine. But she is a creature, and surely a creature lower than ourselves. And a fallen creature—not an evil creature but a good creature corrupted, retaining many beauties but all tainted."[74]

Whichever way the theological speculations of Lewis and other writers go, we humans find ourselves firmly ensconced in nature, and must share her fate, at least in this life, and if Lewis is right, in the next as well. We ought, surely, to show her the same regard we are bidden to show each other, and get on with the task of loving our neighbors and our planet alike, as ourselves. We already have our marching orders; we need not, and perhaps cannot (and Lewis might say that we should not and must not) wait until the Creeds have been rewritten before we begin.

Notes

[1] C.S. Lewis, "William Morris" (1939), *Selected Literary Essays* (Cambridge: Cambridge UP, 1969) 229.

[2] William Morris, "Lectures on Socialism: Art Under Plutocracy," *Selections from the Prose works of William Morris* (Cambridge: Cambridge UP, 1931) 109.

[3] Morris, "Lectures on Socialism" 110.

Notes

[4] William Morris, "Capitalist Morality," *News From Nowhere and Selected Writings and Designs* (Harmondsworth, UK: Penguin, 1962) 156.

[5] Morris, "Lectures on Socialism" 109.

[6] Morris, "Capitalist Morality" 79.

[7] C.S. Lewis, *All My Road Before Me: The Diary of C.S. Lewis, 1922–1927*, ed. Walter Hooper (London: HarperCollins, 1991) 157.

[8] C.S. Lewis, *The Four Loves* (1960; New York: Harcourt Brace, 1988) 14.

[9] C.S. Lewis, *Poems* (London: Geoffrey Bles, 1964) 61.

[10] C.S. Lewis, *The Great Divorce* (1946; London: Harper Collins, 2001) 1.

[11] C.S. Lewis, *The Great Divorce* 1.

[12] C.S. Lewis, *The Great Divorce* 78.

[13] Rev. Ian Bradley, *God is Green: Ecology for Christians* (Toronto, ON: Image/Doubleday, 1992) 12.

[14] Bradley, *God is Green* passim.

[15] Bradley, *God is Green* 52.

[16] Bradley, *God is Green* passim.

[17] Bradley, *God is Green* 90.

[18] Bradley, *God is Green* 91.

[19] C.S. Lewis, "On Living in An Atomic Age," *Present Concerns* (London: Collins, Fount, 1986) 73.

[20] C.S. Lewis, "On Living in An Atomic Age" 74.

[21] C.S. Lewis, "On Living in An Atomic Age" 79.

[22] C.S. Lewis, "Religion and Rocketry," *The World's Last Night and Other Essays* (New York: Harcourt, 1960) 89.

[23] C.S. Lewis, "Religion and Rocketry" 89.

[24] C.S. Lewis, *All My Road Before Me* 224-25.

[25] Rosemary Radford Ruether, *Gaia and God: An Ecofeminist Theology of Earth Healing* (San Francisco, CA: HarperCollins, 1992) 229.

[26] Ruether 229.

[27] Ruether 230.

[28] Ruether 231.

[29] Charles M. Mountain, "The New Testament Christ-Hymn," *The Hymn* 4.1 (Jan. 1993): 23.

Notes

[30] Mountain 23.

[31] Mountain 23.

[32] Mountain 25, note 17.

[33] Ruether 233.

[34] Ruether 233.

[35] Ruether 235.

[36] Ruether 235.

[37] Ruether 236. Quotation from Irenaeus, taken from *Asversus Haereses*, V.2.2, trans. from *Gnosticism: A Source Book of Heretical Writings from the Early Christian Period*, ed. by Robert M. Grant (New York: Harper and Brothers, 1961).

[38] Ruether 240.

[39] Ruether 242.

[40] Ruether 245.

[41] Ruether 245.

[42] Ruether 248.

[43] Ruether 249.

[44] Ruether 250.

[45] Ruether 252.

[46] Ruether 253.

[47] C.S. Lewis, "The World's Last Night" 94-95.

[48] C.S. Lewis, "The World's Last Night" 101.

[49] C.S. Lewis, "The World's Last Night" 104.

[50] C.S. Lewis, "The World's Last Night" 110.

[51] C.S. Lewis, "Weight of Glory," *They Asked for a Paper* (London: Geoffrey Bles, 1962) 209.

[52] C.S. Lewis, "Weight of Glory" 210.

[53] Anne Primavesi, *From Apocalypse to Genesis: Ecology, Feminism and Christianity* (Minneapolis, MN: Fortress, 1991) 83.

[54] Primavesi 83.

[55] John Laurent, "C.S. Lewis and Animal Rights," *Mythlore* 19.1 (Winter 1993): 46.

[56] Laurent 50.

[57] C.S. Lewis, *The Discarded Image: An Introduction to Medieval and Renaissance Literature* (Cambridge: Cambridge UP, 1964) 152-53.

[58] C.S. Lewis, *Discarded Image* 204.

Notes

[59] Primavesi 87.

[60] Primavesi 128.

[61] C.S. Lewis, *Miracles: A Preliminary Study* (1947; London: HarperCollins, 2001) 105.

[62] Primavesi 209.

[63] Primavesi 222.

[64] *The New Oxford Annotated Bible,* eds. Bruce M. Metzger and Roland E. Murphy (New York: Oxford UP, 1991) note to Genesis 4.1–6.

[65] Primavesi 258.

[66] Primavesi 305 note 12.

[67] Primavesi 186, 258.

[68] C.S. Lewis, *The Problem of Pain* (London: Geoffrey Bles, 1940) 57.

[69] C.S. Lewis, *The Problem of Pain* 58.

[70] C.S. Lewis, *The Problem of Pain* 59-60.

[71] C.S. Lewis, *The Problem of Pain* 65.

[72] C.S. Lewis, *The Problem of Pain* 72.

[73] C.S. Lewis, "On Living in An Atomic Age" 79.

[74] *The Letters of C.S. Lewis,* ed. W.H. Lewis (London: Geoffrey Bles, 1966) 301.

7. Lord of the Beasts: Animal Archetypes in C.S. Lewis

Here [in one of the attics] my first stories were written, and illustrated, with enormous satisfaction. They were an attempt to combine my two chief literary pleasures—"dressed animals" and "knights in armor." As a result, I wrote about chivalrous mice and rabbits who rode out in complete mail to kill not giants but cats. [...] The Animal-Land which came into action in the holidays when my brother was at home was a modern Animal-Land; it had to have trains and steamships if it was to be a country shared with him.

——C.S. Lewis, *Surprised by Joy*

In "Lord of the Beasts" Patterson explores the nature of Lewis's "Talking Beasts." She chooses, among others, C.G. Jung, Mircea Eliade, Gertrude Levy, and Carlos Casteneda as interlocutors who best represent the historical anthropomorphization of animals, and to elucidate Lewis's fictional creatures as they are presented in That Hideous Strength *and the Chronicles of Narnia. Patterson also discusses animals in Lewis's fiction in "'Banquet at Belbury': The Company of the Damned," included in* Ransoming the Waste Land Volume I.

"Lord of the Beasts: Animal Archetypes in C.S. Lewis" was first published in the Papers of the Narnia Conference, Palms Park, West Los Angeles, 1969, *edited by Glen GoodKnight (Los Angeles, The Mythopoeic Society: 1970): 24-32.*

The creation and the Passion of Aslan, his Narnian history, and the last judgment, all take place in a world parallel to earth populated by Talking Beasts. The incarnation of the Narnian deity as a lion—"this dazzling golden heraldic Beast on fire with Divine Love,"[1] as Stella Gibbons (1965) describes him, is explained by Mr. Beaver to Lucy in *The Lion, the Witch and the Wardrobe*:

"Is—is he a man?" asked Lucy.
"Aslan a man!" said Mr. Beaver sternly. "Certainly not. I tell you he is the King of the wood and the son of the great Emperor-Beyond-the-Sea. Don't you know who is the King of

Beasts? Aslan is a lion—*the* Lion, the Great Lion." (LWW
141; ch. 8)

Certainly Lewis is here calling upon both traditional Christian symbolism—which uses the medieval notion that a baby lion is born dead
but comes to life after three days when its father breathes upon it, to
associate his lion with resurrection, to make him a symbol of "Christ,
the Lord of Life,"[2] and, even more universally, of the sun—"solar
light, morning, regal dignity, and victory."[3] Andreas Lommel (1966)
muses upon Mesopotamian usages of the solar lion, finding an "allegorical sameness [...] between the majestic and terrible sight of a
lion's glance in real life [...] and the equally terrible sun, whose
mighty morning rays obliterated the stars of the night."[4] These themes
are suggested in the description of the resurrected Aslan in *The Lion,
the Witch and the Wardrobe*:

> There, shining in the sunrise, larger than they had seen
> him before, shaking his mane [...] stood Aslan himself.
> "Oh, Aslan!" cried both the children, staring up at him,
> almost as much frightened as they were glad.
> "Aren't you dead then, dear Aslan?" said Lucy. "Not
> now," said Aslan." (LWW 162; ch. 15)

There is something here that distinguishes these books from any comparable tale of talking animals in the modern canon of children's literature. What is it?

C.G. Jung discusses the traditional role of such animals in his
chapter, "Theriomorphic Spirit Symbolism in Fairy Tales." He calls
them "helpful animals," which "act like humans, speak a human language, and display a sagacity and a knowledge superior to man's. In
these circumstances we can say with some justification that the archetype of the spirit is being expressed through an animal form."[5] Mircea
Eliade refers to the same usage in *The Sacred and the Profane* (1957),
when he remarks "groups of cosmic hierophanies reveal a particular
structure of the sacrality of nature; or, more precisely, a modality of
the sacred expressed through a specific mode of existence in the cosmos."[6] He concludes by quoting Léon Bloy: "Whether life is in men,
in animals, or in plants, it is always Life, and when [...] death comes,
it is always Jesus who departs."[7]

The most complete analysis of this concept may be found in Gertrude Levy's *The Gate of Horn* (1948), which shows how Stone Age religious concepts developed into the framework of ancient and classical religion. She begins with Paleolithic art, with "the beasts whose portrayal at its best has rarely been equalled in any subsequent culture."[8] She attempts to prove that "a participation in the splendour of the beasts [...] was of the nature of religion itself."[9] According to her theory, this close identification was expressed both through art and through the dance, in which men danced wearing animal skins, leaping and perhaps even coupling in imitation of and communion with the "splendour of the beasts." As these concepts developed, animals became associated with the sun, moon, and stellar deities of Neolithic times. Ultimately the splendid beasts of Paleolithic hunting culture became the sacrificial beasts whose symbolism is so familiar to us from the Bible. The men dressed as animals became the animal attendants, who "always appear as servants of the Goddess, bearing offerings in procession, or bringing home her slain and captive beasts, in rare instances even replacing her between the heraldically opposed creatures, and rightly, since they represent a fusion of divinity and worshipper." She continues, "their lineage goes back through many millennia to the masked ceremonies of the Paleolithic caves, and forward to the [...] satyrs and half-human ministrants of the mystery Gods of Greece, and through them to the Drama."[10] These are the "pantomime animals" Lewis mentions in his introduction to *That Hideous Strength*.[11]

Writing of this process in China, Erwin Rousselle (1968) comments: "the gods in their animal forms presided as godparents over the cradle of a kindred mankind."[12] In this period, he continues, "when the gods were still animals and the animals were still men and gods, a wonderful sense of the prodigious permeated human civilization."[13] Later, however, "when the animal was dethroned [...] and the animals were reduced to companions, messengers, attributes of the gods, the prodigious [...] was repressed [...] But, in the secret dreams and visions of our nights, the holy animals still appear to us."[14] These holy animals, called out and unfallen, visited by a God incarnate in their own beast-flesh, are the inhabitants of Narnia.

By contrast, the animal spirits of the New World did not suffer the process of diminishment so poignantly described by Levy and

Rousselle. According to Ruth Underhill (1965), here "they had always had a dual form, human and animal. When mankind arrived and the animals retired to the forests and waters, they kept the ability to put on a human guise when they chose."[15] The concept of the animal–man–spirit was always a continuum for the North American mind. Thus intercourse between these orders continued to be expected and "favored people might visit [the villages of the animals] and be taught some of the wisdom and the magic powers that the man-animals retained."[16] The distinction between "real" events and psychic events was not, and to a degree still is not, made by North American Indians as it is so universally and confidently made in the "Western" culture which is attempting to overwhelm them.

For C.S. Lewis, this distinction was clear but capable of being overcome. He called himself an "Old Western Man" in his first address at Cambridge University, and his own thought was derived from that earlier period in Western culture when those realities drawn from the unconscious mind were accorded equal dignity with the conclusions of consciousness. His genius as a mythmaker perhaps derives from his self-affirmed status as one of the last survivors of this period. He was, of course, perfectly aware of modern psychology. "For Jung," he wrote in an essay on children's books, "fairy tale liberates the archetypes which dwell in the collective unconscious, and when we read a good fairy tale we are obeying the old precept, 'know thyself.'"[17] In his own earliest childhood, Lewis tells us, he wrote and illustrated "with enormous satisfaction" his own stories about "dressed animals [...] and chivalrous mice and rabbits who rode out in complete mail to kill not giants but cats."[18] One can see here the origin of Reepicheep, who is one of the Narnian Beasts most likely to enrage Lewis's detractors.[19] He tells of his discovery of Tenniel's "dressed animals," and finally of "the Beatrix Potter books, and here at last beauty."[20] He is at pains to distinguish between the Animal-Land of his childhood, and Narnia, which had nothing in common "except the anthropomorphic beasts."[21] The former "excluded the least hint of wonder,"[22] while Narnia is imbued with that "wonderful sense of the prodigious" all but lost to the modern mind.

Lewis has mused deeply since the days of his "dressed animals," upon the relationship between beasts and men. He sets out his thoughts in the chapter on "animal Pain" in *The Problem of Pain.*

Atheists naturally regard the co-existence of man and the other animals as a mere contingent result of interacting biological facts; and the taming of an animal by a man as a purely arbitrary interference of one species with another. The "real" or "natural" animal to them is the wild one, and the tame animal is an artificial or unnatural thing. But a Christian must not think so. Man was appointed by God to have dominion over the beasts, and everything a man does to an animal is either a lawful exercise, or a sacrilegious abuse, of an authority by divine right. The tame animal is therefore in the deepest sense, the only "natural" animal— and it is on the tame animal that we must base all our doctrine of beasts.[23]

This concept he works out fictionally in Mr. Bultitude, the redeemed bear of *That Hideous Strength*. Such animals are the beasts of our own world, toward whom we have important religious duties. But they are not the numinous "holy animals" of Narnia.

The talking animal is so much a staple of fairy tales that a child who, approaching the "age of reason," guffaws at Red Riding Hood's resurrection from the belly of the wolf, raises no objection whatever to conversation between the two characters. In the nineteenth century this convention produced two masterpieces: the exquisite watercolor world of Beatrix Potter, and the more deeply shadowed *Wind in the Willows*. A distinction needs to be drawn here, however. The wolf is a wolf, even when he masquerades as Red Riding Hood's grandmother. His capacity to speak is simply part of his nature: in that world, men and animals, generally commune in speech. For Beatrix Potter and Kenneth Grahame the animals approach the line which in the stage version, *Toad of Toad Hall*, is most emphatically crossed: they are so much like men that we can see in them, as C.S. Lewis saw in the Badger, "that extraordinary amalgam of high rank, coarse manners, gruffness, shyness, and goodness," from which, he declares, a child can gain "a knowledge of humanity and of English social history which it could not get in any other way."[24]

The animals become mirrors of man: we see ourselves in whose antics of Krazy Kat and Pogo, to mention two twentieth-century figures in the same tradition. This is the world not of faerie but of fable: Aesop's (for ancient Greece); Bidpai's (for Islam); the medieval Bestiaries (for the West); Fontaine's (for more recent

Europe); even the world of Br'er Rabbit, represent this tendency to didactic rationalization. Although Lewis is aware of this technique, he does not use it himself. His animals talk and they demonstrate moral lessons, but in a special way. They are something more subtle than either the primal world of metamorphosis from which fairy tales arise, or the moralizing menagery which rationalization can, at its worst, make of that world.

In Narnia, only talking beasts are Talking Beasts, a special category of being, called out by Aslan himself, as a "secondary creation," after he has completed his primary creation: "Narnia, Narnia, Narnia, awake. Love. Think. Speak. Be walking trees. Be talking beasts. Be divine waters" (MN 126; ch. 9). This distinction did not probably exist in Lewis's mind when he wrote the first book in the series: it represents a developed Narnian theology, more like that of St. John the Divine than that of St. Mark. Nevertheless the distinction is important. The Talking Beasts of Narnia attain their special status by being called out, becoming, as it were, a chosen people. Aslan pre-exists those Beasts, but he is himself one of them, a Talking Beast, as Bree, the Talking Horse, found out to his astonishment. These Beasts are truly animals, but they have been raised to a new status. They can fall from this exalted position: Aslan tells them, "the Dumb Beasts whom I have not chosen are yours also. Treat them gently and cherish them but do not go back to their ways lest you cease to be Talking Beasts. For out of them you were taken and into them you can return. Do not so" (MN 128; ch. 10).

An example of this is the character of the Lapsed Bear boxed by Prince Corin, in *The Horse and His Boy*. This particular motif reminds one strongly of the notion in George MacDonald's *The Princess and Curdie*, of men who are turning back into animals, so that their hands, to one gifted with special perception, feel like those of the beasts to which they are reverting. This Narnian phenomenon can be read as a reconciliation between the full-scale special creation of man (in line with a fundamentalist interpretation of Genesis), and the interpretation of man as a beast raised from the blind thrust of Evolution to a distinct role of self-consciousness and power (as in Psalm 8: "What is man, that Thou art mindful of him? And the son of man that Thou visitest him? For Thou hast made him a little lower than the angels and hast crowned him with glory and honor.")

There are also men in Narnia, but they are all descendants of humans transposed from Earth: the royal pair of the Cabby and his wife described in *The Magician's Nephew*. Wickedness is also alien to Narnia, as it arrives there in the form of the white witch Jadis, called in by a sin from the dying world of Charn. The Beasts, however, are natives, and they retain this aboriginal flavor throughout. They have about them a paradisical quality which they do not lose, though the direction of the narrative frequently turns elsewhere. When the action returns to Narnia, the Beasts are its citizens, unchanged: "I'm a beast, I am, and a Badger what's more," declares Trufflehunter when Prince Caspian finds Old Narnia in hiding. "We don't change. We hold on" (PC 69; ch. 5).

A brief catalog of the more memorable animals in this population would include Reepicheep, a mouse who achieves the supernal quest and is transported to Aslan's Country, like Elijah in the Chariot, in a tiny skin coracle; the Parliament of Owls; the helpful Eagles; and the fauns, especially Mr. Tumnus, who is the first inhabitant to appear out of the magical snows of a Narnian winter with an armful of parcels and an umbrella. The Old Narnians include the faithful Trufflehunter, and Jewel, the exquisite and valiant Unicorn, who accompanies the last King of Narnia into heaven. Remember the Jackdaw who "is" the First Joke; the splendid Leopards; the Centaurs with their limbs like those of English farmhorses; Fenris Ulf (later somewhat more tamely re-named) the police-state wolf; the pitiful little Christmas dinner-party of squirrels turned to stone by the White Witch; the milk-white lamb in Aslan's Country, the were-dragon who is Eustace Scrubb; the appalling Sea-Serpent; and the divine bird of Narnia's paradise garden. There, in one of the most poignant of all episodes, Digory finds a magic apple that heals his mother's fatal illness as the young Lewis could not do when his own mother died of cancer. Finally, we must recall the lugubrious but delightful Marsh-wiggle, Puddleglum. No doubt this list neglects some special favorite of each of Lewis's readers, for Narnia is full of such Beasts and composite Beings, flashed with jewel-like intensity upon a background of "heathery mountains and [...] thymy downs [...] many rivers [...] splashing glens [...] mossy caverns [...] and the ringing with the hammers of the Dwarfs" (HB 11; ch. 1).

An extraordinary final validation of the psychic accuracy of Lewis's animal creation and its lordly Beast/God/King has recently appeared in the book which is already a classic of its kind: *The Teachings of Don Juan, a Yaqui Way of Knowledge*, in which Carlos Castaneda (1968) describes his apprenticeship to a Yaqui shaman. At his initiation into the use of peyote, he experiences the following sequence of "nonordinary reality":

> All I was capable of seeing was the dog becoming iridescent; an intense light radiated from his body. I saw again the water flowing through him, kindling him like a bonfire [...] I drank until the fluid went out of my body through each pore, and projected out like fibers of silk, and I too acquired a long, lustrous, iridescent mane. I looked at the dog and his mane was like mine. A supreme happiness filled my whole body, and we ran together toward a sort of yellow warmth that came from some indefinite place. And there we played. We played and wrestled until I knew his wishes and he knew mine.[25]

The shaman interpreted this experience as the acceptance of his apprentice by Mescalito, the "Presence" who comes in the sacrament of Peyote. Compare this passage with the first actions of the resurrected Aslan:

> "Oh, children," said the Lion, "I feel my strength coming back to me. Oh, children, catch me if you can!" He stood for a second, his eyes very bright, his limbs quivering, lashing himself with his tail. Then he made a leap high over their heads and landed on the other side of the Table. [...] A mad chase began. Round and round the hill-top he led them, now hopelessly out of their reach, now letting them almost catch his tail, now diving between them, now tossing them in the air with his huge and beautifully velveted paws and catching them again, and now stopping unexpectedly so that all three of them rolled over together in a happy laughing heap of fur and arms and legs. It was such a romp as no one has ever had except in Narnia. (LWW 133; ch. 15)

The divine romp of Carlos Castaneda with the Presence of Mescalito in the "holy animal" of his peyote experience, and the mad chase of the visionary Lucy and the practical Susan with Aslan—the divinity incarnate—cannot take place "except in Narnia," but the reality of the experience shines through the luminous "pantomime animals" as "cosmic heirophanies," showing us the "splendour of the beasts."

Notes

[1] Stella Gibbons, "Imaginative Writing," *Light on C.S. Lewis*, ed. Jocelyn Gibb (London: Geoffrey Bles, 1965) 100-101.

[2] George Ferguson, "Lion," *Signs and Symbols in Christian Art* (New York: Oxford UP, 1954).

[3] J.E. Cirlot, *A Dictionary of Symbols* (New York: Philosophical Library, 1962) 181.

[4] Andreas Lommel, *Prehistoric and Primitive Man* (New York: McGraw-Hill, 1966) 43.

[5] C.G. Jung, "The Phenomenology of the Spirit in Fairy Tales," *The Archetypes and the Collective Unconscious*, 2nd edition, CW (Princeton, NJ: Princeton UP, 1968) 231.

[6] Mircea Eliade, *The Sacred and the Profane* (1957; New York: A Harvest Book, Harcourt, Brace & World, 1959) 155.

[7] Eliade, *The Sacred and the Profane* 159.

[8] G.R. Levy, *The Gate of Horn* (London: Faber and Faber, 1948) 14.

[9] Levy 20.

[10] Levy 225, 227.

[11] He writes: "intending to write about magicians, devils, pantomime animals, and planetary angels" (THS 7; ch. 1).

[12] Erwin Rousselle, "Dragon and Mare, Figures of Primordial Chinese Mythology," *The Mystic Vision*, ed., Joseph Campbell, Bollingen Series XXX (New York: 1968) 103.

[13] Rousselle, "Dragon and Mare" 103.

[14] Rousselle, "Dragon and Mare" 104.

[15] Ruth Underhill, *Red Man's Religion* (Chicago, IL: University of Chicago Press, 1965) 41.

[16] Underhill 41.

[17] C.S. Lewis, "On Three Ways of Writing for Children," *Of Other Worlds* (New York: Harcourt Brace Jovanovich, 1966) 27.

[18] C.S. Lewis, *Surprised by Joy* (1955; New York: Harcourt, Brace, Jovanovich, 1966) 13.

Notes

[19] The writer, at the October, 1968, conference of the Tolkien Society of America, heard one well-known Tolkien enthusiast exclaim, "Help stamp out Reepicheep!" in what appeared to be perfect, (if wry), earnest.

[20] C.S. Lewis, *Surprised by Joy* 14-15.

[21] C.S. Lewis, *Surprised by Joy* 15, note.

[22] C.S. Lewis, *Surprised by Joy* 15, note.

[23] C.S. Lewis, *The Problem of Pain* (London: Geoffrey Bles, 1940) 126.

[24] C.S. Lewis, "Sometimes Fairy Stories May Say Best What's To Be Said" 27.

[25] Carlos Castaneda, *The Teachings of Don Juan, a Yaqui Way of Knowledge* (New York: Ballantine, 1968) 33-34.

8.   "The Bolt of Tash": The Figure of Satan in C.S.
        Lewis's *The Horse and His Boy* and *The Last Battle*

> Once again the day came when the members of the court of
> heaven took their place in the presence of the LORD, and Sa-
> tan was there among them.
>
> ——Job 2.1 (NEB)

> And then she understood the devilish cunning of the enemies'
> plan. By mixing a little truth with it they had made their lie far
> stronger.
>
> ——C.S. Lewis, *The Last Battle*

*In this short paper Patterson summarizes and interprets the represen-
tation of deities in* The Horse and His Boy *and* The Last Battle. *She
compares the Tash of the earlier novel with the Old Testament Baal
and Satan, and the Tash of the final book with the Father of Lies. It is
with his talent for deception that Tash brings about the worldly defeat
of Narnia. Aslan, of course, is understood to be Jesus, and he exer-
cises his ability to turn the defeat into victory.*

  *Patterson provides close studies of the representation of some
of Lewis's other dark fictional deities in "The Holy House of Ungit"
and in "Letters from Hell: The Symbolism of Evil in* The Screwtape
Letters,*" both of which are included in this volume; in "This Equivocal Being': The Un-Man in* Perelandra,*" available in* Ransoming the
Waste Land Volume I; *as well as other papers in both volumes.*

  "'The Bolt of Tash': the Figure of Satan in C.S. Lewis's The
Horse and His Boy *and* The Last Battle*" was first published in* Mythlore *16.4 (Summer 1990): 23-26. It is Patterson's fourth paper on the
representation of evil in Lewis's fiction.*

The Horse and His Boy

   In *The Horse and His Boy* (1954), the young foundling Shasta
discovers that Arsheesh is not his father: "Why, I might be anyone!"
he thought, "I might be the son of a Tarkaan myself—or the son of the

Tisroc (may he live forever)—or of a god!" (HB 10; ch. 1). Shasta has been reared in Calormen, a land to the south of the Kingdom of Narnia, whose god is known as Tash. Shasta decides to run away from his stepfather, and is joined by Aravis; we first hear of Tash from her words: "In the name of Tash and Azaroth and Zardeenah Lady of the Night, I have a great wish to be in that country of Narnia" (HB 39; ch. 3). Aravis has asked for "three days" in which "to do secret sacrifices to Zardeenah" (HB 39; ch.3), as a ruse by which to escape an unwanted marriage. We hear no more of Azaroth, but of Tash we are to learn much: "In the name of Tash the irresistible, the inexorable" (HB 41; ch.3), suggesting that he is a god of mendacity.

The worship of Tash is centered in the great city of Tashbaan, to which the runaway children go. Tashbaan is described baldly by Edmund, one of the Pevensie children who are, as Narnian royalty, on a state visit to the capital of Calormen. He calls it "this devilish city" (HB 70; ch. 5). Edmund is the saved traitor of his family, and of Narnia, whose redemption has been bought at the price of Aslan's life. Best of all his siblings, he knows what devilishness is. Even so, it is in Tashbaan that Shasta first hears the name of Aslan. The good little faun Tumnus, who thinks the youth is Prince Corin of Archenland, comforts Shasta with stories of Narnia, "Who knows?—We might see Aslan himself! (HB 76; ch. 5). Before the book ends, this hope becomes fact for Shasta.

Meanwhile, Aravis, helped by Lasaraleen, creeps into the place of the Tisroc. Almost discovered in this forbidden place, Lasaraleen whispers, "Tash preserve us!" (HB 106; ch. 7). The two girls overhear the plot of Rabadash, son of the Tisroc, to invade Narnia. The Tisroc agrees to this plan: "These little barbarian countries that call themselves free [...] are hateful to the gods" (HB 112; ch. 8), he says self-righteously, and adds that "The High King of Narnia [...] is supported by a demon of hideous aspect and irresistible maleficence who appears in the shape of a Lion (HB 113; ch. 8), a Screwtapeian view of Aslan.

Aravis escapes and joins Shasta, and at last they arrive in Archenland, just ahead of the great army. "'By Tash!'" cries Aravis, ever the Calormene, "It's Rabadash'" (HB 140; ch. 10). At this point a terrible lion, Aslan in the form of a deity closest to the one Aravis has invoked, intervenes to force the horses into a last desperate gallop, and wounds Aravis with a stroke of his claws. Thus chastened, she reaches the peaceful enclosure of the Hermit of the Southern March, while Shasta's reward is another desperate trek still further north to warn the endangered Archenland.

Here he runs into the very arms of King Lune, but as the company rides north, the boy falls behind, and in a gathering fog Shasta overhears Rabadash's battle plans "In the name of Tash the irresistible, the inexorable—forward!" (HB 160; ch. 11). It is all up to Shasta now, but in this terrible situation, he is not alone; a "Person" goes with him. Asked for his name, the Lion three times gives it as "Myself," the equivalent of the Name "I Am," given by Yahweh to Moses. Tash has been evoked by Rabadash but it is Aslan who has come.

The Lion leads Shasta to Narnia, where Rabadash is defeated and providentially suspended by the back of his chain-mail shirt from a hook on the castle wall. He has cried out "The bolt of Tash falls from above" and jumped down from the wall to this unforeseen end. Shasta meanwhile, is discovered and recognized as Prince Corin's twin brother and King Lune's son, and Aravis joins him at court, where the unrepentant Rabadash is still raging and declaring that "The bolt of Tash falls from above! (HB 216; ch. 13). Careful readers will surely be alerted to the imminent arrival of Aslan upon such an invocation, and indeed, Aslan appears, as Rabadash screams curses in the name of Tash. Thus raving, he is turned into a donkey, a proper shape for one who has been making an ass of himself.

In a sense, *The Horse and His Boy* shows us an Old Testament world in which most of the people are polytheists, while the population of Narnia know of the one God incarnated as Aslan. We hear much of Tash and his temple, but we do not see him. He is, perhaps, like Baal, a god known but in abeyance for the Israelites, who follow Yahweh. He is even more like the Adversary as he appears in Job. The Satan or Accuser of Job is "one of the sons of God whose duty is to test person's faithfulness to God,"[1] rather than the character called Satan in the medieval "folk presentation of Christianity"[2] who is the "'counter-principle of Jesus Christ'."[3]

In another sense, the situation in *The Horse and His Boy* is a New Testament one, in which the truth about Aslan and his saving grace has been revealed to Narnia, but not to Calormen. He intervenes whenever he is needed, whether recognized or not. The wish of

Aravis to be in Narnia, made in the name of Tash and other gods, is granted by Aslan. When Lasaraleen calls upon Tash to preserve herself and Aravis, they are indeed preserved, but Aravis is wounded by Aslan soon afterwards, when she invokes Tash for rescue, even as she is again being saved. When Rabadash identifies with Tash in leaping down toward his enemies, we do not doubt that his healing in Tash's temple will be Aslan's work as well.

The Last Battle

The Christian dialectic of good created, marred, and restored by a new good, operates everywhere in *The Horse and His Boy,* but its operation is implicit rather than explicit. In *The Last Battle* (1956) the lines are drawn with more precision. Certainly, it is in a New Testament world that *The Last Battle* takes place. The precise book of that Testament is Revelation. The story begins, drearily, with an Ape—Shift—who is clever in the proper medieval manner, and a donkey—Puzzle—again in the medieval manner, who is not. The two discover a lion's skin in a pool at the western border of Narnia, invoking the medieval symbolism of the West and end-time. Shift, like the Grinch, has a sudden and awful idea. He sets up Puzzle in the lion-skin as a false Aslan, who "has come and is not like the Aslan we have believed in and longed for" (LB 30; ch. 3).

In making a treaty with the invading Calormenes—"our dark faced friends," as the racist Ape expresses it—a new theological concept is introduced in response to a good question asked by a Lamb:

> Please […] I can't understand. What have we to do with the Calormenes? We belong to Aslan. They belong to Tash. They have a god called Tash. They say he has four arms and the head of a vulture. They kill Men on his altar. I don't believe there's any such person as Tash. But if there was, how could Aslan be friends with him? (LB 37; ch. 3)

These words uttered by this symbol of innocence deserve close attention. The god of the Calormenes is described here for the first time, as a theriomorphic god like the ones the Israelites rejected, a metamorphic divinity which combines the attributes of animal and divinity. We can speculate that his description with "the head of a vulture" associates him with death, or at least with the dead. The response of Shift to the Lamb's remarks is immediate. "Tash is only another name for Aslan [...] Tash is Aslan: Aslan is Tash" (LB 38; ch. 3). Tirian, the last King of Narnia, attempts to protest: "He meant to go on and ask how the terrible god Tash who fed on the blood of his people could possibly be the same as the good Lion by whose blood all Narnia was saved" (LB 40; ch. 3). Lewis reminds the reader that there can be no equality between killing one's followers and dying for them.

The captive Tirian calls upon the name of the real Aslan: "Come and help us Now" (LB 49; ch. 4), with the result that he sees, in a vision, the "seven friends of Narnia" (LB 51; ch. 4). A prayer to Aslan is always answered. First to arrive are Jill and Eustace; after releasing Tirian they return to the benighted stable of the false Aslan where the unicorn Jewel is imprisoned. The rescue, when completed, includes another prisoner, Puzzle, and Eustace exclaims, "Where the *devil* have you been to?" (LB 74; ch. 6). Lewis never used this word lightly: Jill has rescued "The false Aslan" (LB 62; ch. 6) and Tirian, not pleased, prepares to execute the "accursed Ass" until Jill pleads for his life.

Is the ass a devil? Certainly the devil is an ass, and this Ass has made an ass of himself in following the lead of the Ape instead of thinking of himself. But there is forgiveness for Puzzle. Tirian, now disguised as a Calormene, stops a procession of Dwarfs and says to their captors, "By the great god Tash, they are very obedient" (LB 78; ch. 7). He has invoked their deity, a thing which, we have seen, cannot be done lightly. He questions the Dwarfs about their obedience and learns that these are "Aslan's orders" (LB, 78; ch. 7). To free the Dwarfs from this delusion, Tirian displays Puzzle in his disheveled lion-skin and declares that *"The light is dawning, the lie broken"* (LB 80; ch. 7). But the result is not what he expects. "We've been fooled once and we're not going to be fooled again" (LB 82; ch. 7), the Dwarf leader declares, and off they march, except for "one single Dwarf," Poggin, who returns.

It emerges that Ginger the Cat has explained Tirian's escape by saying that Aslan has swallowed him up "at one mouthful" (LB 88; ch. 7), "'What devilish policy' said Tirian" (LB 89; ch. 7). "Devilish" indeed. The Cat and the Tarkaan in charge of the Calormene detachment "care neither for Tash nor Aslan." Lewis does not agree with these conspirators. Not only is there a real Aslan—there is a real

Tash. Invoked, perhaps by this ultimate blasphemy, Tash now appears: "At first glance you might have mistaken it for smoke, for it was gray and you could see things through it. But the deathly smell was not the smell of smoke" (LB 92; ch. 8). Lewis has piled image upon image in creating this vision: it is seen in the "shadow" it resembles "smoke"; it is in "the shape of a man" but is also in the form of a "bird of prey"; it leaves a "deathly smell" and withered grass in its wake. This Tash is real, but not corporeal. Unlike Aslan, a living, natural animal at whose presence winter gives way to spring, this being is a spirit, made manifest only as a "cloudy shape." Having learned something, perhaps, from the vision, Tirian decides to put aside his Calormene disguise.

Now he learns that the banner of the Tisroc flies over Cair Paravel, and recognizes that "Narnia is no more" (LB 103; ch. 8). Death has been called by his name and has answered by coming to those who called, and he must and always will come. There are not many children's books which culminate in the deaths of the most attractive protagonists—*Charlotte's Web, At the Back of the North Wind,* and *The Water-Babies* come to mind—and readers of *The Last Battle* do not yet realize that their favorites are in fact going to die.

After a vigil, Tirian and his friends look with undeluded eyes as the Ape announces that a "wicked beast" has "dressed itself up in a lion-skin and is wandering about in these very woods pretending to be Aslan" (LB 115; ch. 9). Jill, in horror, understands "the devilish cunning of the enemies' plan." The devil, after all, is the Father of Lies. Jill asks Tirian, "What do you think is really inside the Stable?" and dares to ask, "Tash himself?" (LB 121; ch. 10). In answer to this, Tirian utters the second most beautiful phrase in the book: "Courage, child: we are all between the paws of the true Aslan."

At this moment Ginger announces that he will go in, and he is followed by Emeth, the good Calormene. "Thou has said that their Aslan and our Tash are all one," Emeth declares, and enters to look upon the face of his god. An armed Calormene stumbles out again and falls to the ground, but it is not Emeth. Tirian now reveals himself to the gathered Narnians, declaring that "Tash is a foul fiend," and the Tarkaan calls upon his warriors invoking "the wrath of Tashlan" which we know by now is a very dangerous thing to do. Almost immediately there is heard "a clucking and screaming as if it was the hoarse voice of some monstrous bird" and Tash himself appears in person.

The first skirmish of *The Last Battle* has now begun, and the Calormenes steadily drive the friends of Narnia toward the Stable door, calling out "Tash! Tash! The great god Tash! Inexorable Tash!" At the battle's height, Tirian flings the Tarkaan into the stable:

> A terrible figure was coming toward them [...] It had a vulture's head and four arms. Its beak was open and its eyes blazed. A croaking voice came from its beak.
>
> Thou has called me into Narnia, Rishda Tarkaan. Here I am. What has thou to say? (LB 151; ch. 12)

This at last is no wraith, but the Lord of Death himself, who pounces upon the Tarkaan like the bird of prey he is. Now, a voice is heard: "Begone, Monster, and take your lawful prey to your own place: in the name of Aslan," and with that, "The hideous creature vanished with the Tarkaan still under its arm" (LB 152; ch. 12). It is the voice of the High King Peter. Servants of Aslan are able to drive out demons in his name. This is the last ever seen of Tash in Narnia. Tirian is now inside the stable and meets the seven friends of Narnia in their eternal form, and they report that Tash has already made away with Shift the Ape. Now Aslan appears, and Tirian flings himself at the Lion's feet to receive the "well done" (LB 167; ch. 13) of the good and faithful servant.

Aslan has come to bring about the end of Narnia, and to take from it into his own land all who will. When all is at an end, there is found "a young Calormene sitting under a chestnut tree beside a cold stream of water. It was Emeth" (LB 183; ch. 14). When he entered the stable so boldly, the Calormene had met not Tash but Aslan, who greeted him with these sweetest of words: "Child, all the service thou has done to Tash, I account as service done to me" (LB 188; ch. 15). This is so,

> "Not because he and I are one, but because we are opposites, I take to me the services which thou hast done to him. For I and he are of such different kinds that no service which is vile can be done to me, and none which is not vile can be done to him." (LB 189; ch. 15)

Perhaps Lewis never wrote more important words. They are also the very last words in *The Last Battle* about Tash. At the conclusion of this passage, as Aslan says, "all find what they truly seek," the story of Tash is at an end. He has no place in Aslan's Country. And there, we, who know more than Lewis at the time he wrote *The Last Battle,* must leave the god of the Calormenes, whether he represents death, or Satan, or the local divinity of an archaic kingdom, or any of the false gods worshipped in our world. Not all mysteries are capable of resolution this side of the stable door.

Notes
[1] Donald Taylor, "Theological Thoughts About Evil," ed. David Parkin, *The Anthropology of Evil* (Oxford: Basil Blackwell, 1985) 34.
[2] Taylor 36.
[3] Lionel Caplan, "The Popular Culture of Evil in Urban South India," *The Anthropology of Evil*, ed. David Parkin (Oxford: Basil Blackwell, 1985) 124.

9.   Letters from Hell: The Symbolism of Evil in
      The Screwtape Letters

"An apology for the devil: it must be remembered that we have heard only one side of the case; God has written all the books."

——Samuel Butler, *Notebooks*

In "Letters from Hell" Patterson analyzes the temptation by the World, Flesh, and Spirit orchestrated by Wormwood with the encouragement of Screwtape in The Screwtape Letters. *She details Lewis's biographical and literary sources for the narrative, including, among others, Thisted's* Letters from Hell *(1885). Her examination of Lewis's representation of evil in this epistolary novel draws attention to the importance of names, and such motifs as the hidden, bureaucracy, animals, the act of devouring, and others. Patterson studies some of Lewis's other dark deities in "'The Bolt of Tash': the Figure of Satan in C.S. Lewis's* The Horse and His Boy *and* The Last Battle" *and in "The Holy House of Ungit'," both included in this volume; in "This Equivocal Being': The Un-Man in* Perelandra" *available in* Ransoming the Waste Land Volume I; *and other papers in both volumes.*

*   "Letters from Hell: The Symbolism of Evil in* The Screwtape Letters" *was first published in* Mythlore *12.1 (Autumn 1985): 47-57. It is Patterson's third paper on the representation of evil in Lewis's fiction.*

————————

    C.S. Lewis's *The Screwtape Letters* is a short epistolary fantasy that includes three compelling interwoven narratives: the life of the young human "patient" from his Christian conversion to his death; the diabolical efforts of his tempter Wormwood and the senior devil Screwtape to capture him for hell; and the role, implicit throughout and made evident in the end, of God in saving him for heaven. The narrative is divided into three phases of temptation, the first by the World, the second by the Flesh, and the third by the Devil (that is, by spiritual means). In the presentation of this most human of all stories, Lewis makes use of the major and classic symbols of evil from the traditions of Western culture, including the animal motif, the fear of being devoured, and, most fundamental of all, the concept of defilement. In sum, he presents evil as defined by the doctrine of *privatio boni*, the absence of good, as he explores the mythic structures of the war in heaven. He describes a bureaucratic hell in which Satan and his fallen angels, unable to create so much as a single pleasure, continually struggle to understand the intentions of their adversary, God. Inaccurate to the last, they occupy the ultimately ridiculous position of created beings rebelling against their creator. From this ignoble posture, they reach out ravenously to draw each human being into the same contradiction. In *The Screwtape Letters*, the tempters meet defeat and the "patient" meets his maker face-to-face: Lewis thus tells the one tale his listeners most want to hear as their own.

Summary of *The Screwtape Letters*

On a human level, *The Screwtape Letters* tells a very simple but poignant story. At the onset of World War II, a young British convert to Christianity undergoes a series of temptations by the World, the Flesh, and the Devil; he meets and falls in love with a young Christian girl, begins to participate in defense work, acquits himself well in his first air-raid, and is killed in a state of grace in his second. The efforts of his personal tempter, one Wormwood, having been reported to a senior devil, Screwtape, elicit letters of advice on the diabolical aspects of the process. From these we follow a second, spiritual level of events in which the emphasis is upon the infernal characters but includes a hint of the divine actions as well.

On the diabolical level, Screwtape advises, scolds, threatens, praises, and finally condemns the efforts of his nephew Wormwood, who, after unsuccessfully trying to betray his uncle and corrupt his "patient," becomes food for Screwtape in the saved soul's place. The work of God meanwhile has drawn the young man into the Church, defended him against temptation, provided him with a girl to love and Christians to befriend him, and taken him, still young and in spiritual health, to himself. This taking, contrary to infernal practice, is not into a state of absorption, but into true and complete selfhood at the heart of Selfhood; the diabolical meal which Screwtape makes of Wormwood is an inverted parody (like the black mass) of the central Christian symbol of the relationship between human and divine: the Eucharist, the sacred meal in which the body and blood of Christ become the food of the faithful. Screwtape never learns what God wants from his creation; the idea that God wants to give himself to his creatures—depicted in so absolute, stunning, and concrete an image as this—obviously cannot occur to the devil. But Lewis uses exactly this image as the operative symbol of his book.

It is instructive to summarize the story with a sentence for each of the thirty-one chapters. There is a young man who has a materialist friend. Even so, he becomes a Christian. He has problems with his mother, a difficult old lady who resents his conversion. He begins a prayer life in which he becomes aware of God's presence. War begins. He feels fear, loss, and self-pity. In particular, he fears the prospect of military service. He does not know he has a tempter who will manipulate his fear toward a false pacifism. He undergoes a period of dryness, a natural result of "undulation" or rhythm in a convert's life. His tempter tries to make use of this. The young man is tempted by the World in the form of a couple who are fashionably liberal. They enjoy laughter but not of the healing kind. Although his soul is in danger, he still continues to attend church and make his communions. As a result, he repents, and undergoes a "second conversion." He gains a new humility and aid from God in keeping his mind off himself.

There is a lull in the war, and he feels a "natural" sense of ease, happily, ever since his conversion, he has attended the same church. A new attempt is made on his soul through appetite, a special form of "delicacy" which he shares with his mother—this is a temptation of the Flesh. His flesh is also tempted toward unchastity; this takes a strong form, playing upon his private obsessions. Through Grace, he falls in love with a virginal Christian girl of a family advanced in holiness. He meets many new, intelligent Christian friends. The girl's only flaw is that she naively sees non-Christians as a little ridiculous. But he is living a new kind of Christian life among truly charitable people. They are "mere Christians" for whom the faith is an end in itself, not a means to an end. The courtship continues; the very enchantment of licit sexual desire increases their charity toward one another. He begins to pray about a problem of distraction in prayer; he begins to make a habit of obedience.

Now the devil prepares his final attack. While the young man's mother and young woman pray for him, he takes up defense work. The anticipation of bombardment awakens temptations to hatred, fear, and despair; but he feels shame at these expressions of incipient cowardice. In his first air-raid, he acquits himself well; he is afraid, and ashamed of his fear, but does his duty anyway. Finally, he is killed in another raid, simultaneously becomes aware of his tempters, of the angels who have protected him, and of Christ himself who greets him, wearing "the form of a Man."

We do not learn the ultimate fate of his mother or his young woman, though they figure prominently in the story. Perhaps the unpleasant old lady will be saved by her son's intercessions, and the girl, made more mature and less naïve by her bereavement, will one day meet him in Heaven, perhaps after a lifetime of marriage to someone else.

I have suggested in this summary, by my division of the narrative into three paragraphs, and by the language I have used, that the subject of *The Screwtape Letters* is tempted by the World, the Flesh, and the Devil. For at least four centuries, Anglicans have prayed that newly baptized babies may "triumph against the devil, the world, and the flesh." These terms refer to spiritual sin, social sin, and physical sin. In terms of the traditional Seven Deadly Sins, these categories might be divided into Pride and Despair (the Devil); Avarice, Envy, and Anger (the World); and Gluttony and Lust (the Flesh). Dorothy L. Sayers wittily entitled an essay "The Other Six Deadly Sins" because so few people have heard of any but the last (Lust), while she concluded that the first (Pride) was the fundament and ruler of the others.

Of *luxuria* (lust), Sayers said briskly that it is indeed a sin; that until recently Caesar agreed with the Church in combating it, but now, no longer needing families, has ceased to care; and people fall into it by "sheer exuberance of animal spirits" but equally easily by "sheer boredom and discontent."[1] Lust, along with *ira* (Wrath) and *gula* (Gluttony), Sayers calls the "warm-hearted, or disreputable sins."[2] The others she acerbically calls "the cold-hearted or respectable sins." These are *avaritia* (Covetousness); *invidia* (Envy); *acedia* (Sloth) of which she says "In the world it calls itself tolerance; but in hell it is called despair"[3]; and *superbia* (Pride), which is "the sin of trying to be God."[4] This last is, of course, the sin of Satan.

Biographical Sources

To Lewis, one need not look past one's own experience to have a knowledge of sin:

> In all but a few writers the "good" characters are the least successful, and every one who has ever tried to make even the humblest story ought to know why. To make a character worse than oneself it is only necessary to release imaginatively from control some of the bad passions which, in real life, are always straining at the leash [...][5]

Indeed, the voice of Screwtape (by intention a character worse than "oneself") is the voice of the young Lewis as revealed in his own early letters: supercilious, mocking, cruelly calculating, belittling, and anxious for position, and certainly he drew upon his own life, his own temptations, in *The Screwtape Letters*.

The character of Wormwood's patient is not quite Everyman. He resides in a town large enough to undergo bombardment, rather than a village or on a farm. He lives with his mother (an echo, surely, of Lewis's surrogate mother, Mrs. Janie Moore), and has several contrasting circles of friends who reflect the intellectual currents of the day, including Christianity. He is an Anglican (not a "mere Christian"), a member of a specific parish of the Church of England. We do not learn how he makes his living but suspect it is not as a laborer. Perhaps he works at a desk in a large bureaucracy, so that Wormwood is his infernal counterpart: a junior tempter for a junior clerk! His private life of relationships with family, friends, and courted girl are depicted, but his life as a worker, which would have occupied most of his daylight hours, is not discussed in the story. The bureaucratic Hell which Lewis has created may have taken its place, setting forth the diabolical aspects of this lifestyle with vigor. It is also possible that the young man, like Lewis's friend Arthur Greeves, had no employment, but lived with his mother on the proceeds of her inheritance, whether from her family or her husband. Although he is of an age for military service, the young man does not volunteer and is not called: he serves instead at home in defense work, and indeed, dies at his post. Perhaps he is slightly disabled, as Greeves reportedly was, by a faulty heart.

Despite these specifics, however, his youth, his lack of particular employment, and his membership in the state church, give him a partially generalized identity. Lewis must have wanted a character specific enough to be believable but general enough to be understandable by the majority of his readers. The book began as a series printed in the *Manchester Guardian* early in World War II, and was intended for readers aware of intellectual currents.

I have suggested above the autobiographical element in the patient's difficult mother: another feature, available to us since the publication of the Lewis-Greeves correspondence, is hinted in the temptations to unchastity. These include references to masturbatory fantasy—"solitary vice" and "personal obsession"—which for the youthful Lewis took the form of imagined sadism. He may also have been unchaste, as he hints in *Surprised by Joy* (his dancing teacher) and *The Pilgrim's Regress* (the brown girl). As far as we know, he never won the love of a virginal Christian girl, but he had a number of friendships with young women of the type he describes in the character of the patient's "young woman," female cousins, and family acquaintances of his Belfast youth, including Jane McNeill. His wife, as befitted his maturity, was a brilliant divorced woman who offered him intellectual equality and experienced sexual partnership. But that lay ahead of him when he wrote *The Screwtape Letters*.

Sources in Literary Fantasy

The book is an epistolary narrative in a form characteristic of a number of Victorian works of fantasy including *Dracula* (1897) by Bram Stoker and *The Moonstone* (1868) by Wilkie Collins. This form was also used by religious writers and Lewis's specific source has been stated to have been *Letters From Hell* (1885) by Waldemar Adolph Thisted. Lewis wrote from Great Bookham, where he was being tutored for Oxford, to his friend Greeves on the 18th of July, 1916: "I wonder what a book called 'Letters from Hell' published at 1/- by Macmillan would be like?"[6] By the 25th of July he had learned that the edition had an introduction by George MacDonald, already known to him from *Phantastes*. When the book so breathlessly awaited was finally read, Lewis wrote to Greeves that he had given it "to a jumble sale for the red cross or something" and that "I am at present enjoying the malicious pleasure of expecting that the buyer will be as disappointed as I was."[7]

The book begins "I felt the approach of death." No wonder the young Lewis had felt attracted to it when he first opened it! But what follows is a dry memoir recorded during a sojourn in hell, interspersed with bizarre visions of symbolic import: a city with a nightly "auto-da-fé," a city of Politicians where the statesmen fall to bickering. These images suggest motifs that reappear in *That Hideous Strength*. All the while, the light slowly fades, as it does in hell in *The Great Divorce*. There is a wronged maiden, who finds her way to heaven, without the protagonist, a hint of the Christian girl in *The Screwtape Letters*, perhaps. Indeed, at the end, the damned soul meets his own mother on the stygian shore and they sink into a final despair, providing at least the germ of the mother in *The Screwtape Letters*. The style is ornate, even elegiac, but the contents are extremely diffuse. Presumably Lewis had chances beyond this to observe the City of Dis: his brother Major Warren Lewis wrote in his diary of a part of Liverpool (the sad seaport to which the child Lewis was ferried at the end of each holiday from Belfast to his terrible school in England): "I, after a siesta, went for a more extended stroll in Birkenhead than I have yet had; it is exactly Hell described by J in the opening chapter of *Grand Divorce* [sic]. How can any government expect content from the inhabitants of such a place?"[8]

But Lewis did, perhaps, derive a very concrete, and finally more important, idea from the Introduction to the book by George MacDonald, who wrote that *Letters from Hell* was "full of truth." In his comments, MacDonald penned this powerful statement:

> [M]en, in defacing the image of God in themselves, construct for themselves a world of horror and dismay; that of *the outer darkness* our own deeds and character are the informing or inwardly creating cause; that if man will not have God, he never can be rid of his weary and hateful self.[9]

In the essay, "Screwtape Proposes a Toast" (1961), which Lewis composed two decades after *The Screwtape Letters*, he makes Screwtape say that the damned would possess "a hard, tight, settled core of resolution to go on being what it is" (ST 191). This consists of "a very small core" (ST 192). Lewis reiterates, and, drawing upon the most terrible image he knew; "almost, in its own way, prim and de-mure; like a pebble, or a very young cancer" (ST 192). In this passage we see in an ultimate nutshell, Lewis's teaching on sin. He was close, by then, to his own death.

The Devil's Point-of-View

Michael Paternoster (1967) points out that while Charles Williams can "manage without a personal devil," his friend "C.S. Lewis [...] clearly does not merely use evil spirits as a literary device but believes in them, and believes that their existence helps to explain the phenomenon of everyday experience."[10] The purpose of the present essay is to examine Lewis's depiction of evil, by using images (as one must for the expression of all psychic or spiritual phenomena) in *The Screwtape Letters*. In this work, and this work only (excepting its very late "chapter" just quoted) evil appears personified in precisely diabolical form. Lewis had already written books with evil characters— *Dymer* (1929), *The Pilgrim's Regress* (1933) and *Out of the Silent Planet* (1938)—and he was to write *Perelandra* (1943) with the Unman as a human being possessed by "macrobes." The White and Green Witches of the Narnia Chronicles (1950–1955) are evil female beings, while Tash is modeled upon a malevolent Near Eastern divinity, and in the last fantasy, *Till We Have Faces* (1956), there are no such characters.

In *The Screwtape Letters*, however, we have devils depicted as themselves, personified as individual spiritual beings. Without trying to define evil in itself, we can agree with Jeffrey Burton Russell's definition in *The Devil* (1977): "evil is frequently and in many societies felt as a purposeful force, and it is perceived as personified [...] Evil is never abstract. It must always be understood in terms of the suffering of an individual."[11] This latter idea is explored by Lewis in *The Problem of Pain*. The being Lewis was depicting is based upon "that old serpent, called the Devil, and Satan, which deceiveth the whole world," who "were cast out with him," as is reported in Revelation 12.9.

This personified evil and the suffering of an individual are precisely what *The Screwtape Letters* is about. To the often-put question of whether he really believed in the devil, Lewis wrote this reply: "if by 'the Devil' you mean a power opposite to God and, like God, self-existent from all eternity, the answer is certainly 'No'." But, he continued, as to whether he believed in devils, "I do. That is to say, I believe in angels, and I believe that some of these, by the abuse of their free will, have become enemies to God and, as a corollary, to us" (ST 6). Interestingly, one of Lewis's critics agrees with him, on aesthetic grounds. Diana Waggoner (1979) remarks that "It is an artistic mistake to invent an evil being who exists purely to do, and to represent 'evil'; it puts the subcreator in the position of a God who deliberately creates the Devil in order to make things more interesting."[12] Screwtape is no invention. He is an image, and stated to be an image, of the diabolical forces so many cultures have detected. As Russell puts it, "The Devil is the hypostasis, the apotheosis, the objectification of a hostile force or hostile forces perceived as external to our own consciousness."[13] This being is "no quaint or outmoded figure, but a phenomenon of enormous and perennial power in, or over, the human spirit."[14]

In the New Testament this figure is called Satan: a Hebrew term carried over from the Old Testament. The word refers to "a being who hinders free, forward movement, therefore an adversary or accuser."[15] The Greek word also used in the New Testament as the equivalent of Satan is Diabolos, which is translated into English as "Devil." Literally, it too means "to throw across." As John Sanford (1981) puts it, "it is as though the diabolos throws something across our path to interfere with our progress."[16] The Satan of the New Testament causes both physical and mental illness, and "strives to turn man from God by inciting him to sin and rebellion."[17] This diabolos or Satan figure is the pattern from which Lewis's Screwtape is cut.

The best commentary on the depiction of evil in *The Screwtape Letters* is by Lewis himself, in the Preface he prepared to a new edition which included the essay "Screwtape Proposes a Toast." Admitting that he believes in angels and consequently in devils, he offers five paragraphs of sophisticated commentary on the depiction of angels and devils in Western art and literature. He summarizes the traditional methods in this pithy and witty remark: "Devils are depicted with bats' wings and good angels with birds' wings […] because most men like birds better than bats" (ST 7). Most tellingly, he states of angels, "They are given human form because man is the only rational creature we know. Creatures higher in the natural order than ourselves

[…] must be represented symbolically if they are to be represented at all" (ST 7).

After referring specifically to the devils in Dante (which "are the best"), Milton (which "have done great harm"), and Goethe (whose Mephistopheles is "the really pernicious image") (ST 8), Lewis remarks (of himself) that "a little man may sometimes avoid some single error made by a great one," and that he hoped "my own symbolism should at least not err in Goethe's way." As to his own method in *The Screwtape Letters*, "I like bats much better than bureaucrats […] the greatest evil is not now done in […] 'dens of crime' [… or] even in concentration camps and labour camps." Rather, "it is conceived and ordered […] in clean, carpeted, warmed, and well-lighted offices." In short, "my symbol for Hell is something like the bureaucracy of a police state or the offices of a thoroughly nasty business concern" (ST 9). Lewis published these words in the England of 1961. Readers of the present, some two decades further on, will have no reason to dispute his choice of symbol and perhaps recognize his remarkable powers of prophecy!

Screwtape, then, is the embodiment of evil conceived as one of a group of fallen spirits. The devils are fallen angels, beings created good but free, who have chosen to rebel against their maker. Lewis, in a book he published in the same year as *The Screwtape Letters*, discussed the meaning of Satan. He states in *A Preface to Paradise Lost* (1942) that "Milton has chosen to treat the Satanic predicament in the epic form and has therefore subordinated the absurdity of Satan to the misery which he suffers and inflicts."[18] *The Screwtape Letters*, then, is a work contra Milton's method: "it is a mistake to demand that Satan […] should be able to rant and posture through the whole universe without, sooner or later, awaking the comic spirit." Screwtape is, and is intended to be, a comic figure: "mere Christianity commits every Christian to believing that 'the Devil is (in the long run) an ass'."[19]

The devil an ass? Why? Because "a creature revolting against a creator is revolting against the source of his own powers."[20] The devil is a created being, as was the adversary, Satan, in the Old Testament. The rebellion of such a being is ultimately laughable because what is attempted is in the end impossible. Why, then, would a spiritual being of the highest created order turn to such hopeless rebellion? Lewis has an answer—quoting *Paradise Lost* I, 98—Satan suffers "a sense of injur'd merit." *A Preface to Paradise Lost* is dedicated to Charles Williams, whose thoughts on Milton influenced Lewis just as his thoughts on Dante influenced Sayers. In his *Preface to The Poetical Works of Milton* (1940) Williams stated: "much of *Paradise Lost* can be felt to revolve, laughingly and harmoniously, round the solemn and helpless image of pride."[21] This is the sin of Pride, which goes at the head of the list in Sayers's comments on the Seven Deadly Sins, raised to it ultimate level. As Williams puts it, "He is full of injured merit [...] He is the full example of the self-loving spirit."[22]

Charles Williams's commentary, which provided Lewis with his central insight into *Paradise Lost*, contains one of Williams's most famous aphorisms: "Hell is always inaccurate."[23] This is the theme of *The Screwtape Letters*, as Hell struggles and fails to comprehend the divine intentions. It is a self-willed failure: having gotten the basic order of the premise—creator-created—wrong, how could an accurate conclusion be drawn from it? Lewis calls this inaccuracy "this doom of Nonsense," and uses the same theme in his banquet scene in *That Hideous Strength*.

But what was this war in heaven, this spiritual rebellion in high places, to do with earth and humankind? What interest has the devil in us? Lewis explains this in his summary of Milton's Satan:

> He begins by fighting for "liberty," however misconceived; but almost at once sinks to fighting for "Honour, Dominion, glorie and renoune." Defeated in this, he sinks to that great design [...] of ruining two creatures who had never done him harm [...] This brings him as a spy into the universe, and soon not even a political spy, but a mere peeping Tom leering, and writhing in prurience as he overlooks the privacy of two lovers [...] as "the Devil,"—the salacious grotesque, half bogey and half buffoon, of popular tradition. From hero to general, from general to politician, from politician to secret service agent, and thence to a thing that peers in at bedroom or bathroom windows, and thence to a toad, and finally to a snake—such is the progress of Satan.[24]

In my epigraph, I quote a famous utterance of Samuel Butler's, complaining that we do not hear Satan's side of the matter. Mark Twain also took this whimsical viewpoint in an essay: "It may be that

I lean a little his way, on account of his not having a fair show. All religions issue bibles against him, and say the most injurious things about him, but we never hear *his* side." These statements are, of course, tongue-in-cheek. They imply that such an inverted point of view is intrinsically comic, just as Lewis says.

I referred above to several works in the epistolary manner from the Victorian era. In fact, the Edwardian period yields even more precise counterparts to Lewis's method in *The Screwtape Letters*, and though there is no evidence he read them, a description of two such works, popular religious treatises purporting to give the devil's point of view, may give a sense of the attitudes which informed Lewis's youth. They have just that jaunty, comic element which characterizes nearly all popular works on religion. Lewis's ability to take this stance and yet write works of surpassing power is what I suppose most infuriates his critics.

In *Sermons by the Devil* (1904), the Rev. W.S. Harris explains his plot:

> The part that Satan plays in the drama of a human life is often larger than a person will admit. Each one of us is not only acting, but we are constantly acted upon by one or the other of two great influences. The Good Spirit endeavors to lead us to the skies, and its angels are ever willing to minister to any real needs. The Evil Spirit, either openly or under cover, seeks to destroy our mind with the untruth by preaching to us his black sermons of death.[25]

Each "sermon" is a little drama in which a human character undergoes temptation (countered by responses from "a good angel"). Advising parents in child-rearing, for example, Satan suggests: "Constantly tell him, by your actions and your words, that religion is not intended to give a man greater liberty than he would otherwise enjoy, but, on the contrary it often tends to narrow a man down to a set of hard rules."[26] In "An Essay Delivered to the Devil and his Cabinet by a Theological Specialist," the essayist cheerfully reports that "You will all agree with me that things are drifting in the right direction."[27] He proposes a series of guidelines for modern pastors, concluding with words that could have been uttered by Screwtape: "If you cannot succeed with the speculative argument, then try the sensational fad.

There are not a few who can be turned off at this angle, and instead of putting a little spice into the sermon they can be persuaded to make it nearly all spice."[28]

A similar book, by the Rev. J.R. Miller, *The Devil of Today* (1903) is written in the form of an allegory, with characters including not only Satan and A Guardian Angel, but Miss Sincere, Widow Faith, Mr. Hypocrite, and Evangelist, as well as pastors like the Rev. Mr. Good and the Rev. Mr. Please-All. Satan is provided with aides: Deception, Belial, Faultfinder, and Heresy. The book begins: "In my vision it was morning."[29] In a typical passage Satan and Heresy discuss attacks on the Bible: "'Let us bend our united energies towards confusing the faith of Christians in their old book,' added the fiend."[30] Forthwith, Mr. Hypocrite gives Miss Sincere a book "in the hope of liberalizing her simple faith. He spoke glibly of the sidelights recently discovered by modern investigation and science, which had somewhat changed the landmarks of historic faith." At the conclusion of the book, Miss Sincere and Widow Faith are last seen entering Heaven: "Standing within the doorway with their guide, they beheld before them a cloud in which shone the glory of the world invisible, and within it were a host of celestial beings, chanting the song of the triumphant."[31] The resemblance of this image to the last chapter of *The Screwtape Letters* will be apparent.

The Temptations

In discussing the human plot of Lewis's book we reduced it to a series of sentences summarizing chapters. Insights into the diabolical world of Screwtape can be gained by applying a similar method. In Chapter I, Screwtape writes to Wormwood, the "patient's" tempter. Thereafter, he expresses anger and promises penalties for Wormwood's performance in letting his patient become a Christian. Glubose, the tempter of the patient's mother, is introduced. Screwtape criticizes Wormwood's ideas. He scolds his nephew and invokes the views of Scabtree, a diabolical theorist. Wormwood, who has inquired, is told to keep himself secret from his patient. The younger tempter mistakenly thinks his man is losing his faith; Screwtape blames Slubgob, head of the Training College. Triptweeze reports that the patient has new worldly friends. Screwtape congratulates Wormwood on this development; he tells him he is making "excellent progress," but when the patient repents, Screwtape blames Wormwood for it.

The senior tempter recommends fear or overconfidence as a new approach. He says Wormwood's record so far is not good: the patient still attends the same church. Screwtape accuses Wormwood of ignorance on the subject of Gluttony, referring to Glubose again. He makes additional slighting remarks about Slubgob, and in the next letter he anxiously insists that he didn't *mean* that God really loves humans or that Slubgob is incompetent, but he tells his nephew to hide his letters anyway. He expresses impatience that God helps defend the patient against attacks on his chastity, and declares that Satan will surely win this soul through conquest. The Secret Police now visit Screwtape after Wormwood has informed on him. When confronted with the patient's newly-met "young woman," a sweet Christian girl, Screwtape becomes so overwrought that he turns into a centipede and is signed for by Toadpipe.

World and Flesh having failed, Screwtape proposes corruption through the spirit. He advises on how to corrupt through the courtship, and wishes that Slumtrimpet, the tempter of the girl, would curb her sense of the ridiculous. Screwtape remarks that Wormwood is doing very little good in his efforts, and insists on reports, not on war itself, but on its effects on the patient. He foresees that Germany will soon bombard the town. When this comes to pass, while Wormwood has enjoyed the bombardment, the Secret Police report on the patient's performance (most unsatisfactory from the diabolical point of view). Screwtape openly warns Wormwood: "Bring us back food or be food yourself." And in Letter XXXI he rapturously and ravenously greets his nephew, because, having lost the patient, he will now become a meal in hell.

The Importance of Names

In the story outline above, we learn the names of eight devils:

Wormwood: the patient's tempter
Screwtape: His Abysmal Sublimity, Under Secretary, T.E., B.S., etc., and Wormwood's uncle
Glubose: the tempter of the patient's mother
Scabtree: a high-ranking diabolical theorist
Slubgob: the head of the Training School

Triptweeze:	who informs upon Wormwood to Screwtape
Toadpipe:	Screwtape's secretary who signs for him when he turns into a centipede
Slumtrimpet:	the tempter of the patient's "young woman"

Lewis's talent for inventing names is richly exercised in these characters: Wormwood's is the only one directly and entirely derived in its precise form not only from nature itself, but from the Bible.

Wormwood is a substance used because of its content of santonin, as a vermifuge (to expel worms), and to give its characteristic flavor to absinthe. Referring to any of the genus *Artemisia*, and in particular to the Eurasian perennial *Artemisia absinthum*, Wormwood is a dark green oil with a bitter taste. In its secondary definition it means any "bitter, unpleasant," or, significantly, "mortifying experience." References to Wormwood—Deuteronomy 29.18, Proverbs 5.4, Jeremiah 9.15, 23.5, Lamentations 3.5, 13, and Amos 5.7—in the Old Testament relate both to the bitterness of it, literally and figuratively, and to its use in intoxicating substances. The Proverbist says of the "strange woman" (a Near Eastern temple prostitute): "her end is bitter as wormwood," and the Lamentations speak of being made "drunken with Wormwood." These are the senses of the famous New Testament image in Revelation 8.11: "And the name of the star is called Wormwood; and many men died of the waters, because they were made bitter." Wormwood, in other words, poisons his patient's mind, or tries to. Perhaps Screwtape's most significant advice is that since God made the pleasures it is the intent of hell to diminish or spoil them: Wormwood is to embitter his patient's simple joys and render all his experiences into wormwood. This is the thrust of the temptations against chastity, in which the object must be a corrupted figure, like the strange woman of Proverbs, for the patient's sexual attraction to his "young woman" only serves God's will. Indeed, this sweetly natural physical attraction is so contrary to Screwtape's wishes that he metamorphoses to a centipede in contemplation of the girl in all her purity.

Wormwood's name also invokes echoes of wood-worm, wormy wood, worminess and woodenness. These suggest images of hidden weakening, of borings from within in old houses, furniture, and artifacts. Old wood is generally full of worm-holes in England,[32] and the wood-worm was a threat in British experience both to the wooden pilings of docks and to the wooden ships that docked there. I cannot agree with Norman Bradshaw (1983) that this choice of name has some special resonance for Lewis because of an obsession he purportedly had with worms, attributed by Bradshaw to Lewis's imagining of the "worm-like action of devouring the body" in the cancer which consumed his mother.[33] Lewis was quite capable of using cancer as an image in itself, as we have seen. One need not be the victim of an obsession to feel the resonance of these images, which are—at least for the literate—a part of the inheritance of Western culture. Not only is the word "Wormwood" deeply fixed in the vocabulary of the Old and New Testament, so too is the concept of the devouring worm, in its spiritual sense. Mark 9.44, 46, and 48 reiterates Christ's terrible refrain upon hell: "where their worm dieth not, and the fire is not quenched." Furthermore, the worm—that is, the maggot which devours carrion—is a symbol of bodily corruption and a reiterated figure in European thought. Both devouring and defiling are ancient operative images of evil, as will be shown below.

The rest of the eight diabolical names are clever portmanteaux, combinations of images of Lewis's own coinage: Screwtape, Glubose, Scabtree, Slubgob, Triptweeze, Toadpipe, and Slumtrimpet. Most of these words have an unpleasant sense—"trip" must refer to tripping up, not taking a trip—and invoke a variety of things people don't like. As Lewis says, "I aimed merely at making them nasty" (ST 12). He elaborates:

I fancy that *Scrooge, screw, thumbscrew, tape-worm,* and *red tape* all do some work in my hero's name, and that *slob, slobber, slubber,* and *gob* have all gone into *Slubgob.* (ST 12)

Following Lewis's method we may suggest the possible association of the other diabolical names:

Glubose:	glue, glucose, glub, verbose
Scabtree:	scab, scabby, tree, crab, scrabble, scabies, crabtree
Triptweeze:	trip, tweezer, tease, tip, teazle, tweeze
Toadpipe:	toad, pipe, peer, tape, toper
Slumtrimpet:	slime, slim, trumpet, slum, trim, trip, scrimp, slip, lump, limpet, slump, limp

Screwtape's infernal titles include two given by initial only—
"T.E., B.S."—for which I suggest Tempter Emeritus and Banished
Spirit as possible meanings which are not ribald. When Screwtape
proposes his toast at the "Annual dinner of the Tempter's Training
College" (under the direction of Dr. Slubgob), he addresses his audi-
ence as "Mr. Principal, your Imminence, your Disgraces, my Thorns,
Shadies, and Gentledevils." The only other specific spiritual beings of
whom we learn the titles are Satan himself: "Our Father Below," and
God, called by Screwtape "the Enemy." But we do learn of a number
of infernal institutions, as befits a bureaucratic hell: "the office," the
Secret Police, the House of Correction for Incompetent Tempters, the
Philological Arm, the Infernal Police, and the Training College. And
hell itself gets two titles: the Miserific Vision, and the Kingdom of
Noise. Appropriately, Screwtape swears by Beelzebub.

On the other hand the names of human subjects are few—in
addition to the Name of Jesus, we read of Paul, Apollos, Maritain,
Hooker, Thomas Aquinas, and Socrates—all eminent warriors who
have forced the infernal forces to take account of them. "Fr. Spike" is
presumably a soubriquet: this is not the *Inferno*, in which Dante
placed everybody he disliked or disapproved of. The human characters who actually appear in the story are not named at all: the patient
(ironically called after the inmate of a hospital or mental institution),
his mother, his young woman, a worldly couple, and a Christian family. Perhaps the "Christian" names of humans are not generally known
to devils, having been given in Baptism in the presence of the Trinity,
which would have been a suffocating cloud of silence to the newly-
assigned tempter. Only in "Screwtape Proposes a Toast" do we learn
the names of any human inmates or friends of hell: Farinata, Henry
VIII, Hitler, Messalina, Casanova, Rousseau, and Hegel. Only Aristotle is mentioned in what we would regard as a favorable sense, and
that twice. Screwtape has to look up everybody in records and dossi-
ers; apparently only an individual tempter is in contact with an individual human: devils are not omnipresent as God is. Screwtape looks
up churches "in the office" where presumably a diabolical file of them
is kept.

Spiritual Realities: Images of the Diabolical

Lewis is at pains to indicate that his infernal subject is spiritual: "You, being a spirit" (ST 120; Ltr. 27), Screwtape writes in one letter to Wormwood. He uses a delicately disguised synonym in the suggestion of spirits. When Wormwood (an agent of one form of liqueur, remember) writes that he is "delirious with joy" over the new war, Screwtape tartly retorts: "You are not delirious; you are only drunk" (ST 36; Ltr. 5). Wormwood has "tasted that wine which is the reward of all our labours—the anguish and bewilderment of a human soul" (ST 36; Ltr. 5). His success with his patient will be rewarded with "a brim-full living chalice of despair and horror and astonishment which you can raise to your lips as often as you please" (ST 36; Ltr. 5). And Screwtape at the infernal banquet notes that a few bottles of the "old sound vintage *Pharisee*" (ST 156) have been preserved, with its mingled flavor of "Dark fire" (ST 157). The reference to a toast (an offering of wine) reminds us that wine in other hands is an element of the sacrament, but the life-blood *it* contains is divine and is partaken by a human soul, not the other way around as in hell's inverted parody.

Hiddenness, a trait of the spiritual, is to be sought by devils: "Our policy, for the moment, is to conceal ourselves" (ST 42; Ltr. 7). Indeed, "If any faint suspicion of your existence begins to arise in his mind, suggest to him a picture of something in red tights, and persuade him that since he cannot believe in that [...] he therefore cannot believe you" (ST 42-43; Ltr. 7). The laughter aroused by this image is of course not a pleasant sound; laughter is "disgusting and a direct insult to the realism, dignity, and austerity of Hell" (ST 56; Ltr. 11). Screwtape is offended by the patient's young woman because she is "the sort of creature who'd find ME funny!" (ST 99; Ltr. 22). The hiddenness of the diabolical world may be an imitation of their blinded perception of the Divine: Grace is experienced by them as "the asphyxiating cloud which prevented your attacking the patient on his walk from the old mill" (ST 63; Ltr. 13). When the soul of his patient slips away from him into the Presence of God, "You reeled back dizzy and blinded" (ST 136; Ltr. 31)—but "what is blinding, suffocating fire to you, is now cool light to him [...] and wears the form of a Man" (ST 137; Ltr. 31).

The bureaucratic image, of a nether hierarchy, or as Lewis reverses it, "Lowerarchy," receding downwards in reflection of the upward-seeking altitudes of Heaven, is drawn in part from Dante's *Commedia Divina*, but the modern touches are Lewis's own. Hell seems to be an institution devoted to data: what fun Lewis could have had with the idea of an infernal computer! In the effort to understand what the Enemy (God) is *really* up to, "more and more complicated theories, fuller and fuller collections of data, richer rewards for researchers who make progress, more and more terrible punishments" (ST 88; Ltr. 19) for failure are needed. Is there an academic of the eighties who has not already visited these halls? Certainly, this bureaucratic nightmare will be a familiar habitat to many of its inmates; of those who care more for "meetings, pamphlets, policies, movements, causes, and crusades" than for "prayers and sacraments and charity" (ST 34; Ltr. 7), Screwtape says "I could show you a pretty cageful down here" (ST 45; Ltr. 7).

The end of all the endeavors of hell is two-fold: first, "Our war aim is a world in which Our Father Below has drawn all other beings into himself" (ST 47; Ltr. 8). This is a perversion of the saying of Jesus, "I, if I be lifted up, from the earth, will draw all men unto me" (John 12.32). When people are drawn unto Jesus they find themselves members of the Church which is His Body, a One which is nonetheless many. If every being were drawn *into* Satan there would be only one being, because he would have eaten all the others. The second end is to comprehend the purposes of God, which though rejected by Satan nonetheless preoccupies him. Indeed, "if we ever came to understand what He means by Love, the war would be over and we should re-enter Heaven" (ST 88; Ltr. 19). To gain this end, or rather, to find out what God is *really* up to, since Screwtape declares that "He cannot really love: nobody can" (ST 88: Ltr. 19); the Lowerarchy labors to produce its complicated theories. And they imagine that God for His part hasn't "the least inkling of that high and austere mystery to which we rise in the Miserific Vision" (ST 100; Ltr. 22), the vision being the intention of Satan to absorb all things into himself. As Lewis puts it, "His dream is of the day when all shall be inside him and all that says 'I' can say it only through him" (ST 10).

The suggestion above that an understanding of God's true purpose would return the fallen angels to Heaven is the one clear spot in his cloudy vision. The idea that even fallen demons can be redeemed seems to be a peculiarly Anglican notion. Roger Lloyd, in his Christian fantasy *The Troubling of the City* (1962) depicts the archdemon Vitrios of the Select College of dark spirits (surely modeled after Lewis's creation). He is sent to earth in human form (causing him to feel "diminished" and "chafed").[34] With the aid of the familiar demons of Winchester—mandrill, Vilifor, Snirtle, and Sloombane—and a group of vivified gargoyles, he attempts to subvert the city. At the climax of the book there is a confrontation of St. Swithun and these adversaries at Winchester Cathedral. First, a gargoyle repents and is forgiven: "As he stood there, the scarred stone body, the mis-shapen face, the broken nose, the scornful eyes all seemed to be peeled from him, like a dirty scab from a healed cut."[35] This image must be modeled upon the climactic freeing of Wormwood's patient from his diabolical infestation, "as if a scab had fallen from an old sore" (ST 172). Then Vilifor, an "original fient"—one of the company of angels who fell from Heaven along with Lucifer—steps forward. He repents of "the supreme sin of rebellion,"[36] and, quickening, transfiguring as he goes, he runs into the outstretched arms of "the Christ of the great reredos"[37] which gather him into "enfolding light." This, too, echoes Lewis's image of the encounter of Wormwood's patient with "Him," the "cool light" which "wears the form of a Man." Lloyd has transferred the image of a saved soul to the image of saved demon, a risky but attractive conjecture to those (like George MacDonald) with a taste for Universalism.

As Lewis himself has suggested, his images of the diabolical are drawn from the wellsprings of Western culture despite his use of modern dress (or more accurately, modern organizational technique and modern technology). In his study of mythology devoted to *The Powers of Evil* (1975), Richard Cavendish lists three major supernatural beings associated with evil: the Devil, Death, and Fate. Motifs used in expressing the evils include "the connection between evil and the animal world, for instance, the dread of being devoured, the contradictory attitudes to the dead, the links between death, evil, and sex, the fear of disorder, [and] the refusal to believe in chance."[38] From this list, Lewis had chosen only two. The first is his use of one animal motif, the centipede. In contemplating the patient's "young woman," Screwtape writes (via his secretary) that "I find I have inadvertently allowed myself to assume the form of a large centipede" (ST 101; Ltr. 22). Lewis indeed made use of a personal obsessive fear.

The image is given full force in *Perelandra* (1943). As Ransom confronts the Un-man for the final time, his adversary, crawling out of a hole, is followed by "a huge, many legged, quivering deformity"—described in horrible detail and containing every feature that is detestably insectile. When the Un-man dies, this apparition is rendered merely an "animated corridor train." Lewis says "All that he had felt from childhood about insects and reptiles died that moment" (PER 154; ch. 14). This passage was an exorcism for Lewis of his own childhood "insect fears," first evoked by a nursery book illustration of Tom Thumb threatened by a stag beetle with a moveable mandible, as he tells us in *Surprised by Joy*.[39] In *The Silver Chair* (1953) the centipede of *The Screwtape Letters* (1942) recurs: on reaching the domain of the Green Witch, the children and their guide confront a huge bow-shaped bridge, richly carved with "mouldering faces and forms of giants, minotaurs, squids, centipedes, and dreadful gods" (SC 86; ch. Ch. 6).

As Cavendish has suggested, it is not the animal form per se that creates revulsion, but the idea of metamorphosis. The human turned cockroach of Franz Kafka's story is a well-known example. Screwtape himself hints at a Miltonic source for his experience: in Book X, ll. 505-546 of *Paradise Lost*, the assembled demons metamorphose into serpents and thus greet Satan with unexpected hisses:

> A greater power
> Now rul'd him, punisht in the shape he sinn'd,
> According to his doom. (ll.515-517)

What sins Screwtape has committed in the shape of a centipede, we are not told, and perhaps do not wish to enquire!

The second motif used by Lewis from Cavendish's catalogue of mythological evils is the fear of being devoured. Cavendish chronicles a number of these images: the vultures of Catal Huyuk (before 6000 BCE) who are accompanied by headless corpses; Am-mut, the "eater of the dead" and Baba the "Eater of Shades" from ancient Egypt, and a Coptic Christian hell with a ditch of seven-headed scorpions and a giant snake which "chewed on the dead five days a week [... but] took the weekend off"[40] (suggesting the refrigerium depicted

221

by Lewis in *The Great Divorce*). The Delphic demon Eurynomus ate the flesh of corpses, and Hesiod's Tartarus, a "gigantic yawning throat," received the descending dead,[41] while various earthly giants and ogres (including Polyphemus) eat people in Greek mythology as they do in that of other branch of Indo-european peoples, the Norse, from which Lewis drew many of his images in the Narnian chronicles.

Hell, too, with its yawning hell-mouth[42] so commonly depicted in medieval drama and the art derived from it, and the Devil himself, as "a huge, devouring monster," partake of this image. Indeed at the nethermost pit of hell, frozen in the icy sea, Dante's Satan forever devours (with the mouths of his three heads) three archetypal traitors including Judas. Cavendish even quotes a secular image from Carlyle's *Sartor Resartus*: the universe itself is perceived as "the boundless jaws of a devouring Monster, wherein I, palpitating, waited to be devoured."[43]

In his use of this very image in *The Screwtape Letters*, Lewis is perfectly clear: Screwtape says to Wormwood: "Bring us back food, or be food yourself" (ST 131; Ltr. 30). The event is depicted entirely in spiritual terms: that is, we read of the hungry anticipation of one spirit as he prepares to devour another. Screwtape, having addressed Wormwood as "My dear, my very dear, Wormwood, my poppet, my pigsnie" (that is, my delicious bitter drink, my doll, my pixie), announces, "I think they will give you to me now; or a bit of you. Love you? Why, yes. As dainty as morsel as even I grew fat on." Lewis, of course, knew perfectly well what he was doing. He wrote in his Preface of 1961: "I feign that devils can, in a spiritual sense, eat one another; and us. Even in human life we have seen the passion to dominate, almost to digest, one's fellow; to make his own intellectual and emotional life merely an extension of one's own—to hate one's hatreds and resent one's grievances and indulge one's egotism through him as well as through oneself" (ST 10). There is evidence that some of Lewis's students in the late 1930s thought that he was trying to do this to them! He continues, "On earth this desire is often called 'love'. In Hell I feign that they recognise it as hunger" (ST 10).

As I have hinted above, this theme of devouring has an awful and macabre application often expressed in the figure of the devouring worm. I wish I could write that today most people are only familiar with the action of maggots upon carrion through experiences like my childhood examination of a dead bird, in which I made the horrified discovery of the cheerfully active "worm"-life within. Unfortunately, many people in today's world understand well enough the effect, through the production of corpses left for discovery by various malignant and warring states. Maggots are not, strictly speaking, worms, but infant flies, which offer carrion the same service they offer excrement. Beelzebub, the only historical devilish name invoked by Screwtape, means "the Lord of the Flies," and works of literature from Golding's novel of that name to studies of the *Amityville Horror* have exploited this fact.

Consumption by worms is a natural figure reiterated in the Bible: In Exodus 16.24 manna kept too long against God's wish "bred worms," and in Deuteronomy 28.39, vineyard keepers are warned that they shall plant but never drink of these grapes, "for the worms shall eat them." These images, of corrupted bread and wine, as it were, are followed by more solemn pictures: Job, presumably describing the nastier results of gangrene, complains that "my flesh is clothed with worms" (Job 7.5) and the action of moth larvae is not neglected: Isaiah 51.8 says of those opposed to his hearers that worms "shall eat them like wool." Specific images of maggots consuming the dead appear in Job, including the ironic phrase, "the worm shall feed sweetly on him" (Job 24.29). God prepares a worm to smite the gourd giving shade to Jonah (Jonah 4.7) and Herodis "eaten of worms" in Acts 12.23. But these are all natural images which occur every day and are but one part of the characteristic honesty and openness about natural phenomena which makes the Bible the vigorous document that it is.

It is the supernatural image not of bodily death but of spiritual death which Screwtape depicts. As Jesus says in Matthew 10.28—"fear not them which kill the body, but are not able to kill the soul but rather fear him which is able to destroy both body and soul in hell." This is Screwtape's wish.

Probably the most important study of my subject is Paul Ricoeur's *The Symbolism of Evil* (1967). Ricoeur proposes a theme not mentioned by Cavendish, which is a third major image in *The Screwtape Letters*. This is the symbolism of "defilement," which Ricoeur calls one of the "Primary Symbols." The Old Testament begins its discussion of evil with symbols: "the preferred language of fault appears to be indirect and based on imagery."[44] Ricoeur states, "Sin, as alienation from oneself, is an experience even more astonishing, disconcerting, and scandalous, perhaps, than the spectacle of nature, and for this reason it is the richest source of interrogative thought."[45] In this long-lasting sequence of questions, the idea of defilement is more archaic than the idea of sin. Defilement is "spoken of under the symbol of a stain or blemish."[46] It is "the idea of a quasi-material something that infects as a sort of filth, that harms by invisible properties, and that nevertheless works in the manner of a force in the field of our undividedly psychic and corporal existence."[47] Ritual washing of hands or feet in Judaism, Christianity, and Islam, together with the washing away of sins in Baptism, are based upon this primitive viewpoint. Ricoeur suggests that we feel we have left this concept behind,[48] but that in the area of sex it is still functional: sex is considered the "primordial defilement."[49] Even so, it is a *symbolic* stain: "Defilement is not a stain, but like a stain."[50]

Lewis uses this image, and one of its related motifs, in the climactic scene of *The Screwtape Letters*, as Screwtape describes the saved soul's release from Wormwood.

> Just think (and let it be the beginning of your agony) what he felt at that moment; as if a scab had fallen from an old sore, as if he were emerging from a hideous, shell-like tetter, as if he shuffled off for good and all a defiled, wet, clinging garment. By Hell, it is misery enough to see them in their mortal days taking off dirtied and uncomfortable clothes and splashing in hot water and giving little grunts of pleasure—stretching their eased limbs! What, then, at this final stripping, this complete cleansing? (ST 135; Ltr. 31)

The ruling image here is of defilement by mud or bodily excretions, but there is the addition of the image of the scab (injury) and the tetter (skin disease): one thinks of poor Job sitting upon his dungheap and scratching his afflicted skin with a potsherd! The commonplace phrase, "raddled whore," which Lewis uses in the same chapter, is based on the sores caused by venereal disease, but any skin disease was a figure of defilement in the Bible, especially the forms of psoriasis and other diseases lumped together as the whiteness of "leprosy" in both Testaments.

The image of defilement is given a final expression in *The Screwtape Letters* as Lewis introduces his famous hint of the possibility of Purgatory, which he was to express even more clearly in *The Great Divorce*. Michael Paternoster in his study of the afterlife, *Thou Art There Also* (1967) makes considerable use of quotations from C.S. Lewis, and of *The Screwtape Letters*: "the tempter says of the victim who has escaped: 'Pains he may still have to encounter, but they *embrace* those pains.'"[51] He regards Lewis as an example of "Modern popular religious writers" who seem to take the doctrine of Purgatory "for granted."[52] Lewis was to use the figures of Purgatory as the cleansing of defilement with vigor in other places, but his mention of it following his paean to final cleanliness is powerfully suggestive.

Spiritual Realities: The Psychic Realm

So far we have addressed these images as depictions of spiritual reality; as Lewis says in his Preface to later editions, "this is all only myth and symbol" (ST 11). One aspect of the spiritual realm must be its role in psychic reality, the contents of the human mind. In the human psyche, as described by Sanford, a Christian writer who uses the categories of C.G. Jung, there are a number of forces short of absolute or totally personified Evil, which must be dealt with. Most important is the Old Testament adversary of Job, a created being who, because God has made him precisely for the purpose which he performs, apparently shows the "dark side of God," who comes to humans as an "adversary" or "dark power" which may be destructive but "cannot be said to be intrinsically evil."[53] This idea can be found in the writings of George MacDonald and Charles Williams, both of whom influenced Lewis. This is not a God who is really a devil, or a devil who is really a God. This is the action of God who, like a surgeon must wound in order to heal.

An idea related to this but not the same, is the "happy fault," the *felix culpa*—the evil depicted in the Gospels which is sent by God to "some Divine Purpose." Jesus predicts woe for the perpetrators of such evil, but while this "evil is really evil, there is nevertheless an overriding Purpose, which it must serve."[54] The primary image in this category is, of course, the Resurrection as the result of the Crucifixion.

Again, there is "the human Shadow," an aspect of the personality which seems to act out evil when split from the whole, but which can be made conscious and lose its satanic character. In Jungian thought, the Shadow is the part of one's own personality which one dare not or cannot see, those traits which appear "dark" because we do not know we have them. They are a figure for the invisibility or the cloak of darkness which shrouds the entire unconscious from us, and when we begin to come to terms with this adversary, we can begin to "see" what has been hidden before.

In another sense, the devil image can be understood as "a personification of the power drive of the ego." This, too, turns out to be a force of the personality which may be necessary for ego differentiation. (In Jungian thought the Ego is not the center of personality but one aspect of it.) Finally, "the devil becomes a kind of collective shadow figure [...] whose darkness compensates a too rigid and one-sided conscious attitude."[55] All of these elements are relative, apparent evils, not true evil.

But Sanford does not deny the existence of evil. He turns to the doctrine of the *privatio boni* suggested by Aristotle and favored by Origen, Augustine, Aquinas, and, indeed, by C.S. Lewis. In Sanford's words: "The basic idea of the doctrine [...] is that good alone has substance, and that evil has no substance of its own, but exists by means of a diminution of the good."[56] Jung seems to have thought that the origin of evil would have to be sought in God Himself, and that the Christian idea of a God who is solely good is too one-sided. Sanford sets forth the objection of Jung to the doctrine of *privatio boni*, and, in the true spirit of a Jungian disciple, argues with his teacher in "A Critique of Jung's View of the Privatio Boni." Sanford defines evil thus: "We can say that intrinsic evil is a force of destructiveness that destroys wholeness."[57] He defends the *privatio boni* as a doctrine which affirms both the reality of evil and the ultimate power of God, and concludes by emphasizing the "basic optimism in the Christian attitude toward evil."[58]

The concept of evil as a diminution of, or a corruption of good, is made clear in *The Screwtape Letters*. As Screwtape says, "No natural phenomenon is really in our favour" (ST 74; Ltr. 15) and "Nothing is naturally on our side." Indeed, "Everything has to be *twisted* before it's any use to us (ST 100; Ltr. 22)." Even the organization of hell is a parody of Heaven, and the tempter an inverted version of the guardian angel. Only at the end of *The Screwtape Letters* does Screwtape admit the presence of angelic adversaries: as the patient died, "he also saw Them" (ST 136; Ltr. 31).

But there is a further application of this doctrine, which is reflected in George MacDonald's declaration in *Weighed and Wanting* (1882): "He who is parted from God has no original nothingness with which to take refuge. He is a live discord, an anti-truth. He is a death fighting against life."[59] In the early 1960s a brilliant addition was made to the theology of evil by Brother Dunstan Jones of the Anglican religious order, the Community of the Resurrection, in his essay, "Creation and the Fall." He begins by suggesting that the Fall is related to Creation not as a single event perpetuated, through Satan, in humankind, but begins much earlier in the process revealed by the fossil record. He finds a specific motif which runs through the Bible—"*Creation through conflict.*"[60] Discussing this idea and its Near Eastern mythological antecedents, he links it with creation out of "nothing,"[61] an idea which is the invention of Judaism.

In Jewish thought, the Creation is revealed by God as being *ex nihlio*. When, then, comes the Fall? Not only humankind, but the entire Creation suffers in the creation process, which when apprehended in time, is on-going. The corruption is not based in materiality, for everything made by God is good (Genesis 1.31). Even the corrupt spirits began as good, since God made them too. But Creation is not a "point in time," to use a current barbarism—it is an event outside of time and hence ever-present. All resistance to God is resistance to creation *sub specie aeternitatis*—"If then the world or some of its parts resist their creation, they resist their creation in the timeless acts of their being created."[62] This resistance takes the form of "the determination to un-be." Brother Dunstan continues: "Sin then is basically the determination to resist creation [...] This rebellion in its fullness we attribute to spiritual creatures."[63] Indeed, "God's perfect intention for the creation is not attained except by overcoming the resistance of some creatures to their own creation and their corrupting of the rest of creation through this resistance."[64]

It is the spiritual effort to break the will to be in a single human that is depicted in *The Screwtape Letters*. When this effort is overcome, the soul "could stand upright and converse with spirits before whom you, a spirit, could only cower" (ST 136; Ltr. 31), Screw-tape angrily tells Wormwood. The soul has faced death and in dying it has become a free citizen of Heaven.

Notes

[1] Dorothy L. Sayers, "The Other Six Deadly Sins," *The Whimsical Christian* (New York: Macmillan, 1978) 158.

[2] Sayers, "The Other Six Deadly Sins" 159.

[3] Sayers, "The Other Six Deadly Sins" 176.

[4] Sayers, "The Other Six Deadly Sins" 177.

[5] C.S. Lewis, *A Preface to Paradise Lost* (1942; London: Oxford UP, 1961) 100.

[6] C.S. Lewis, *They Stand Together*, ed. Walter Hooper (London: Collins, 1979) 123.

[7] C.S. Lewis, *They Stand Together* 151.

[8] W.H. Lewis, *Brothers and Friends*, ed. Clyde S. Kilby and Marjorie Lamp Mead (San Francisco: Harper and Row, 1982) 188.

[9] George MacDonald, "Preface" to *Letters From Hell* by Waldemar Adolph Thisted (New York and London: Funk and Wagnalls, 1885) with a Preface by George MacDonald, vi-vii. I am happy to say that I found this book at jumble sale myself!

[10] Michael Paternoster, *Thou Art There Also* (London: SPCK, 1967) 127-28.

[11] Jeffrey Burton Russell, *The Devil* (1977; New York: Meridian, 1979) 17.

[12] Diana Waggoner, *The Hills of Faraway* (New York: Meridian, 1979) 63.

[13] Russell, *The Devil* 34.

[14] Russell, *The Devil* 35.

[15] John A. Sanford, *Evil: The Shadow Side of Reality* (New York: Crossroad, 1981) 36.

[16] Sanford 36.

[17] Sanford 37.

[18] C.S. Lewis, *A Preface to Paradise Lost* 95.

[19] C.S. Lewis, *A Preface to Paradise Lost* 95.

[20] C.S. Lewis, *A Preface to Paradise Lost* 96.

Notes

[21] Charles Williams, "John Milton," *The Image of the City*, ed. Anne Ridler (London: Oxford UP, 1958) 28.

[22] Williams "John Milton" 30.

[23] Williams "John Milton" 30.

[24] C.S. Lewis, *A Preface to Paradise Lost* 99.

[25] W.S. Harris, *Sermons by the Devil* (Elkhart, IN: Mennonite Publishing, 1904) 3. Also found in a jumble sale!

[26] Harris, *Sermons by the Devil* 92.

[27] Harris, *Sermons by the Devil* 247.

[28] Harris, *Sermons by the Devil* 257.

[29] J. R. Miller, *The Devil of Today* (no loc: publisher unknown, 1903/06) 41. This book was lent to me by Jane Urquhart, and is gratefully acknowledged. Editor's note: The author indicated here is evidently the Christian author James Russell Miller (1840–1912). He wrote numerous books, but I have been unable to locate this one, thus the references given to it here are unverified.

[30] Miller, *The Devil of Today* 242.

[31] Miller, *The Devil of Today* 454.

[32] And in Canada: during the writing of this paper, the table being used was unexpectedly discovered to be undergoing attack by a colony of woodworms.

[33] Norman Bradshaw, "The Extraordinary Being," *The Canadian C.S. Lewis Journal* (Spring 1983): 12. As for Bradshaw's assertion that "an obsession with 'the vermicular' […] and 'the Worm' […] was hammered home so persistently, in both 'Screwtape' books" (12), I searched *The Screwtape Letters* for the word "worm" outside of Wormwood's name, and could not find it.

[34] Roger Lloyd, *The Troubling of the City* (London: George Allen and Unwin, 1962) 15.

[35] Lloyd, *The Troubling of the City* 206.

[36] Lloyd, *The Troubling of the City* 208.

[37] Lloyd, *The Troubling of the City* 211.

[38] Richard Cavendish, *The Powers of Evil* (London: Routledge and Kegan Paul, 1975) viii.

[39] C.S. Lewis *Surprised by Joy* (1955; New York: Harcourt, Brace Jovanovich, 1966) 9.

Notes

[40] Cavendish, *The Powers of Evil* 112-13.

[41] Cavendish, *The Powers of Evil* 116.

[42] Cavendish, *The Powers of Evil* 156.

[43] Cavendish, *The Powers of Evil* 157.

[44] Paul Ricoeur, *The Symbolism of Evil* (Boston, MA: Beacon Press, 1967) 9.

[45] Ricoeur, *The Symbolism of Evil* 8.

[46] Ricoeur, *The Symbolism of Evil* 9.

[47] Ricoeur, *The Symbolism of Evil* 25-26.

[48] Ricoeur, *The Symbolism of Evil* 26.

[49] Ricoeur, *The Symbolism of Evil* 29.

[50] Ricoeur, *The Symbolism of Evil* 36.

[51] Paternoster 64; quotation from ST 137; Ltr. 31.

[52] Paternoster 64.

[53] Sanford, *Evil* 126.

[54] Sanford, *Evil* 127.

[55] Sanford, *Evil* 127.

[56] Sanford, *Evil* 135.

[57] Sanford, *Evil* 145.

[58] Sanford, *Evil* 151.

[59] Quoted from Chapter 35 of George MacDonald, *Weighed and Wanting* (1882) in Rolland Hein, *The Harmony Within* (Grand Rapids, MI: Eerdmans, 1982) 47 note 3.

[60] Dunstan Jones, "Creation and the Fall," *Mirfield Essays in Christian Belief* (London: The Faith Press, 1962) 125.

[61] Jones, "Creation and the Fall" 125.

[62] Jones, "Creation and the Fall" 136.

[63] Jones, "Creation and the Fall" 137.

[64] Jones, "Creation and the Fall" 138.

Bibliography

Alpers, Paul J. *The Poetry of the Faerie Queene*. Princeton, NJ: Princeton UP, 1967.

Andersen, Hans Christian. *The Snow Queen*. 1844. Gutenberg ebook # 442.

Baltazar, Eulalio P. *The Dark Center: A Process Theology of Blackness*. New York: Paulist Press, 1973.

Begg, Ean. *The Cult of the Black Virgin*. London: Routledge and Kegan Paul [Arkana], 1985.

Blount, Margaret. *Animal-Land*. New York: Avon, 1977.

Bradley, Ian. *God is Green: Ecology for Christians*. Toronto, ON: Image/Doubleday, 1992.

Bradshaw, Norman. "The Extraordinary Being." *The Canadian C.S. Lewis Journal* (Spring 1983): 1-16.

Brady, Charles A. *America* (27 October 1956). Cited in Walter Hooper. *C.S. Lewis, A Companion and Guide*. London: HarperCollins, 1996.

Briffault, Robert. *The Mothers*. New York: Atheneum, 1977.

Briggs, Katherine. *A Dictionary of Faeries*. London: Allen Lane, 1976.

Caplan, Lionel. "The Popular Culture of Evil in Urban South India. *The Anthropology of Evil*. Ed. David Parkin. Oxford: Basil Blackwell, 1985. 110-27.

Carnell, Corbin Scott. *Bright Shadow of Reality: C.S. Lewis and the Feeling Intellect*. Grand Rapids, MI: William B. Eerdmans, 1974.

Castaneda, Carlos. *The Teachings of Don Juan, a Yaqui Way of Knowledge*. New York: Ballantine, 1968.

Cavendish, Richard. *The Powers of Evil*. London: Routledge and Kegan Paul, 1975.

Chadwick, Nora. *The Celts*. Harmondworth, UK: Penguin, 1970.

Cirlot, J.E. *A Dictionary of Symbols*. New York: Philosophical Library, 1962.

Coleman, Simon, and John Elsner. *Pilgrimage Past and Present: Sacred Travel and Sacred Space in the World Religions.* London: British Museum Press; and Cambridge, MA: Harvard UP, 1995.

Cosman, Madeleine P. *Medieval Holidays and Festivals*. New York: Charles Scribners and Sons, 1981.

Cox, John D. "Epistemological Release in *The Silver Chair.* " *The Longing for a Form: Essays on the Fiction of C.S. Lewis*. Ed. Peter J. Schakel. Kent, OH: Kent State UP, 1977. 159-70.

Cunningham, Richard B. *C.S. Lewis, Defender of the Faith*. Philadelphia, PA: Westminster Press, 1967.

Dante Alighieri. *The Divine Comedy of Dante Alighieri, The Florentine. Cantica I, Hell*. Trans. Dorothy L. Sayers. Harmondsworth, UK: Penguin, 1949.

Davidson, H. R. Ellis. *Gods and Myths of Northern Europe.* Harmondsworth, UK: Penguin, 1964.

—— *Scandinavian Mythology*. London: Hamlyn, 1969.

Donaldson, Mara E. *Holy Places are Dark Places: C.S. Lewis and Paul Ricoeur on Narrative Transformation*. Lanham, MD: University Press of America, 1988.

Downing, Christine. *The Goddess: Mythological Images of the Feminine*. New York: Crossroads, 1981.

Dumezil, Georges. *Gods of the Ancient Northmen*. Berkeley, CA: University of California Press, 1973.

The Elder Edda. Trans. Paul B. Taylor and W.H. Auden. New York: Viking Books, 1970.

Eliade, Mircea. *The Sacred and the Profane*. 1957. New York: A Harvest Book, Harcourt, Brace & World, Inc., 1959.

—— *Shamanism: Archaic Techniques of Ecstasy*. Princeton, NJ: Bollingen Foundation, Princeton UP, 1970.

Eliot, T.S. *Four Quartets*. London: Faber and Faber, 1959.

232

Fanon, Frantz. *Black Skin, White Masks.* 1952. English trans. New York: Grove Press, 2008.

Ferguson, George. *Signs and Symbols in Christian Art.* New York: Oxford UP, 1954.

Ford, Paul F. *Companion to Narnia.* San Francisco, CA: Harper and Row, 1980.

Foster, Robert. *Tolkien's World from A to Z: The Complete Guide to Middle-Earth.* 1971. Revised and Expanded Edition. New York: Random House, 1978.

Friedrich, Paul. *The Meaning of Aphrodite.* Chicago: University of Chicago Press, 1978.

Galland, China. *Longing for Darkness: Tara and the Black Madonna.* New York: Penguin, 1990.

Gibbons, Stella. "Imaginative Writing." *Light on C.S. Lewis.* Ed. Jocelyn Gibb. London: Geoffrey Bles, 1965. 86-101.

Gimbutas, Marija. *The Goddesses and Gods of Old Europe 6500-3500 BC.* Berkeley, CA: University of California Press, 1982.

—— *The Language of the Goddess.* San Francisco, CA: Harper and Row, 1989.

Glover, Donald E. *C.S. Lewis: The Art of Enchantment.* Athens, OH: Ohio UP, 1981.

Goldsmith, Barbara. *Little Gloria; Happy at Last.* New York: Dell, 1981.

GoodKnight, Glen. "Lilith in Narnia." *Narnia Conference Proceedings.* 1969. Ed. Glen Goodknight. Los Angeles, CA: The Mythopoeic Society, 1970. 15-19.

Goody, Jack. *The Culture of Flowers.* Cambridge: Cambridge UP, 1993.

Gould, Stephen Jay. *Time's Arrow, Time's Cycle.* Cambridge, MA: Harvard UP, 1987.

Green, Roger Lancelyn and Walter Hooper. *C.S. Lewis, A Biography.* London: Collins, 1974.

Hansen, Harold A. *The Witches Garden.* Santa Cruz, CA: Unity Press, 1978.

Harris, W.S. *Sermons by the Devil*. Elkhart, IN: Mennonite Publishing, 1904.

Harrison, Jane. *Prolegomena the Study of Greek Religion*. First Edition 1903. London: Merlin Press, 1962.

Harvey, John. *Medieval Gardens*. Beaverton, OR: Timber Press, 1981.

Hein, Rolland. *The Harmony Within*. Grand Rapids, MI: Eerdmans, 1982.

Henderson, Philip. *William Morris: His Life, Work and Friends.* London: Thames and Hudson, 1967.

Herbert, J. "Hindu Mythology." *Larousse World Mythology*. Ed. Pierre Grimal. London: Hamlyn, 1965.

Hilen, Andres. *Longfellow and Scandinavia, A Study of the Poet's Relationship with the Northern Languages and Literature*. New Haven, CT: Yale UP, 1947. Yale Studies in English 107. Archon Books, 1970.

Holyer, Robert. "The Epistemology of C.S. Lewis's *Till We Have Faces*." *Anglican Theological Review* 70.3 (July 1988): 233-55.

Howard, Thomas. *The Achievement of C.S. Lewis.* Wheaton, IL: Harold Shaw, 1988.

Huxley, Aldous. *The Doors of Perception and Heaven and Hell.* 1954. Harmondsworth, UK: Penguin, 1959.

Jacob, Dorothy. *A Witch's Guide to Gardening*. New York: Taplinger, 1964.

James, E.O. *Seasonal Feasts and Fasts*. London: Thames and Hudson, 1961.

Johnson, Buffie. *Lady of the Beasts: Ancient Images of the Goddess and Her Sacred Animals*. New York: Harper & Row, 1988.

Jones, Dunstan. "Creation and the Fall." *Mirfield Essays in Christian Belief.* London: The Faith Press, 1962.

Jung, C.G. "The Phenomenology of the Spirit in Fairy Tales." *The Archetypes and the Collective Unconscious*. 2nd Edition. CW. Princeton, NJ: Princeton UP, 1968. 207-54.

Karkainen. Paul A. *Narnia Explored*. Old Tappan, NJ: Fleming H. Revell, 1979.

Kerenyi, Karl. *Goddesses of the Sun and Moon*. Irving, TX: Spring Publications, 1979.

Kilby, Clyde S. *The Christian World of C.S. Lewis*. Grand Rapids, MI: Wm. B. Eerdmans, 1964.

Kramer, Samuel Noah. *Mythologies of the Ancient World*. Garden City, NY: Anchor Books, 1961.

—— *Sumerian Mythology*. Philadelphia, PA: University of Pennsylvania Press, 1969.

Larson, Gerald James, Pratapaditya Pal, and Rebecca P. Gowan. *In Her Image*. Santa Barbara, CA: University of California Press, 1980.

Laski, Marghanita. *Ecstasy, A Study of Some Sacred and Religious Experiences*. London: The Cresset Press, 1961.

Laurent, John. "C.S. Lewis and Animal Rights." *Mythlore* 19.1 (Winter 1993): 46-50.

Laurentin, Rene. *Bernadette of Lourdes*. Minneapolis, MN: Winston Press, 1979.

Levy, G.R. *The Gate of Horn*. London: Faber and Faber, 1948.

Lewis, C.S. *The Allegory of Love*. 1936. New York: Oxford UP, 1958.

—— *All My Road Before Me: The Diary of C.S. Lewis, 1922-1927*. Ed. Walter Hooper. London: HarperCollins, 1991.

—— *A Preface to Paradise Lost*. 1942. London: Oxford UP, 1961.

—— *The Discarded Image: An Introduction to Medieval and Renaissance Literature*. Cambridge: Cambridge UP, 1964.

—— *The Four Loves*. London: Geoffrey Bles, 1960.

—— *The Great Divorce*. London: Geoffrey Bles, 1946.

—— *Letters to Malcolm, Chiefly on Prayer*. 1963. New York: Harcourt, 2002.

—— *Mere Christianity: A Revised and Amplified Edition*. 1952. HarperSanFrancisco, 2001.

—— *Miracles: A Preliminary Study*. 1947. London: HarperCollins, 2001.

—— *Of Other Worlds*. "On Three Ways of Writing for Children. Ed. Walter Hooper. New York: Harcourt Brace Jovanovich, 1966. 22-34.

—— "On Living in an Atomic Age." *Present Concerns*. London: Collins/ Fount, 1986.

—— *The Pilgrim's Regress*. 1933. Grand Rapids, MI: William B. Erdmans, 1981.

—— *Poems*. London: Geoffrey Bles, 1964.

—— *The Problem of Pain*. London: Geoffrey Bles, 1940.

—— *Spenser's Images of Life*. Cambridge: Cambridge UP, 1967.

—— *Spirits in Bondage: A Cycle of Lyrics*. 1919. London: Harcourt Brace Jovanovich, 1984.

—— *Studies in Medieval and Renaissance Literature*. Collected by Walter Hooper. Cambridge: Cambridge UP, 1966.

—— *Surprised by Joy: The Shape of My Early Life*. 1955. New York: Harcourt, Brace, Jovanovich, 1966.

—— *They Stand Together: The Letters of C.S. Lewis to Arthur Greeves 1914-1963*. Ed. Walter Hooper. London: Collins, 1979.

—— "The Weight of Glory." *They Asked for a Paper*. London: Geoffrey Bles, 1962.

—— "William Morris" (1939). *Selected Literary Essays*. Ed. Walter Hooper. Cambridge: Cambridge UP, 1969. 219-31. Reprinted from C.S. Lewis, *Rehabilitations and Other Essays*. London: Oxford UP, 1939.

—— "Williams and the Arthuriad." *Arthurian Torso*. London: Oxford UP, 1948. 93-200.

—— *The World's Last Night and Other Essays*. New York: Harcourt, 1960.

Lewis, W.H. *Brothers and Friends*. Eds. Clyde S. Kilby and Marjorie Lamp Mead. San Francisco, CA: Harper and Row, 1982.

Lindholm, Dan. *Stave Churches in Norway*. London: Rudolf Steiner Press, 1969.

Lloyd, Roger. *The Troubling of the City*. London: George Allen and Unwin, 1962.

Lommel, Andreas. *Prehistoric and Primitive Man*. New York: McGraw-Hill, 1966.

Longfellow, Henry Wadsworth. Rev. "Frithior's Saga (The Legend of Frithiof) by Esaias Tegnér." *The North American Review* 45.96 (July 1837): 149-85.

The Mabinogion. Trans. Lady Charlotte Guest. John Jones, Cardiff, 1977.

MacDonald, George. *At the Back of the North Wind*. 1868. Gutenberg ebook #225.

—— "Preface." Waldemar Adolph Thisted by *Letters From Hell*. New York and London: Funk and Wagnalls, 1885. v-ix.

—— *The Princess and the Goblin*. 1872. Gutenberg ebook #708.

—— *Weighed and Wanting*. 1882.

Macey, Samuel L. *Patriarches of Time: Dualism in Saturn-Cronus, Father Time, the Watchmaker God, and Father Christmas*. Athens, GA: University of Georgia Press, 1987.

Mascall, E.L. *A Dictionary of Christian Theology*. Ed. Alan Richardson. 1969. London: SCM Press Ltd., 1972.

McGillis, Roderick F. "George MacDonald and the Lilith Legend in the XIXth Century." *Mythlore* 6.1 (Winter 1979): 3-11.

Miller, J.R. *The Devil of Today*. No loc.: Publisher Unknown, 1903/06.

Monaghan, Patricia. *The Book of Goddesses and Heroines*. New York: E.P. Dutton, 1981.

Mookerjee, Ajit. *Kali: The Feminine Force*. New York: Destiny Books, 1988.

Moorhouse, Geoffrey. *The Missionaries*. London: Eyre Methuen, 1973.

Morris, William. "Capitalist Morality." *News From Nowhere and Selected Writings and Designs*. Harmondsworth, UK: Penguin, 1962.

—— "Lectures on Socialism: Art Under Plutocracy." *Selections from the Prose works of William Morris.* Cambridge: Cambridge UP, 1931.

Mountain, Charles M. "The New Testament Christ-Hymn." *The Hymn* 4.1 (Jan 93): 23.

Moynihan, Elizabeth B. *Paradise as a Garden.* Princeton, NJ: Princeton UP, 1979.

Murrin, Michael. "The Multiple Worlds of the Narnia Stories." *Word and Story in C.S. Lewis.* Eds. Peter J. Shakel and Charles A. Huttar. Columbia, MO: University of Missouri Press, 1991. 232-55. Reprinted from VII: *An Anglo-American Literary Review* 3 (1982): 93-112.

Myers, Doris T. *C.S. Lewis in Context.* Kent, OH: Kent State UP, 1994.

Neumann, Erich. *The Great Mother.* Bollingen Series XLVII. Princeton, NJ: Princeton UP, 1955.

Newall, Venetia. *An Egg at Easter: a Folklore Study.* London: Routledge and Kegan Paul, 1971.

The New Oxford Annotated Bible. Eds. Bruce M. Metzger and Roland E. Murphy. New York: Oxford UP, 1991.

Nilsson, Martin P. *A History of Greek Religion.* New York: Norton Library, 1964.

Norwood Jr., W.D. "C.S. Lewis's Portrait of Aphrodite." *The Southern Quarterly* 8 (1970): 237-72.

Patterson, Nancy-Lou. [Including her major *Mythlore* papers, the papers she wrote and which she also cited in papers included in *Ransoming the Waste Land*, and other major papers that specifically address the work of the Inklings.]

—— "'A Bloomsbury Blue-Stocking': Dorothy L. Sayers' Bloomsbury Years in Their 'Spatial and Temporal Content [sic]." *Mythlore* 19.3 (1993): 6-15.

—— "'A Comedy of Masks': Lord Peter as Harlequin in *Murder Must Advertise*." *Mythlore* 15.3 (1989): 22-28.

—— "'All Nerves and Nose': Lord Peter Wimsey as Wounded Healer in the Novels of Dorothy L. Sayers." *Mythlore* 14.4 (1988): 13-16.

—— "'Always Winter and Never Christmas': Symbols of Time in Lewis's Chronicles of Narnia." *Mythlore* 18.1 (Autumn 1991): 10-14. [See *Ransoming the Waste Land Volume II.*]

—— "An Appreciation of Pauline Baynes." *Mythlore* (Autumn 1980): 3-5.

—— "Angel and Psychopomp in Madeleine L'Engle's 'Wind' Trilogy." *Children's Literature in Education* 14.1 (1983): 195-203.

—— "Anti-Babels: Images of the Divine Centre in *That Hideous Strength.*" *Mythcon II, Francisco Torres, Santa Barbara, CA, 1971.* Ed. Glen Good Knight. Los Angeles: The Mythopoeic Society, 1971. 6-11. [See *Ransoming the Waste Land Volume I.*]

—— "Archetypes of the Mother in the Fantasies of George MacDonald." *Mythcon I, Harvey Mudd College, Claremont, Ca., 1970.* Glen GoodKnight. Los Angeles: The Mythopoeic Society, 1970. 14-20.

—— "Artist's Statement about the Cover: The Merry Party." *The Lamp-Post of the Southern California C.S. Lewis Society* 19.4 (Winter 1995-96): 4-6.

—— "'A Ring of Good Bells': Providence and Judgement in Dorothy L. Sayers' *The Nine Tailors.*" *Mythlore* 16.1 (1989): 50-52.

—— "Art in the English Classroom: An Interdisciplinary Approach." *English Quarterly* 6.4 (Winter 1973): 345-49.

—— "Artist's Statement on This Month's Cover." *The Lamp-Post of the Southern California C.S. Lewis Society* 8.4 (December 1994): 4.

—— "'Banquet at Belbury': Festival and Horror in *That Hideous Strength.*" *Mythlore* (Autumn, 1981): 7-14, 42. [See *Ransoming the Waste Land Volume I.*]

—— "Beneath That Ancient Roof: The House as Symbol in Dorothy L. Sayers' Busman's Honeymoon." *Mythlore* 10.3 (1984): 39-46.

—— "'The Bolt of Tash': the Figure of Satan in C.S. Lewis's *The Horse and His Boy* and *The Last Battle*." *Mythlore* 16.4 (Summer 1990): 23-26. [See *Ransoming the Waste Land Volume II*.]

—— "Bright-Eyed Beauty: Celtic Elements in Charles Williams, J.R.R. Tolkien, and C.S. Lewis." *Mythlore* 10.1 (Spring 1983): 5-10.

—— "Cat o' Mary: The Spirituality of Dorothy L. Sayers." *Studies in Sayers: Essays Presented to Dr. Barbara Reynolds on her 80th Birthday*. Dorothy L. Sayers Society, 1994. 28-32.

—— "'Changing, Fearfully Changing' [Polarization and Transformation in Dorothy L. Sayers's Strong Poison]." *University of Waterloo Courier* (Sept. 1985): 11-17.

—— "Charles Williams." *Modern British Essayists. Second Series*. Ed. and Foreword Robert Beum. Detroit, MI: Gale, 1990. 316-25.

—— "C.S. Lewis and the Dragon." *The Lamp-Post of the Southern California C.S. Lewis Society* 27.1 (Spring 2003): 21-25.

—— "Death by Landscape." *Niekas* 45 (July 1998): 22-25.

—— "'Eve's Sharp Apple': Five Transgressing Women in the Novels of Dorothy L. Sayers." *The Sayers Review* III.3 (April 1980): 1-24.

—— "'The Glorious Impossible': Mystery and Metaphor in the Fantasies of Madeleine L'Engle." Archives, University of Waterloo.

—— "The Green Lewis: Inklings of Environmentalism in the Writing of C.S. Lewis." *The Lamp-Post of the Southern California C.S. Lewis Society* 18.1 (Mar. 1994): 4-14. [See *Ransoming the Waste Land Volume II*.]

—— "Guardaci Ben: The Visionary Woman in C.S. Lewis' Chronicles of Narnia and *That Hideous Strength*." *Mythlore* in 6.3 (Summer; 1979): 6-10; and 6.4 (Autumn 1979): 20-24. [See *Ransoming the Waste Land Volume I*.]

—— "'Halfe Like a Serpent': The Green Witch in *The Silver Chair*." *Mythlore* 11.2 (Autumn 1984): 37-47. [See *Ransoming the Waste Land Volume II*.]

—— "*Homo Monstrosus*: Lloyd Alexander's Gurgi and the Shadow Figures of Fantastic Literature." *Mythlore* 3.3 (1976) / *Tolkien Journal* (1976): 24-8.

—— "The Holy House of Ungit." *Mythlore* 21.4 (Winter 1997): 4-15. [See *Ransoming the Waste Land Volume II*.]

—— "The Host of Heaven: Astrological and Other Images of Divinity in the Fantasies of C.S. Lewis. Part I. The Fields of Arbol." *Mythlore* 7.3 (Autumn 1980): 19-29. "Part II." *Mythlore* 7.4 (Winter 1981): 13-21. [See *Ransoming the Waste Land Volume I*.]

—— "'This Equivocal Being': The Un-Man in C.S. Lewis's *Perelandra*." *The Lamp-Post of the Southern California C.S. Lewis Society* 19.3 (Fall 1995): 6-24; 19.4 (Winter 1996) 7-19. [See *Ransoming the Waste Land Volume I*.]

—— "Images of Judaism and Anti-Semitism in the Novels of Dorothy L. Sayers." *The Sayers Review* II.2 (June 1978): 17-24.

—— "The 'Jasper-Lucent Landscapes' of C.S. Lewis." *The Lamp-Post of the Southern California C.S. Lewis Society.* Part I. 22.1 (1999): 6-24. "Part II." 23.2 (1999): 16-32. Part III 23.4 (1999): 7-16. [See *Ransoming the Waste Land Volume II*.]

—— "The Jewels of Messias: Images of Judaism and Antisemitism in the Novels of Charles Williams." *Mythlore* 6.2 (Spring 1979): 27-31.

—— "Kore Motifs in *The Princess and the Goblin*." *For the Childlike: George MacDonald's Fantasies for Children*. Ed. Roderick McGillis. Metuchen, NJ: Scarecrow, 1992. 169-82.

—— "Letters from Hell: the Symbolism of Evil in *The Screwtape Letters*." *Mythlore* 12.1 (Autumn 1985): 47-57. [See *Ransoming the Waste Land Volume II*.]

—— "Lord of the Beasts: Animal Archetypes in C.S. Lewis." *Narnia Conference, Palms Park, West Los Angeles, 1969*. Ed. Glen GoodKnight. Los Angeles: The Mythopoeic Society, 1970. 24-32. [See *Ransoming the Waste Land Volume II*.]

—— "'Miraculous Bread … Miraculous Wine': Eucharistic Motifs in the Fantasies of C.S. Lewis." *Mythlore* 22.2 (Summer 1998): 28-46. [See *Ransoming the Waste Land Volume I*.]

—— "Narnia and the North: The Symbolism of Northerness in the Fantasies of C.S. Lewis." *Mythlore* 4.2 (1976): 9-16. [See *Ransoming the Waste Land Volume II.*]

—— "On The 'Lady Alice' Quadrangle in *That Hideous Strength.*" *The Lamp-Post of the Southern California C.S. Lewis Society* 9.4 (1986): 22. [See *Ransoming the Waste Land Volume I.*]

—— "Ransoming the Wasteland: Arthurian Themes in C.S. Lewis's Interplanetary Trilogy, Part I." *The Lamp-Post of the Southern California C.S. Lewis Society* 8.2-3 (November 1984): 16-26. "Part II." 8.4 (December 1985): 3-15. [See *Ransoming the Waste Land Volume I.*]

—— "'Some Kind of Company': The Sacred Community in *That Hideous Strength.*" *Mythcon XVI, Wheaton College, Wheaton, Ill., 1985.* Ed. Diana Pavlac. The Mythopoeic Society, 1985. 247-70. Rpt. in *Mythlore* 13.1 (1986): 8-19. [See *Ransoming the Waste Land Volume I.*]

—— "Some Women in C.S. Lewis's *That Hideous Strength.*" *The Toronto Pilgrimage C.S. Lewis Society* 1.1 (Jan.1994): 1-7. [See *Ransoming the Waste Land Volume I.*]

—— "Thesis, Antithesis, Synthesis: The Interplanetary Trilogy of C.S. Lewis." *CSL: The Bulletin of the New York C.S. Lewis Society* 16.8 (June 1985): 1-6. [See *Ransoming the Waste Land Volume I.*]

—— "Trained Habit: The Spirituality of C.S. Lewis." *The Canadian C.S. Lewis Journal* 87 (Spring 1995): 37-53.

—— "Tree and Leaf: J.R.R. Tolkien and the Visual Image." *English Quarterly* 6.4 (Spring 1974): 10-26.

—— "The Triumph of Love: Interpretations of the Tarot in Charles Williams' *The Greater Trumps.*" *Mythcon III, Regency Hyatt House, Long Beach, Ca., 1972.* Ed. Glen GoodKnight. Los Angeles, CA: The Mythopoeic Society, 1974. 12-32.

—— "The Unfathomable Feminine Principle: Images of Wholeness in *That Hideous Strength.*" *The Lamp-Post of the Southern California C.S. Lewis Society* 9.1-3 (1986): 3-38. [See *Ransoming the Waste Land Volume I.*]

—— "Why We Honor the Centenary of Dorothy L. Sayers (1893–1957)." *Mythlore* 19.3 (1993): 4-5.

Patai, Raphael. *The Hebrew Goddess*. New York: Avon, 1978.

Paternoster, Michael. *Thou Art There Also*. London: SPCK, 1967.

Price, Meredith. "All Shall Love Me and Despair, the Figure of Lilith in Tolkien, Lewis, Williams, and Sayers." *Mythlore* 9.1 (Spring 1982): 3-7, 26.

Primavesi, Anne. *From Apocalypse to Genesis: Ecology, Feminism and Christianity*. Minneapolis, MN: Fortress, 1991.

Prymer-Kensky, Tikva. *In the Wake of the Goddess: Women, Culture and the Biblical Transformation of Pagan Myth*. New York: Fawcett Columbine, 1992.

Ricoeur, Paul. *The Symbolism of Evil*. Trans. Emerson Buchanan. Boston, MA: Beacon Press, 1967.

Rousselle, Erwin. "Dragon and Mare, Figures of Primordial Chinese Mythology." *The Mystic Vision*. Ed. Joseph Campbell. Bollingen Series XXX. New York: 1968.

Ruether, Rosemary Radford. *Gaia and God. An Ecofeminist Theology of Earth Healing*. San Francisco, CA: HarperCollins, 1992.

Russell, Jeffrey Burton. *A History of Heaven*. Princeton, NJ: Princeton UP, 1996.

—— *The Devil*. 1977. New York: Meridian, 1979.

Sammons, Martha E. "Time." *A Guide Through Narnia*. Wheaton, IL: Harold Shaw Publishers, 1979. 63-64.

Sanford, John A. *Evil: The Shadow Side of Reality*. New York: Crossroad, 1981.

Sauvageat, A. "Finland-Ugria: Magic Animals." *Larousse World Mythology*. Ed. Pierre Grimal. London: Hamlyn, 1973.

Sayers, Dorothy L. *The Letters of Dorothy L. Sayers*. Volume 2. Selected and Edited by Barbara Reynolds. Cambridge: The Dorothy L. Sayers Society, 1997.

—— "The Other Six Deadly Sins." *The Whimsical Christian*. New York: Macmillan, 1978.

Schakel, Peter J. *Reading With the Heart: The Way into Narnia.* Grand Rapids, MI: Eerdmans, 1979.

—— *Reason and Imagination in C.S. Lewis: A Study of Till We Have Faces.* Grand Rapids, MI: William B. Eerdrnans, 1984.

Sir Gawain and the Green Knight, Pearl, and Sir Orfeo. Trans. J.R.R. Tolkien. London: George Allen and Unwin, 1975.

Spenser, Edmund. *The Faerie Queene.* Volume I. Introduction by Graham Hough. London: The Scolar Press, 1976.

Sturleson, Snorri. *The Prose Edda.* Trans. Jean I. Young. Berkeley, CA: University of California Press, 1954.

Taylor, Donald. "Theological thoughts about evil." Ed. David Parkin, *The Anthropology of Evil.* Oxford: Basil Blackwell, 1985. 26-41.

Thisted, Waldemar Adolph. *Letters From Hell.* Preface by George MacDonald. New York: Funk and Wagnalls, 1885.

Thompson, Dorothy Burr, and Ralph E. Griswold, *Garden Lore of Ancient Athens.* Princeton, NJ: American School of Classical Studies at Athens, 1963.

Tolkien, J.R.R. *The Monsters and the Critics.* Ed. Christopher Tolkien. London: George Allen and Unwin, 1983.

Trachtenberg, Joshua. *Jewish Magic and Superstition: A Study in Folk Religion.* New York: Atheneum, 1970.

Underhill, Ruth. *Red Man's Religion.* Chicago: University of Chicago Press, 1965.

Volsunga Saga. Trans. William Morris. New York: Collier Books, 1962.

Walker, Barbara G. *The Woman's Dictionary of Symbols and Sacred Objects.* San Francisco: Harper and Row: 1988.

Waggoner, Diana. *The Hills of Faraway.* New York: Atheneum, 1978.

Watts, Alan W. *Myth and Ritual in Christianity.* Boston, MA: Beacon Press, 1968.

Webster's New Collegiate Dictionary. Springfield, MA: G. and C. Merriam, 1956.

Whitaker, Chris. "Group Discussion Report of ROKE, Baton Rouge, La. (Feb. 19 1974)." *Mythprint* 10.5 (Nov. 1974): 5, 13 ff.

Williams, Charles. *The House of the Octopus*. London: Edinborough House Press, 1945.

—— "John Milton." *The Image of the City*. Ed. Anne Ridler. London: Oxford UP, 1958.

—— *The Region of the Summer Stars*. London: Oxford UP, 1950

—— *Shadows of Ecstasy*. New York: Pellegrini and Cudahy, 1950.

Williams, Georgiana L. "*Till We Have Faces*: a Journey of Recovery." *The Lamp-Post* 18.4 (December 1994): 5-15.

Zohary, Michael. *Plants of the Bible*. Cambridge: Cambridge UP, 1982.

Index

215; Psalms 76, 82, 90, 93, 119, 154, 157, 161, 188; Revelation 42, 98, 110, 130, 154, 157-158, 160-161, 171, 196, 208, 215; Samuel 92; Sirach 78; Song of Solomon 79, 97, 159; Timothy 98; Wisdom 78

Bidpai (Sanskrit fables) 187

bird imagery and symbolism 84; bird's head masks 84; bird cults 84

Bism 46, 53, 55, 141

black mass 202

Blake, William. "Milton" 156-157

blasphemy 88, 198

Bles, Geoffrey 3

blood imagery, symbolism, and mythology 81, 83, 85, 95, 97, 218

blue, symbolism of color 155, 159-160, 162, 176

The Book of Common Prayer 67n6, 84-85; Morning Prayer 85

Bookman (periodical) 8

Br'er Rabbit 188

Bracton College 124-125

Bradley, Ian. *God is Green* 169-170

Bragdon Wood 124-125

bread imagery and symbolism 76-77, 84, 223

Bree 11-14, 20, 141-145, 188

bridges, symbolism and mythology 51-52

British Green Party 169

Brute (*TWHF*) *see* Shadowbrute

Buddha 15; Buddhism 79; Black Tara 79

Bultitude, Mr. 129, 187

Butler, Samuel. *Notebooks* 201, 211

Cain and Abel 177-178

Cair Paravel 47, 52, 133, 198

Calormen 11, 13, 15, 141, 143, 194-199; Calormenes 12, 16, 20, 22-23, 142, 144, 148, 151, 196; Calormene religion 52, 148-149, 193-200

Canaan 89

cancer imagery and symbolism 208, 216

cardinal directions, symbolism 14-18; *see also* North, South, East, West

Carlyle, Thomas. *Sartor Resartus* 222

Carroll, Lewis 109, 130; *Alice in Wonderland* 126

Casanova 217

Caspian, Prince 48-50, 67n5, 133-136, 139, 141, 189

Cassandra imagery 51

Casteneda, Carlos 22; *The Teachings of Don Juan* 190

Catal Huyuk 221

Celtic mythology 8, 49

Centaurs in Narnia 189

centipedes 51-52, 214-215, 220-221

Ceres (Roman goddess) 78

Charity (*caritas*) 80, 119, 203, 219

Hathor (Egyptian goddess) 78, 82

Heaven 34, 36, 121, 130, 138, 150, 156, 158, 161, 169, 201, 204, 207, 219, 226

Hebrew (language) 112, 160, 209

Hecate 78

Hegel, Georg Wilhelm Friedrich 217

Hel (Norse goddess) 51, 62, 65

Helen, Queen 147, 189

Helios (Greek god) 56

Hell 34, 36-37, 55, 59, 111, 121-122, 130, 156, 158, 169, 205, 207, 210, 216, 219, 222-223, 226

Hellenistic thought 171

Henry VIII 217

Hermit of the Southern March 13, 144, 161, 195; dwelling place 143-144, 161

hermitages, hidden chapels, and eremitical motifs 113

Herodotus 89

Hesiod 222

hierarchy 175, 219

hieros gamos (sacred marriage) 24

hijab 84

Hiroshima 170

history 41

Hitler, Adolf 9, 217

Hogg, James. "Kilmeny" 138

Holger the Dane 39

Holy Ghost 88

Holy Tree (TWHF) 90; compared to Cross 90

Holy Week 132

Homer 82. *Iliad* 5, 53; *Odyssey* 56; Homeric hymns 83

honey and bees, imagery and symbolism 88, 93-94

hope 119

Hopkins, Anthony xvi*n*2

horizon, imagery and symbolism 57

The Horse and His Boy. 11-16, 20, 24, 29n78, 47, 52, 82, 116, 141-145, 188, 193-196; working title, 3-4

hot and cold, symbolism 17

house, imagery and symbolism 135-136, 146, 161-162; "low pillared house," pillars 161

Housman, A.E. *A Shropshire Lad* 135

hrossa 175

human sacrifice 89, 152, 196

humours, theory of 176

Huxley, Aldous 18, 22; "Heaven and Hell" (in *The Doors of Perception and Heaven and Hell*) 110-111, 114, 119-120, 128, 151

Hwin 12, 82, 142-143

Iceland 5, 13, 15; Icelandic literature 5-6

immanence 156, 161

immortality 120, 174

impotence 61

Inanna (Sumerian)/Ishtar (Babylonian) 46, 49, 64-65, 82, 89

India 16

Indo-European mythology 82

162, in Plymouth 115, wounded 115; at Oxford after WWI 117, 161-162; at Cambridge 186; visits to "Ladies at Wantage" 161, walks and walking tours in England 94, 118, 135; travel to France 162, to Greece 162, character before conversion 205; as an atheist 114; conversion to Christianity xii, 4, 7, 91, 114, 121, 127, 175; Whipsnade Zoo and conversion 121; as Anglican 205; religious beliefs and spirituality 41, 94, 147; preferences in worship 162

Beliefs and opinions: Accusations of racism 20; attitude towards domesticated animals and Heaven 150; animal rights 170, 176; attitude towards hierarchy 175; attitude towards mythology xii-xii; attitude toward source criticism x; belief in angels and devils 208-209; attitude towards natural beauty 113-115; towards English landscape 115-116; towards Irish landscape 118; love of nature 167, 169; environmental thought 167-179; Castlereagh Hills, significance to Lewis 120, 141; awareness of modern psychology 186; dislike of rapid travel, preference for trains 125-126

Lewis, Warren 94, 114, 118, 183, 207
light, imagery and symbolism 86, 111, 117, 154, 160
lilies, imagery and symbolism 137
Lilith 58, 61, 65, 78; Lilith imagery and mythology 58
Lindburgh baby kidnapping 68n10
Lindsay, David. *A Voyage to Arcturus* xiv-xv
The Lion, the Witch and the Wardrobe 11, 32-35, 37-39, 62, 115, 131-133, 141, 148-149, 183-184
lions, imagery and symbolism 183-184, 196; in Mesopotamian myth 184
Liverpool 207
Lloyd, Roger. *The Troubling of the City* 220
locus amoenus 109, 111, 132, 134, 136, 143, 150, 154; *see also* Paradise, gardens
Logos 171
Loki 62
London 145-146, 168
Lone Islands 135
longaevi 37, 63
Longfellow, Henry Wadsworth. Journal 9; *The Saga of King Olaf* 7, 10; "Tegnér's Drapa" 7-10
Lord's Prayer 47
Lot's wife 37
love 57, 101, 219, 222; goddesses of 58, 64, 80; god of

Nancy-Lou Patterson. "The Destruction of Edgestow." First published as the cover of *Mythlore* 16.2 (Winter 1989). Further publication prohibited.

www.ingramcontent.com/pod-product-compliance
Lightning Source LLC
Chambersburg PA
CBHW020657270326
41928CB00005B/168

* 9 7 8 1 9 8 7 9 1 9 0 5 9 *